The Better Teacher's Toolbox

The Better Teacher's Toolbox

Practical Ideas for Any Teacher to Become a Better One

LARRY FERLAZZO

KATIE HULL SYPNIESKI

JB JOSSEY-BASS™

A Wiley Brand

Library of Congress Cataloging-in-Publication Data is Available:

ISBN 9781394171644 (Paperback)
ISBN 9781394171651 (ePDF)
ISBN 9781394171668 (ePub)

Cover Design: Wiley
Cover Image: © Bokeh Art Photo/stock.adobe.com
Author Photos: © Katie Hull Sypnieski, © Larry Ferlazzo

Printed and bound by CPI Group (UK) Ltd, Croydon, CR0 4YY

C9781394171644_170426

Contents

Acknowledgments ix

About the Authors xi

Introduction .... **xiii**

1. Relationships, Relationships, Relationships **1**
What Is It? 1
Why We Like It 3
Supporting Research 4
Application 6
What Could Go Wrong 16
Chapter Summary 19
Technology Connections 19

2. Student Agency, NOT Student Empowerment **21**
What Is It? 21
Why We Like It 22
Supporting Research 23
Application 24
What Could Go Wrong 36
Chapter Summary 37
Technology Connections 38

3. Differentiated Instruction **39**

What Is It? 39
Why We Like It 41
Supporting Research 42
Application 42
What Could Go Wrong 66
Chapter Summary 67
Technology Connections 67

4. Tech Has Its Place, but Also Has to Be Kept in Its Place **71**

What Is It? 71
Why We Like It 71
Supporting Research 72
Application 73
What Could Go Wrong 86
Chapter Summary 86
Technology Connections 87

5. Developing Classrooms That Promote Self-Motivation **89**

What Is It? 89
Why We Like It 91
Supporting Research 92
Application 93
What Could Go Wrong 105
Chapter Summary 105
Technology Connections 105

6. Emphasizing Students' Assets, Not Deficits **107**

What Is It? 107
Why We Like It 108
Supporting Research 109
Application 110
What Could Go Wrong 119
Chapter Summary 120
Technology Connections 120

7. Strategies for Maximizing Learning **121**

What Is It? 121
Why We Like It 121
Supporting Research 122
Application 122

What Could Go Wrong..139

Chapter Summary..140

Technology Connections...140

8. Classroom Climate and Culture 143

What Is It?...143

Why We Like It...144

Supporting Research..144

Application..145

What Could Go Wrong..159

Chapter Summary..160

Technology Connections...161

9. Providing Effective Student Feedback..................................163

What Is It?..163

Why We Like It...164

Supporting Research..164

Application..165

What Could Go Wrong..183

Chapter Summary..184

Technology Connections...184

10. Cultural Responsiveness, Not Cultural Tokenism.......................187

What Is It?..187

Why We Like It...188

Supporting Research..189

Application..189

What Could Go Wrong..198

Chapter Summary..199

Technology Connections...199

11. Teacher Self-Care and Sustainability.................................201

What Is It?..201

Why We Like It...202

Supporting Research..202

Application..202

What Could Go Wrong..210

Chapter Summary..212

Technology Connections...212

Index 215

Acknowledgments

Larry Ferlazzo

I'd like to thank my wife and family for all their support over the years while I've been teaching and writing. Of course, I'd also like to thank Principal Jim Peterson and all my former colleagues and students at Luther Burbank High School— I learned so much from them during the twenty-three years I worked there. And a big thank you to Katie Hull Sypnieski, who has been a friend, colleague, and co-author for many, many years.

Katie Hull Sypnieski

I am grateful to all the students I've had over the years for their determination, creativity, and for helping me grow as an educator and human. Thank you to my colleagues for their support, especially Larry Ferlazzo, my co-author, co-teacher, and dear friend. Finally, to my family, especially David, Drew, Ryan, and Rachel, who have supported me in this process. I love you all!

Larry and Katie

We need to offer thanks to Amy Fandrei and Pete Gaughan at Jossey-Bass for their patience and guidance in preparing this book, and previous ones, and to Jennifer Borgioli Binis at Schoolmarm Advisors for her assistance in developing our manuscript submission.

About the Authors

Larry Ferlazzo taught English, Social Studies, and International Baccalaureate Theory of Knowledge classes for twenty-three years to English language learners and English proficient students at Luther Burbank High School in Sacramento, California.

He is the author, co-author, or editor of 14 books on education, including *The ELL Teacher's Toolbox, The ESL/ELL Teacher's Survival Guide,* and *Navigating the Common Core with English Language Learners*. He's also been *Education Week*'s teacher advice columnist for fifteen years.

His articles have also appeared regularly in *The New York Times* and in *The Washington Post*. Larry was a community organizer for nineteen years prior to becoming a high school teacher. He is married and has three children and five grandchildren.

Last, but not least, he has been a dedicated, though mediocre, pickleball and basketball player for many years.

Katie Hull Sypnieski has taught English language learners of all proficiency levels and English proficient students in the Sacramento City Unified School District for nearly thirty years. She has served as a teaching consultant with the Area 3 Writing Project housed at the University of California, Davis for the past twenty-five years.

She has co-authored three books on teaching ELLs and has co-edited three books on education. She has published articles and instructional videos for *Education Week*. In addition, she has co-authored articles for *Edutopia, The New York Times Learning Network*, and ASCD's *Educational Leadership*.

Katie lives in Sacramento with her husband and three children.

Introduction

"Better" comes from the Old English word *betera*, which, according to Etymonline. com, means "of superior quality or excellence." It also means "improved in health, more healthy."

Those two definitions encapsulate our reasons behind writing this book and our hopes for it. We believe the instructional strategies we recommend in it—based on our many decades of experience in the classroom—can be used by teachers to both improve their practice and make their lives more healthy or at least less stressful.

This book is the latest in the Jossey-Bass "Toolbox" series. We've previously written two editions of The ELL Teacher's Toolbox and have edited other books for Math, Science, and Social Studies teachers.

We felt a good addition to the series would be this one, which offers advice to all teachers, regardless of their level of experience, no matter what subject or grade level. Though most of what we write here is geared to middle and high school students, as that's where our professional experience lies, our conversations with colleagues have shown much of it is adaptable to younger grades.

As is the case in all our books, Figures and other resources are freely available for download with no registration required in order to access them. Just visit wiley.com/go/betterteacherstoolbox or use the QR code at the end of this Introduction, and it is also located at the end of every chapter. Each chapter follows the same structure: What it is, why we like it, supporting research, ways to apply it in your classroom, a brief discussion of what could go wrong, and links galore in a technology connection. Finally, we provide a short summary of each chapter; basically what we'd say if you asked us for advice about the chapter topic and we only had a few minutes to chat in the faculty lunchroom.

We should never say never, but this is likely the last education book either of us will write. We've always felt it was important for active practitioners to offer views directly from the classroom. Now that Larry has retired (he co-authored this book in the summer following his retirement), he no longer has that connection (though he remains a volunteer tutor.)

But, at least for now, you can continue to read Larry's education writing at his resource-sharing blog and at his Education Week column. He's hopeful he can convince Katie to contribute there. And he's beginning work on a novel set during the Mexican-American War—there's probably a novel inside every teacher!

As far as Katie is concerned, she is going to try to actually enjoy her weekends and summers!

And we hope that the ideas in this book help enhance your teaching *and* provide you more time to also enjoy *your* weekends and summers!

https://www.wiley.com/go/bettereacherstoolbox

CHAPTER 1

Relationships, Relationships, Relationships

What Is It?

Building a positive *public* relationship with students means teachers work at creating a connection where children feel that educators view them as more than just bodies in their class. Rather, they feel like their teachers care for them as human beings and are interested in their lives, dreams, and challenges, as well as being interested in how well they learn the curriculum. And, in a healthy classroom, students reciprocate that to the best of their ability.

This is a *public* relationship, not a *private* one. Public relationships (between students and teachers, teachers and administrators, etc.) have clear boundaries and are not unconditional while our private relationships (with friends and family) may not have those distinctions. In a public relationship, the "currency" can be reciprocity and accountability, while in a private relationship the "currency" is love. The dangers of a professional blurring those boundaries are obvious.

The teacher/student relationship is a public one—a caring one, a relationship that requires patience and understanding—but, nevertheless, a public one necessitating respect, communication, and boundaries, as this next story illustrates.

One year, Larry had a student (we can call him John) with an enormous number of challenges. Larry put a great deal of time and energy into supporting John, including purchasing books of John's own choosing to read, working with him to develop alternative assignments that would be more fun and accessible, and providing occasional snacks between classes. John made great progress during the first six weeks of the school year and was a delight to have in class. However, things suddenly began to go dramatically downhill. Larry made a routine request of Larry and John shouted back, "You don't care about me and you just want to kick me out of class!" Larry asked him to step out in the hall.

This is what Larry said to him in a calm voice:

> I felt hurt by what you said. I feel like I've bent over backward to support you and help you succeed (I then gave examples). I don't need thanks, but I expect respect. And I haven't been feeling very respected by you over the past few weeks. You've raised your voice at me, refused to do work, and distracted other students. I will be a helpful and supportive teacher to you, as I am with all the students in my class. But I don't feel like continuing to go out of my way for someone who doesn't show me respect. I want to emphasize that I will be a helpful and supportive teacher to you, but I'm just not going to continue to go the extra mile.

John began to react negatively, but Larry quickly ended the conversation and they returned to class. Afterward, however, John returned to being respectful and hardworking, and they were able to resume their healthy and public relationship. John ended up having a very successful year.

A private relationship is marked by unconditional, unwavering support. By not ignoring John's behavior and clearly communicating his boundaries, Larry kept their relationship public. The bottom line, as educator author Rick Wormeli has put it, is we teachers can be very friendly with students, but need to stop at being friends—at least until after they graduate![1]

Of course, as in most things in our world, it's not always either/or, and there can be a great deal of nuance in a teacher/student relationship. Nevertheless, keeping the idea of public/private relationships in mind has helped us both maintain more of a personal/professional "equilibrium."

In addition to the public/private dynamic, there is another choice about the kind of relationship teachers need to make about our relationship with the young people in our classrooms. Arizona State University researcher Victoria Theisen-Homer has characterized it as the difference between "instrumental" and "reciprocal."[2,3] During Larry's years as a community organizer, he would frame it similarly,

---

[1] Ferlazzo, L. (2011, October 25). Response: Can teachers be friends with students?—Part One. *Classroom Q & A with Larry Ferlazzo*.

[2] Theisen-Homer, V. (2021). Preparing teachers for relationships with students: Two visions, two approaches. *Journal of Teacher Education*, 72(3), 271–283. https://doi.org/10.1177/0022487120922223

[3] Sparks, S. D. (2019, March 12). Why teacher-student relationships matter. *Education Week*.

though use the terms "transactional" versus "transformational."[4] Larry (and we believe Professor Theisen-Homer) would say transactional teachers tend to look at the world through a lens of punishment, rewards, and or exchange ("horse trading") for motivation, while transformational leaders focus on listening, collaboration, and leading by example.

Classroom dynamics, though, do not always allow for either/or approaches. Yes, having a better teacher-student relationship will likely improve compliance, and we all know that we need a lot of that in our classes. But do we really always just want to look at our students through the lens of how we can best get them to do what we want? That kind of viewpoint seems a bit soulless and empty and is not likely to lead to teacher-energizing stories that we can't wait to tell our families that night.

Having a healthy emphasis on reciprocal/transformational relationships, where we demonstrate genuine curiosity about our students' lives and what they know and think, and where we can often collaborate and learn together—now, those are the kinds of relationships that have powered the two of us in our decades of teaching.

We're not trying to sell a pie-in-the-sky view of the classroom—sometimes you've just got to get students to sit down and do the assignment, and positive relationships help.

But don't forget that at its heart, learning is transformational, not transactional, and genuine relationships can help. Our students are smart, and most of them will detect the difference.

Why We Like It

We often use two quotations to explain why we value teacher-student relationships so highly.

One is from education researcher Robert Marzano, who wrote: *if the relationship between the teacher and the students is good, then everything else that occurs in the classroom seems to be enhanced.*[5]

In our experiences, and in the experiences of many teachers with whom we have been in contact, truer words have never been spoken.

> *Where those positive relationships exist, there are fewer class disruptions, more time focused on learning, a more joyful classroom atmosphere, and, not to mention but not to be ignored, far less teacher stress.*

[4] Ferlazzo, L. (2010, November 8). Being "transactional" versus being "transformational" in schools. *Huffpost.*

[5] Marzano, R. (2007). *The Art and Science of Teaching: A Comprehensive Framework for Effective Instruction.* ASCD. Page 150.

The other quote, perhaps a more well-known one, is from the late, great teacher Rita Pierson, who said: *Kids don't learn from people they don't like.*[6]

Her observation has gotten pushback from people, some who we would suggest have difficulty seeing the forest for the trees (we might also suggest they spend more time in classrooms). Of course, *some* students can learn *some* things from *some* people they don't like *in certain circumstances.*

But we would bet dollars to donuts that most teachers would agree that the vast majority of students tend to learn far, far less from people they don't like. In fact, recent research, albeit done in the workplace, finds that employees who like their supervisors "will be happier at work, go above and beyond what is required of them, experience greater well-being, and perform at a higher level."[7]

Supporting Research

There's more research recognizing the importance of teacher-student relationships for learning than you can shake a stick at.

In a meta-analysis of 100 studies, educational researcher Robert Marzano found that the quality of a teacher-student relationship was the "keystone" of effective classroom management.[8] An even bigger, and more recent, study examining 70 years of research found that positive teacher-student relationships have "large significant relations with eight clusters of student outcomes: academic achievement, academic emotions, appropriate student behavior, behavior problems, executive functions and self-control, motivation, school belonging and engagement, and well-being."[9] And yet another review of literature found that positive teacher-student relationships had significant impacts on student engagement, grade, attendance, behavior, and drop-out rates.[10]

In fact, some research has found that the teacher-student relationship can have an even greater influence on high school student success than parental

---

[6] Pierson, R. F. (2013, May). *Every kid needs a champion* [TedTalk].

[7] McAllister, C., Moss, S., Martinko, M. (2019, October 19.) *Why likable leaders seem more effective.* Harvard Business Review.

[8] Marzano, R. J., & Marzano, J. S. (2003). The key to classroom management. *Educational Leadership, 61*(1), 6–13.

[9] Emslander, V., Holzberger, D., Ofstad, S. B., Fischbach, A., & Scherer, R. (2025). Teacher-student relationships and student outcomes: A systematic second-order meta-analytic review. *Psychological Bulletin, 151*(3), 365–397. https://doi.org/10.1037/bul0000461

[10] Quin, D. (2017). Longitudinal and contextual associations between teacher–student relationships and student engagement: A systematic review. *Review of Educational Research, 87*(2), 345–387. https://doi.org/10.3102/0034654316669434

relationships.[11] Obviously, this conclusion won't apply in all situations (though multiple researchers suggest that the influence of other adults increases in adolescence) but, nevertheless, it does reinforce the importance of the teacher-student relationship.

Though research shows that positive teacher-student relationships benefit all students, it appears that they may be particularly important for boys, who may experience more academic and behavioral challenges than girls.[12]

The student academic success from "looping" (teachers staying with the same students for more than one year) has been primarily attributed to positive teacher-student relationships.[13]

One important research finding that educators, particularly those of us who are white, should keep in mind is that teachers tend to have weaker relationships with immigrant youth and students of color (the study didn't appear to have enough teachers of color in the studied group to determine if this especially applied to white teachers, but it doesn't seem to us be a big stretch to reach that conclusion).[14] "Homophily" describes the research-backed perspective that people tend to feel more connected to others who are like themselves, and many of us teachers are obviously not immune from it.[15] But being aware of this shortcoming is the first step toward actively doing something about it!

More than one study has found that the extent that teachers enjoyed teaching their classes was directly connected to how much they enjoyed the relationships with their students.[16] The two of us can emphatically echo these findings!

The *2025 Report Card: Student Perspective on U.S. Schools*, a Gallup-Walton Family Foundation survey, found that students gave an average grade of a B for "quality of relationships with your teachers." That isn't bad, but nearly a third of students gave it a C or below.[17] There's room for improvement available to all teachers.

[11] Sethi, J., & Scales, P. C. (2020). Developmental relationships and school success: How teachers, parents, and friends affect educational outcomes and what actions students say matter most. *Contemporary Educational Psychology, 63*. https://doi.org/10.1016/j.cedpsych.2020.101904

[12] Reichert, M. C., & Hawley, R. (2014, May 6). What relationships mean in educating boys. *Education Week*.

[13] Barshay, J. (2018, May 21). Two studies point to the power of teacher-student relationships to boost learning. *The Hechinger Report*.

[14] Reichert and Hawley, R. (2014).

[15] Homophily. (n.d.). *Wikipedia*. https://en.wikipedia.org/wiki/Homophily

[16] Sparks (March 12, 2019).

[17] Walton Family Foundation Gen Z Research. (2025). Walton family foundation. www.gallup.com/analytics/651674/gen-z-research.aspx

Application

In this section, we'll share 17 specific ways (not in order of any kind of priority) teachers can begin to develop positive relationships with students. In addition, since we think it's also important and can't think of a better place in this book to put it, we've added a short section on how to encourage students to develop positive relationships with their classmates—this type of environment can support the development of a classroom "community."

Of course, we teachers are human, as are our students. Sometimes we can follow all the "right" steps, and relationships still go south. We offer some recommendations on how to get back on the right track in those situations in the "What Could Go Wrong" section of this chapter.

MAKE STUDENTS LOOK GOOD

When your students do something well, ask if you can record a quick video on their phone for their family where you can praise their child and make sure other students hear you making the recording. Do this regularly and you will have an enormous amount of capital in your relationship banks to enhance what happens in your classroom. And you'll soon have students asking *you* to make recordings.

And when you see one of your students in the hallway talking to their friends, give them a shout out about what a great job they're doing. Larry likes to barge in when one of his students is walking with someone or a group, and says something like "Excuse me, did you know that Abigail wrote a great essay in our class today? She's a superstar!" They'll look embarrassed but, trust us, they love it—at least 99% of the time!

USE PERSONAL GREETINGS

Studies point to the value of greeting students by the door and its value in creating a sense of belonging.[18] More power to teachers who can pull it off, but we think this finding is a good example of education researcher Dylan Wiliam's adage about education research: "Everything works somewhere; nothing works everywhere."[19]

We agree that individually greeting students each day is important, and actually saying their name in the process is critical—some students may never hear their name said in a positive way during the school day otherwise. However, we'd rather be in the front ensuring that students start work on the warm-up as soon as they sit

---

[18] Terada, Y. (2018, September 11). Welcoming students with a smile. *Edutopia*.

[19] Wiliam, D. (2018, December 12). Dylan Wiliam's guide for clear education thinking. *Flypaper*.

down. We can still easily greet each student individually from the front in a cheerful and personalized manner.

CORRECTLY USE STUDENTS' NAMES

Speaking of student names, try to memorize them as soon as possible. As part of that, be sure to ask them what they want to be called—some students have preferred nicknames (Larry once called a student "Prince" for an entire year because he was testing if Larry would actually call students whatever they wanted to be called) and some have preferred names because of their gender identity. We also make a point of inviting students, if they desire, to share their preferred pronouns.

If you have issues with that last point, as we've said in our previous books, get over yourself and remember the Civil Rights refrain, "keep your eyes on the prize." Which, in this case, is a positive teacher-student relationship.

Retrieval practice (see Chapter 7: Strategies for Maximizing Learning) works for students, and it works for us—during the first days of school we'll go around the room saying each student's name asking for corrections. Making it a priority communicates to students that we truly value them as people. And carry a clipboard with the seating chart everywhere for reference and as a reminder. Be sure to visit the Technology Connections for links to more strategies on learning students' names, including having them record their own names for you.

Larry takes it a step further. After the first two weeks of school, he announces that if he forgets or mispronounces a student's name, they will receive a fruit snack. After that announcement, students constantly ask him to tell them their names. It's probably the only time in their lives they actually *want* to have their names mispronounced or forgotten, and it's good practice for Larry.

USE HUMOR. CAREFULLY

The use of appropriate humor can make a huge positive difference in teacher-student relationships.[20]

We want to emphasize the word *appropriate*.

Teacher self-deprecating comments are *in* (we love using this type of humor! Larry highlights his mediocre basketball skills often, especially the time he and two other faculty lost 12-to-0 in a three-on-three game against starters on the school team).

---

[20] Cooper, K. M., Hendrix, T., Stephens, M. D., et al. (2018). To be funny or not to be funny: Gender differences in student perceptions of instructor humor in college science courses. *PLOS ONE, 13*(8), e0201258. https://doi.org/10.1371/journal.pone.0201258

Over-exaggerated reactions to minor student misbehavior instead of a direct reprimand are *in* ("Oh, noooooooo, say it ain't so! You are not watching YouTube on your Chromebook!"). And, only *after* solid teacher-student relationships are built, gentle sarcasm done with a genuine smile can be *in* ("I will put that cellphone on the floor and do a dance on it if you don't put it away").

Weaponizing sarcasm, on the other hand, is definitely out, out, out! Put-downs and snide comments hurt teacher-student relationships and student learning.[21]

BE GENEROUS WITH PRAISE

A number of studies have found that it's not unusual to find that "reprimands"—pushing students to pay attention or get on-task—outnumber praise comments.

We certainly "get" why that is often the case, and we're sure we have had many days where our negative comments have far outnumbered the positive ones. However, narrowing down this "praise-to-reprimand ratio" can lead to better teacher-student relationships and a better classroom environment.[22]

Be conscious of your ratio, make your positive comments specific ("I appreciated how focused everyone was during the lesson" or "That's great to see everyone immediately picking up their book and starting to read") as opposed to general ("You were a good class today"), and try to make reprimands private—no one likes to be embarrassed publicly (we try to bend down and whisper to students or pass them a sticky note). Moderation is the key—both in praise and in negative comments.

Researchers haven't found any kind of ideal ratio as the best one.[23] Use a clipboard to keep track if you need one. We just periodically reflect on our actions and often invite students to weigh in on how we're doing in this area with an anonymous Google Form survey.

DEMONSTRATE PERSONAL VULNERABILITY

As odd as it may sound, it's not unusual to find that some students have a difficult time viewing teachers as ordinary people. Every teacher who has encountered a student outside of school—at a store, restaurant, in a park—can attest to sometimes seeing a shocked expression on our students' faces when they see that we have lives outside of the school context.

[21] Sparks, S. D. (2018, May 11). Students learn less when they sense teacher hostility. *Education Week.*

[22] Ibid.

[23] Caldarella, P., Larsen, R. A. A., Williams, L., Downs, K. R., Wills, H. P., & Wehby, J. H. (2020). Effects of teachers' praise-to-reprimand ratios on elementary students' on-task behaviour. *Educational Psychology,* 40(10), 1306–1322. https://doi.org/10.1080/01443410.2020.1711872

Though we need to avoid the oversharing that is not unusual among many on social media and maintain a public relationship, that does not mean we can't carefully share personal moments that humanize us at appropriate times individually or class-wide. When a student has been grieving the loss of a parent, in addition to listening and offering support, Larry has shared that he lost his father at an early age. And Larry telling his students that he was born with anosmia (the complete loss of smell) and that he has never smelled anything in his entire life has never failed to be a year-long source of fascination for every one of his classes. And telling deprecating stories about our mistakes and mishaps are always hits!

Listen, none of our lives are interesting enough that our students want to hear about every aspect of them (though we have known teachers who do, indeed, overshare, and are encouraged to do so by some students who want to avoid doing classwork). But demonstrating our personal vulnerabilities and sharing our many mistakes can build trust and perhaps help students feel more comfortable about risking making their own errors.[24]

PRACTICE COMMON COURTESY

We are not royalty and students are not our subjects, notwithstanding one day when a student asked Larry why he had to do something and Larry jokingly responded, "Because I'm King." His principal happened to be walking by at the same moment and pointed out to Larry and his students, in the same joking manner, that Larry wasn't the King, the principal was.

Words and phrases like:

- Sorry
- Please
- Thank you
- What do you think?

should be some of the most frequent things your students hear you say. They cost you nothing and can gain you much, but they must be said sincerely.[25] No one likes hearing these comments in a sarcastic tone and no one likes a suck-up.

[24] Romney, A. C., & Holland, D. V. (2023). The vulnerability paradox: Strengthening trust in the classroom. *Management Teaching Review, 8*(1), 84–90. https://doi.org/10.1177/2379298120978362 and (Reichert & Hawley, R., 2014)

[25] Ferlazzo, L. (2013, October 8). The best resources on the importance of saying "I'm Sorry." *Larry Ferlazzo's Website of the Day*; Ferlazzo, L. (2019, January 15). Saying "Thank you" so students. *Larry Ferlazzo's Website of the Day*.

These actions, as most of ours should be, are useful models for our students.

LISTEN AND RESPOND TO WHAT YOU HEAR

Listening to students is a not-to-be-underestimated way of strengthening teacher-student relationships.[26] But equally important is *responding* to what you hear from them.

Introductory Letters

Some years, depending on workload and class make-ups, we write introductory letters about ourselves, share them on the first day of school, and ask students to use them as models to write their own letters about themselves to us. That night, we write a short response on a sticky note and put it on each letter. It could be something like "the Warriors are my team, too" or a question like "Are you going to join the school soccer team?" We pass them out the next day and many students are surprised that we actually read what they wrote.

Weekly Google Form Survey

We use a weekly Google Form survey to learn how students are doing. If students indicate they aren't feeling good about school or their personal life, we make a point of immediately checking in with them and asking if there is some way we can help or send students to see the counselor. When they make narrative comments on the survey about events in their lives, we mention it to them.

These are the questions on the survey, which ask students to rank their answers 1-5 for most, though not all, of their responses:

1. How are you feeling about our class today?
2. How are you feeling about school in general today?
3. How are you feeling about your personal life today?
4. Did you meet the goal you set for yourself in last week's survey?
5. What goal do you want to set for yourself this week?
6. Is there a specific change that could make this class a better one for you?
7. Is there anything else that you think would be helpful for Mr. Ferlazzo to know about how you or your family are doing?

[26] Kincade, L., Cook, C., & Goerdt, A. (2020). Meta-analysis and common practice elements of universal approaches to improving student-teacher relationships. *Review of Educational Research, 90*(5), 710–748. https://doi.org/10.3102/0034654320946836

Short anonymous Google Forms asking specific questions about lessons ("Rate one-to-five how helpful this graphic organizer was to you") or anonymous sticky notes ("Rate one-to-five how well you think you understand this concept") can be excellent formative assessment tools—if teachers act on the responses.

The same goes for anonymous class evaluations we try to do every quarter. If students say on them that your Google Classroom could be better organized, tell them you'll make changes and actually *do it.*

Here are the questions Larry used on one of his recent class evaluations, again asking students to use a 1–5 ranking to respond to several of them[27]:

- How did you generally feel about this class?

- How interesting was the content of this class?

- How fair was the grading for this class?

- How did you feel about the quantity of work that was required for this class?

- How did you feel about Mr. Ferlazzo's teaching ability?

- How much did you feel that Mr. Ferlazzo cared about you as a person?

- What was the most interesting thing you learned in this class?

- What was the best thing about this class?

- What was the worst thing about this class and how do you think it could be improved?

If you're not going to take what students say seriously and act on their opinions, it's better not to ask at all.

That doesn't mean you have to agree with or to everything they say or want. But it does mean you need to acknowledge what they say and, if you are not going to act on their wants, explain your rationale.

Of course, there are also other important ways to listen to students besides surveys or sticky notes. Making time in class (or before-or-after-class) for short thirty second conversations where you ask how students are doing, check in with students who look "down" or distracted by asking "How are you doing?" or "Are you doing okay?," or just give students compliments accompanied by questions. (Larry's bald and has fun complimenting students on their hair after asking them if they recently got a haircut or their hair styled.) Remember the adage that it's better to be *interested* instead of being *interesting.*

Finally, looking for opportunities in the moment for class feedback is another strategy. Whether it's asking students how much time they need to complete an assignment, if they want their small groups to be two people or three, or if they

---

[27] *The ESL/ELL Teacher's Survival Guide,* Ferlazzo & Hull Sypnieski, page 482. Used with permission.

prefer to do writing on their Chromebook or by hand—providing low-stakes choices where you can live with either one indicates you're openness to their ideas and your willingness to see them as people whose agency you value (see Chapter 2: Student Agency, NOT Student Empowerment).

START EARLY

You've probably heard the old—and ridiculous—adage for teachers "don't smile until Christmas."

Most teachers' experiences will tell you tell you that's a recipe for disaster, and research confirms that this is the case.[28] People will respond better when you are positive early on in the year and, by the way, the same research supports the position that it's better to be more critical later in the year. We're all more likely to listen to critique after we've developed a level of trust with people and believe they know what they're doing and have our best interest at heart.

BE CAREFUL WHAT YOU SAY OUTSIDE THE CLASSROOM

Never, ever, ever write negatively about students, their families, (or, for that matter, your colleagues) and only do it rarely verbally.

We get it—sometimes we have to blow off steam—we're just human. But nothing good will ever come from putting anything negative on social media or even in writing in private text chats. When Larry was a community organizer, his advice was always, "Never put anything in writing that you are not comfortable seeing on the front page of the local newspaper."

When we are verbally venting to our spouse or to our closest friend, though, it's always important to try and remember the following mantra: "They're not bad students, they're good students who are having bad days (or weeks)."

Even when we have to write comments about a student for an office referral or for a counselor evaluation, we are like the old TV series *Dragnet:* "Just the facts." But we still try to include positive comments also, even in a disciplinary referral adding a note like, "He's really been working hard lately."

It's unlikely that students or their families will see or hear your comments, even if you ignore our advice. But odds are at least one will, and that may lead to an irreparable relationship. More importantly, we think it's a safe bet that teachers regularly talking negatively about their students will reinforce destructive beliefs, which will likely carry over to attitudes in the classroom.

[28] Lavitt, J., Coutifaris, C., & Green, P. (2025, April 25). Research: When leaders express positivity early on, employees perform better. *Harvard Business Review*.

ATTEND STUDENT EVENTS

We get it—staying after-school or returning to school in the evening to watch a student participating in an athletic event, awards ceremony or theater production can feel like *a lot* after a day of teaching.

Nevertheless, the collateral that a teacher can build in the "relationship bank" with students by taking this time is incalculable.

It can be challenging if you have 160 students in your classes—you obviously can't attend all their events. Truthfully, our goal is to go to five events a year—one every two months. With family and other commitments, we just can't fit in more.

But even just attending those few events makes a difference.

HAVE SUPPORTIVE "HARD" CONVERSATIONS

Part of our jobs, and part of any positive relationship, is having "hard" and candid conversations. Whether it's because we suspect a student might have used Artificial Intelligence to write their essay, or because they're way behind on their class work, or because they're being disruptive in class—no teacher has any shortage of these conversations on their everyday list.

When we approach these conversations, we always try to keep this question from education writer Marvin Marshall in mind: Will what I am about to do or say bring me closer or will it push me away farther from the person with whom I am communicating?[29]

In order to increase the odds of the conversation bringing us closer, we try to implement the process to have honest and kind conversations that has been developed by Dr. Taya Cohen and Dr. Emma Levine.[30] It has four key elements:

1. Be specific. Don't say, "You're always disruptive." Instead, say "Today you were disruptive when you poked Juan in the head."

2. Explain how that behavior affects the entire class. "When you did that, Juan reacted and the whole lesson had to stop for five minutes. I wasn't able to teach during that time, and students weren't able to learn."

3. Communicate respect for the student. "You're one of the sharpest students in the class, and I appreciate that you generally take your work seriously."

4. Develop a plan forward and necessary changes. "What can you do to make sure something like this doesn't happen again and what can I do to support you?"

---

[29] Ferlazzo, L. (2009, November 20). The best piece of classroom management advice I've ever read. *Larry Ferlazzo's Website of the Day*.

[30] Devlin, E., & Jenks, J. (2025, June 22). Gregg Popovich is a coaching legend. He's also a master of tough conversations. *The New York Times*.

This strategy has generally worked well in our conversations, but not always. In the **What Could Go Wrong?** section we share some ideas of how to handle things when they don't.

TRY YOUR BEST NOT TO HOLD GRUDGES

Some of our students can act in pretty annoying ways.

We teachers can also come across sometimes as pretty annoying, too. In fact, one year *The Washington Post* picked up a blog post Larry wrote summarizing one of his class's annual anonymous end-of-year evaluation. The headline? "NEWS BREAK (not breaking news): Teacher asks students to grade him. One wrote: 'I give Mr. Ferlazzo an A at being annoying.'"[31]

And, in fact, some of our students can sometimes act in cruel ways.

Our students are also kids.

As hard as it sometimes may be, we always try to greet students with a smile and say we're happy to see them, no matter what they might have said or done the previous day.

That doesn't mean we shouldn't "call them" on what they did and share how it made us feel.

But, as the saying goes, "You never know what someone is going through." We try to keep that in mind when interacting with our students and *try* to view each day as a new beginning.

TEACH ENGAGING LESSONS

Positive teacher-student relationships are very important to the life of a classroom.

But the primary "business" of school is learning, so teachers want to make sure their classes are challenging and engaging and that students want to be there (most of the time, at least).

Teaching good lessons also demonstrates to students that you are competent, are interested in them growing and learning, and, ideally, trying to connect at least some topics to their hopes and dreams. All of those will only deepen teacher-student relationships.

Other chapters in this book discuss lesson plans in detail. It's important for us to remember education researcher Robert Marzano's point that positive teacher-student relationships can make everything go better in the classroom. However, they won't turn a bad lesson plan into a good one. Or, as the saying goes, good teacher-student relationships won't let you put lipstick on a pig lesson plan.

[31] Strauss, V. (2019, January 18). NEWS BREAK (not breaking news): Teacher asks students to grade him. One wrote: 'I give Mr. Ferlazzo an A at being annoying.' *Answer Sheet.*

NOTICE WHEN STUDENTS ARE ABSENT

Noticing when students aren't there can be as important as interacting with them when they are present.

At the beginning of class, we quickly ask students who have the phone numbers of missing students and ask them to send a text telling them he misses them and hopes they are okay. Students jump at the chance to do it—both because they think it's fun and because they get a moment to check their phone for other things!

If no one has a student's number, we'll just email the missing student later in the day.

It makes a difference!

CONSIDER LOOPING

"Looping" is a strategy where students stay with the same teacher for longer than one year, and research clearly shows relationships and student learning benefits from it.[32]

It's sometimes used in elementary schools, though it does create a burden on the teacher to learn an entirely new curriculum.

At Larry's high school, which had Small Learning Communities where approximately 300 students would stay with the same twenty-or-so teachers during their four-year career, they did a variation of looping where often teachers would have the same students every other year. He can attest to how much this kind consistency contributed to a strong sense of relationships and community.

CREATE CONDITIONS FOR STUDENTS TO DEVELOP RELATIONSHIPS WITH THEIR CLASSMATES

Positive teacher-student relationships are critical to any successful classroom. But it will only take a class so far if students are not in positive relationships with each other!

Here are a few ways to encourage those connections and build a sense of belonging:

- Find something you have in common with another person can help students feel connected.[33] A "Human Scavenger Hunt" is a common activity teachers do at the beginning of the school year to get acquainted. Just search it online and you'll find many examples.

---

[32] Will, M. (2022, June 21). Looping: Here's what happens when students have the same teacher more than once. *Education Week*.

[33] Markman, A. (2012, March 8). It is motivating to belong to a group. *Psychology Today*.

- Have students work together in small groups of two-or-three on assignments. We assign partners at the beginning of the year so that everyone has a chance to work with everybody else and then give students more freedom to choose in the second half.

- In "Warm-Ups," we often will have a personal question ("What's the time you were happiest in your life?") along with an academic question or activity about what we're learning. Students can then share their responses in small groups.

- Provide periodic opportunities at the beginning or ending of class for students to share positive news in their lives.[34]

- Once a week or so, create a few minutes at the end of class for students to compliment a classmate for something they did or said. In this situation, as in most, the teacher obviously will want to model examples.

What Could Go Wrong

We think there are five primary challenges teachers may face in building positive relationships with students.

1. *Maintaining relationship-building as a priority.*
   In the midst of all the other things that vie for our attention, and making sure we actually connect to *each* of our students. One of the tools we used at the beginning of our teaching careers was a clipboard with the seating chart and putting a checkmark next to the name of each student we did something with to strengthen our relationship.

2. *Handling students who want to connect with you on social media.*
   Some districts have strict prohibitions against doing so, and we generally tell students we'll be happy to connect with them there *after* they graduate. Larry makes exceptions for his Newcomer English Language Learner students, who have tended to like to communicate on Facebook—always for school-related questions. We are both pretty liberal with giving our personal cellphone numbers to students and their families (though that practice is not necessarily one we would recommend for everybody) and, of course, it's easy to share messages on Google Classroom or Remind (or other similar apps). The main rule we have, however, is all personal communication through these avenues are either school-related or related to the student's well-being (if a student has been in an accident, lost a loved one, etc.).

[34] Barker, E. (1999, August). What's an easy way to strengthen your relationships? *Barking Up the Wrong Tree.*

3. *Knowing what to do when none of your attempts at building a positive relationship with a student are successful.*

Then what? We think a good framework of how to handle this can be found in a Harvard Business Review podcast titled "How to Repair a Broken Relationship at Work."[35] We've generally used these strategies before we read the article, but here are some things to keep in mind that relate to the classroom:

- First, think about what you like about the student or, at least, focus on what you want from the relationship. Remember the adage—the student isn't bad, they are just having a bad day or a series of them.

- Focus on empathy to ask yourself some questions about why the student is behaving that way—what do I not know, how could they be seeing things? How could they be seeing me and what I do in a negative way?

- Ask them questions, not just the surface level questions, but deeper ones— what gives them joy? Acknowledge things aren't great and that you want to change things. Focus on what you have in common—whether it's their passing the class or liking basketball.

- Give things to the student without overtly asking or expecting anything back—in effect, a gesture of goodwill. This can trigger reciprocation, where they feel they are obligated to return the favor or kindness. This could be giving the student extra time to complete an assignment, or if they're missing a lot of them, tell them you're giving them a break and not going to count several of them and they don't have to make it up, or offering to purchase a book of their choice for them. Larry buys small gifts when he's traveling internationally to specifically give them to students in this situation around holidays or their birthday.

In reflecting on both of our teaching careers, there has only been one student who we've had in class for the entire school year with whom we were not able to repair a relationship, and that was a student Larry had very early in his career. But fixing a broken relationship is not a linear experience—there are always many ups and downs along the way, and it takes a *lot* of energy.

Another strategy that can work in this situation is called "2 by 10." Though we haven't specifically used it, the strategy does make sense to us and research seems to back it up as a way to turn around a challenging teacher-student relationship.[36]

---

[35] Gallo, A. (2024, November 27). How to Repair a Broken Relationship at Work (No. 86). *HBR.* [Podcast].

[36] Kilkenny, P. (2008). Assuming the best. *Educational Leadership, 66*(1).

The strategy is simple in theory, though could be a bit challenging logistically. It's a matter of the teacher identifying a student with whom they have a challenging relationship and then have a two-minute conversation with them about anything for ten consecutive days.

It certainly can't hurt, as long as the conversation is not about the student's behavior or missing assignments. Using those times for inquiring about how their day went, complimenting them on their clothes or hair, asking what they like to do in their free time, etc., can only help.

Another option is to check with the student's other teachers to see if there is at least one who does have a good relationship with them. If that's the case, that teacher could possibly share "tips" on what has helped them develop a connection.

4. *Know when it's time to bring in more support.*
   If teachers have solid positive relationships with their students, it's likely students will share some of their personal struggles. Avoid being a "trauma detective," and know when you need to bring in counseling or administrator support.[37]

5. *Accept your colleagues may not be supportive of your efforts.*
   This challenge is probably not a huge one to you working with your students, but developing a school-wide emphasis on relationship building can only help everybody.

A study may point a way for how teachers can handle this issue. Basically, middle school math teachers spent a little more than an hour reading about research highlighting the value of thinking about—and listening to—students' perspectives and the importance of relationship-building, along with reading short essays by students sharing how individual teachers had made an impact on their lives. Then, teachers were asked to share ideas on how they now develop relationships with students and what they could do in the future.[38]

School suspensions substantially decreased after this professional development.

We can't see anything negative coming from a professional development session like this, and it certainly would be more valuable than what a lot of us have to deal with when it comes to district-dictated PD.

---

[37] Venet, A. S. (2023, October 9). Trauma-informed teachers need trauma-informed administrators. *Unconditional Learning.*

[38] Ferlazzo, L. (2022, April 8). Intriguing research suggests relatively simple exercise with teachers might reduce student suspensions. *Larry Ferlazzo's Website of the Day.*

Chapter Summary

If we only had a few minutes to chat in the teacher faculty room, here's what we'd want you to remember about relationships:

Technology Connections

We tend not to approach building positive teacher-student relationships methodically. With our years of experience, we generally just know when to use the different strategies discussed in this chapter.

However, we also recognize that this is not how everyone works and it took us a long time to get there.

If you feel that you'd be more comfortable with a more methodical approach to relationship-building—that still includes the use of many of the ideas discussed in this chapter, we'd encourage you to read more about the "Establish, Maintain, and Restore" approach.

There is substantial research demonstrating its success. You can read more at "The Best Resources For Learning About The 'Establish-Maintain-Restore' Classroom Management Approach" (https://larryferlazzo.edublogs.org/2022/08/01/the-best-resources-for-learning-about-the-establish-maintain-restore-classroom-management-approach/).

Learn more about relationship building in general at:

- *The Best Resources On The Importance Of Building Positive Relationships With Students* https://larryferlazzo.edublogs.org/2011/03/08/the-best-resources-on-the-importance-of-building-positive-relationships-with-students/
- *The Best Resources Exploring The Use Of Praise In The Classroom* https://larryferlazzo.edublogs.org/2022/04/15/the-best-resources-exploring-the-use-of-praise-in-the-classroom/
- *6 Teacher-Tested Tips for Getting Students' Names Right* https://www.edweek.org/leadership/6-teacher-tested-tips-for-getting-students-names-right/2023/07

CHAPTER 2

Student Agency, NOT Student Empowerment

What Is It?

We believe that helping students develop "agency," which is often defined as the ability to be *proactive* in responding to your circumstances, is an important part of classroom—and life—success. It's about creating opportunities for students to develop self-confidence and skills that allow them to shape their lives—in the present and in the future. We want students to feel—and actually be—orchestrators of their lives, or at least as much as they can be. We don't want them to feel powerless in the face of what might be happening to and around them.

Students with agency tend to demonstrate it through confidence in their ability to achieve goals (self-efficacy), perseverance, exhibition of curiosity, metacognitive skills, motivation, and self-control.[1]

These descriptions of student agency are, more-or-less, what you'll typically hear in the education world. Unfortunately, some miss what we consider another key component—recognizing that there can be forces actively opposing their agency (racism, sexism, ageism, ableism, economic inequity, etc.) and the need for us educators to prepare students with the tools of public life to fight back against them. We do not feel like we are doing our jobs as educators if when teaching

---

[1] Zeiser, K., Scholz, C., & Cirks, V. (2018). *Maximizing Student Agency: Implementing and Measuring Student-Centered Learning Practices*. American Institute for Research. Page 6.; Brandt, W. C. (2024). *Measuring Student Success Skills: A Review of the Literature on Student Agency*. National Center for the Improvement of Educational Assessment.

students about a growth mindset, for example, we don't also prepare them how to act in a world where some in power have a fixed mindset and feel life is a zero-sum game. In other words, students may not have control over all aspects of the world they inhabit—no matter how much self-confidence, curiosity, and perseverance they demonstrate. However, they can control how they respond to life's challenges, and we can help them increase the odds of their being successful in doing so.

We should also point out that some like to use the word "empowerment" in the context of student agency. We dislike that word—no one really "gives" anyone power. Instead, we can help create the conditions where they *take it* and support them as they do so.

A nationally representative poll released by the Brookings Institution of 65,000 students in 2025 found that only 33% of 10th graders reported "they get to develop their own ideas" in school. 29% said "they get to learn things they are interested in."[2] Maybe those statistics indicate we teachers should consider creating the conditions for student agency a higher priority?

The word "agency" comes from the Latin *agentia* which means "effective, powerful" and "agere," meaning "to set in motion, drive forward."[3] This chapter will share many different ways we can help our students be effective, powerful, and forward moving.

Why We Like It

We think supporting student agency is important for several reasons.

One, it makes teaching more interesting to us! How many educators really aspire to act like a "sage on stage" and operate what educator Paulo Freire described as the "banking model" of schooling where students just wait patiently for teachers to "deposit" information into them?[4] Classrooms can be so much more alive when students view themselves as co-creators of their learning.

Two, as the supporting research section—and our own experience—shows, students learn more as they develop agency. They, like most of us, are practitioners of the IKEA Effect—we tend to value something more if we help create it.[5]

[2] Rebecca Winthrop, Youssef Shoukry, & David Nitkin. (2025). The disengagement gap: Why student engagement isn't what parents expect. *Brookings.*

[3] Agency. (n.d.). *Etymonline.*

[4] Banking Model of Education. (n.d.). *Wikipedia.*

[5] Norton, M. I., Mochon, D., & Ariely, D. (2012). The IKEA effect: When labor leads to love. *Journal of Consumer Psychology, 22*(3), 453–460. https://doi.org/10.1016/j.jcps.2011.08.002

Third, while Choice Theory is imperfect—as are most theories about human behavior—power is a basic need for many of our students, and its lack of fulfillment can be the source of many classroom management challenges.[6]

It's been our experience that if we don't create constructive avenues for them to feel and exert their power through student agency, many may choose to demonstrate it in inappropriate ways.

Finally, more opportunities for everyone in the entire school can result from increased student agency.

We have seen many examples in our teaching careers of students, after being in our classes for a while, deciding to start extracurricular clubs, including a debate club for Afghan girls, organizing to create a community garden and a program to provide computers and Internet access to low-income families, and bringing in attorneys to have immigration law clinics for their families. Not to mention the *many* times students have made suggestions that have made our lessons better ones!

What's *not* to like about student agency?

Another lesson Larry learned as a community organizer that he carried into the classroom is the concept that power is not a finite pie; if students gain some power, it doesn't necessarily mean that teachers will have less. The more power is distributed, the bigger the entire pie becomes, *and students may take actions that no one has thought of previously as they develop their sense of agency.*

Supporting Research

Student agency, sometimes referred to as agentic engagement when specifically referring to actions in the classroom, has been found by researchers to have many benefits.

The greater the sense of student agency, the more likely they are in class to demonstrate curiosity, offer suggestions, volunteer, and succeed in achieving their learning goals.[7] In addition, they tend to have higher grades, better relationships with their peers, and, an outcome not to be underestimated, are happier than those students who don't feel a sense of agency.[8]

Students who feel greater agency have also been found to better *transfer* what they learn in the K-12 classroom to their college experience and professional lives.[9]

---

[6] Elvin, G. & Lionel, M. (2011). Choice theory: An effective approach to classroom discipline and management. *Journal of Adventist Education, 73*, 21.

[7] Reeve, J., Jang, H.-R., Shin, S. H., Ahn, J. S., Matos, L., & Gargurevich, R. (2022). When students show some initiative: Two experiments on the benefits of greater agentic engagement. *Learning and Instruction, 80*, 2. https://doi.org/10.1016/j.learninstruc.2021.101564.

[8] Anderson, J. & Winthrop, R. (2025, January 2). Giving kids some autonomy has surprising results. *The New York Times.*

[9] Zeiser, et al. (2018).

The vast majority of recommendations we share in the Application section are ones that are included in the studies we've referenced here, though a few are ones that we've discovered (and that Larry has adapted from his organizing career) that clearly support student agency.

Application

We discussed some of these strategies in our previous book, *Navigating the Common Core with English Language Learners*, 2016.

GOAL-SETTING

Having students set their own goals is not an uncommon activity in many classes. However, many educators—including us—have spent more time having students focus on "performance" or "outcome" goals ("Get an A in class"; "Become a video-game designer") and less on what research has found to be far more effective for leading to achievement—prioritizing "process" goals ("read for twenty minutes each day"; "each week analyze the strengths and weaknesses of one video game").[10]

Yes, it's important for students to identify their ultimate goals. They have some control over them, but there are also a number of external factors at play that they may not be able to control. On the other hand, they have complete control over their process goals.

Students identifying process goals and regularly evaluating their progress on achieving them is one way for them to reinforce their sense of agency, as well as for working towards their performance and outcome goals. Those latter goals may be far into the future, while their process goals are here and now.

This does not mean we want to discourage students from imagining their future selves. There is great value to having students see themselves in the near and far future.[11] Rather, it's a question of priority and emphasis—what can they do now, next week, and regularly to help them get there?

Our outcome goal was to create this book. But that aspirational goal would have been useless and de-motivating without a process goal of finishing a chapter every two weeks. The same holds true with our students.

Links in the Technology Connections section will lead you to many different kinds of goal sheets that we and other teachers have used over the years. Again, focus

---

[10] Williamson, O., Swann, C., Bennett, K. J. M., et al. (2024). The performance and psychological effects of goal setting in sport: A systematic review and meta-analysis. *International Review of Sport and Exercise Psychology, 17*(2), 1050–1078. https://doi.org/10.1080/1750984X.2022.2116723

[11] Ellison, K. (2025, January 5). What connecting to your future self can mean to your present. *The Washington Post.*

on process, and create regular opportunities for self-and-group reflection—and readjustment. No goal is immutable.

TURNING OPERATIONS INTO OPPORTUNITIES

Another skill from community organizing that transfers to the classroom is holding discussions with the goal of "turning operations into opportunities" as a tool for leadership development. In other words, organizers often considered the different work tasks they were doing that might be considered more routine, like calling leaders to remind them of events, preparing newsletters, doing research, etc. Then, they thought about volunteers who they were working with who might have leadership potential and approached them to see if they would like to take over these "operations" and turn them into "opportunities." These transitions would then function as unofficial leadership tests to see if they could then move up to additional responsibilities.

We teachers have numerous operations that we can turn into opportunities for our students, including taking attendance if allowed, organizing potlucks, categorizing classroom libraries, etc. When Larry's Theory of Knowledge classes have weekly mentors for ninth-graders, each period has a "Lead Mentor" for coordination. When we have peer tutors assisting students, we have "Lead Peer Tutors."

These "opportunities" are not just a matter of dumping tasks onto students. They are important jobs where students are given some latitude for deciding exactly how they are done, after initial guidance is provided by us. And we invite them to offer ideas on how the tasks can be restructured or improved.

PEER TUTORING AND MENTORING

Students teaching their classmates or younger students is an activity that has been key to our teaching.

One way we've done this is in our English Language Learner classes where older students receive credit for working each day as peer tutors assisting new immigrants in their academic classes. Extensive research, and our own experience, documents how this kind of tutoring helps both the tutor and the person being tutored.[12]

But peer tutoring doesn't have to be that formalized. If students complete their work early in our class, we often give them a choice—they can read, do extra credit, or help another student who is still working on the assignment. Nine times out of ten, students will choose to work as a tutor, and we emphasize that if they want to

---

[12] Ferlazzo, L. (2023, February 4). The best resources on peer tutors. *Larry Ferlazzo's Website of the Day*.

be able to continue being a tutor, they can't just hang out with their buddy—they need to help someone who needs it. We monitor as best we can while circulating throughout the room, and have found that, at most, a very occasional reminder might be needed.

Another version of peer tutoring is when an English Language Learner is in a class primarily composed of English-proficient students, a teacher might pair them with a classmate, sometimes referred to as a "buddy," who might or might not speak the ELL student's primary language. This combination, only done with the permission of both parties, can help everybody.

Yet another kind of peer tutoring is a variation of the Dialogue Journal idea. Traditionally, dialogue journals are used as back-and-forth conversations between students and teachers. In English Language Learner classes, they're often used for student writing practice. Instead of the teacher explicitly correcting the student's incorrect grammar or spelling, they "recast" their mistakes. For example, if an ELL student writes, "We go to San Francisco last week," the teacher might write, "It sounds exciting that you went to San Francisco last week" in their reply. The idea of direct corrections might make students feel more intimidated by the prospect of writing.

The peer tutoring part of this comes into play when, instead of having the dialogue journals between ELL students and us, they are between them and another class of English-proficient students or more advanced ELLs. Then it's the responsibility of those "sibling classes" to engage in dialogues and recasts with the ELL students. Believe us, our ELL students tend to be much more motivated to write to an authentic audience of another student instead of us. And, once again, the students in the sibling class get grammar practice, too!

Of course, in all of these situations, we provide training and guidance to students about tutoring expectations, including the difference between giving the answers and guiding their "tutees" to finding them on their own with assistance, the importance of positive affirmation over harsh critique, and technology-assisted and non-tech assisted strategies for communicating across languages. Demonstrating good examples *and* bad examples are very effective forms of training. In one situation, Larry used the good example of saying "How can we do this better?" and the bad example of saying, "You did this wrong." It worked well for our students, but remember what we discussed in Chapter 1 and use examples that work with the relationship you have with your students.

Peer *mentoring*, though somewhat similar to peer *tutoring*, is a different kettle of fish. In peer mentoring, older students are paired with younger ones to provide regular emotional support. For example, as mentioned earlier, Larry's IB Theory of Knowledge classes would go to a different ninth-grade class once a week and walk around the school with them for ten minutes. Mentors received training on providing support, and each week asked their mentees about their highs and lows from the previous seven days (and was there anything they could have done to make their low a little better). In addition, they were given a focus question each time, like "What is your goal for the next month?" and "What is your biggest worry right now?"

We also encourage students to do a home-based version of this kind of tutoring/ mentoring. We offer extra credit to students who sit with younger siblings or cousins and read story books to them. They just have to write down the name of the book or story they read, how long it took, and how their sibling/cousin reacted to them. As with practically everything we do, we first provide an example of how to read to a child.

Links in the Technology Connections section will lead you to lots of practical materials about both peer tutors and peer mentors.

TEACHING OTHERS

This "teaching others" strategy is different from the one-on-one or one-on-two peer tutoring and peer mentoring discussed in the previous section.

In this context, "teaching others" means organized activities where the entire class is, in some way or form, teaching everybody else.

In effect, everybody is a teacher.

This could take several forms.

One is the use of the well-known jigsaw technique. In this strategy, which education researcher John Hattie offers as one the most effective available to teachers, an individual student or a small group is tasked with teaching smaller parts of a bigger concept or story (different parts of a historical figure's biography, separate sections of a larger article, certain elements of a scientific concept) to their classmates, either in small groups or to the entire class.[13]

Another is structured peer review. Research has shown that peer review tends to be very effective for enhancing student learning.[14] We've used it primarily in student writing, with classmates providing structured (and supportive!) feedback, and when practicing for presentations. Here, as in most of our class activities, we often provide a written guide and share in writing and verbally both helpful and not-so-helpful peer feedback.

And a third version is having individual students or small groups instruct the entire class. In this activity, usually done near the end of the school year, we let small

---

[13] Ferlazzo, L. (2017, June 15). This is interesting: Hattie says jigsaw strategy hits a homerun. *Larry Ferlazzo's Website of the Day*.

[14] Double, K. S., McGrane, J. A., & Hopfenbeck, T. N. (2020). The impact of peer assessment on academic performance: A meta-analysis of control group studies. *Educational Psychology Review, 32*(2), 481–509. https://doi.org/10.1007/s10648-019-09510-3

student groups choose any topic within reason and they have to develop an instructional unit utilizing the primary teaching strategies we've used during the school year (inductive teaching [see Chapter 3: Differentiated Teaching], Read Alouds, games for reinforcement, etc.). Though they have to create a full unit, they usually just actually teach one lesson because of time constraints.

Most teachers are familiar with the "Gradual Release of Responsibility" model—I do, We do, You do. We think that, when logistically possible, the more educators can add a fourth step, "Teach It," the better for everyone.

Links in the Technology Connections section will lead you to more detailed practical tips on how to implement all these strategies.

STOP JUST TELLING STUDENTS WHAT TO DO

A recent study found that students will be more likely to use retrieval practice (pushing yourself to remember something that is not in front of you) as a study strategy if you explain to them the reasoning behind it and why it works.[15]

We'll be covering the use of retrieval practice later in this book, but that is not why we're bringing it up here.

Really, the far more important point this study makes is that our students, like us, are more likely to do something if we're shown it's in our self-interest to do so OR, even if it's not in our direct self-interest, we're more likely to do it if someone has taken the time to respect us by explaining a logical reason for their request.

Whether it's related to getting students to use retrieval practice, or getting English-language-learner students to reduce their use of Google Translate when writing, or encouraging students to choose to work in more diverse small groups, our students deserve these explanations—even if it might be more time-consuming than just telling them what to do.[16]

SELF-TALK

One of Larry's toddler granddaughters, when initially facing difficulty accomplishing a task, likes to say out loud, "I can do it," which is a phrase she learned from the popular preschool show hosted by Ms. Rachel.

Some research suggests that it might be more effective and create less anxiety by referring to ourselves as "You" or our name instead of "I," but that's always seemed

---

[15] Fan, T., Hui, L., Luo, L., & De Bruin, A. B. H. (2024). Improving the use of retrieval practice for both easy and difficult materials: The effect of an instructional intervention. *Educational Psychology Review, 36*(4), 115. https://doi.org/10.1007/s10648-024-09945-3

[16] Phillips. K. W. (2025, March 31). How diversity makes us smarter. *Scientific American.*

a bit odd to us, so we don't necessarily highlight that part when teaching about positive self-talk.[17]

We do, however, emphasize that any way students want to do it, self-talk can work and is entirely in their control. There are plenty of videos of successful celebrities demonstrating how they use it, and showing one or two of them helps move adolescents off the idea that it might be a strange thing to do.

Inviting students to publicly share moments when they've either used positive self-talk or when they could see themselves use it in the future is a good way to help introduce the idea. And, again, teachers can model their own usage, which, for example, Larry does a lot when playing basketball and pickleball. We emphasize that using it does not always mean we'll be successful (and Larry's basketball and pickleball track record clearly demonstrates this reality). But we also emphasize that research finds that it does, indeed, increase the odds of success.[18]

STUDENT LEADERSHIP TEAMS

In some of our classes, we organize "Student Leadership Teams." We first invite a small handful of students who have shown some leadership potential (see the earlier section on "Turning Operations into Opportunities") and ask them if they'd like to meet with us monthly to review how the class is going and discuss if any changes should be made. We also explain that additional responsibilities would include taking the lead when they are in small groups to ensure that everyone is participating and basically acting as co-teachers.

After a month or two, we then make an open invitation to anyone in the class who would like to join the team, after explaining its purpose and responsibilities.

We've generally found that students on the teams take it very seriously, including ones who we might have not ordinarily expected to "step up." But it's an example of the old community organizing adage, "If you don't give people the opportunity to say no, you also don't give them the opportunity to say yes."

METACOGNITIVE REFLECTION

The common teacher definition of metacognition is "thinking about your thinking," and there are many different strategies for teaching about it in the classroom. In fact, the Technology Connections section has a link that will lead you to many of them.

[17] Wong, K. (2017, June 8). The benefits of talking to yourself. *The New York Times*.

[18] Haas, S. (2016, June 30). Thinking "I can do better" really can improve performance, study finds. *Science Daily*.

When students have done good work, we ask them to reflect on why it was so good and what they did to make it happen.

When students aren't as successful, we ask them to reflect on why they think that was the case, what they did, and what they could have done differently.

For us, though, we just try to keep it short and simple. In fact, we often don't even use the word "metacognition."

We explain how we apply these questions regularly to our own practice, and give concrete examples of how we've been able to use this kind of reflection to be better teachers, parents, pickleball players, etc.

And, though we generally take the lead and ask students to write and share their answers to these questions, we invite students to take the initiative to apply them outside of our class, too. Quite a few have told us that they have done just that.

TEACHING STUDENTS WHAT LEARNING CAN PHYSICALLY DO TO THEIR BRAINS

Helping students see that the effort of their learning results in actual physical change of their brain is another way for students to see that they do have control of their lives.

You can find links to short lessons and videos we do on this in the Technology Connections section or just search "How does learning something new physically change the brain?" online (you could also add on to the search "lesson plan.") Many accessible resources are available, including videos showing how the brain creates neural connections when learning something new.[19] Learning about this "neuroplasticity" can have a powerful impact on some students.

PROVIDING STUDENTS CHOICE

Providing students choice whenever possible increases agency, engagement, and motivation.

These could be "procedural" choices like if they can complete an assignment on a laptop or with pen and paper. (Remember to check in with students to take stock of which approach is actually better for their learning!) Organizational choices might be where to sit or with whom students want to work in small groups. Cognitive choices are another option, which might be choosing which topics to explore in a project-based learning assignment or developing their own ideas for homework

---

[19] Bleakman, E. & Okereke, M. (2024, October 16). *Brain growth: Neuroplasticity in the classroom*. USA Science Festival. https://usasciencefestival.org/video/brain-growth-neuroplasticity-in-the-classroom/

assignments. All are good strategies, though researchers have found cognitive choice to be more effective in promoting longer-lasting student autonomy and agency.[20]

We'll talk more about this topic in Chapter 6: Emphasizing Students' Assets, Not Deficits where students can motivate themselves.

DEMOCRATIC CITIZENSHIP

Horace Mann, one of the country's earliest advocates for public education, felt that schooling was critical to active citizenship and democratic participation.[21] Creating the conditions for student agency to grow supports that vision, and students don't have to wait until after graduation to make democratic citizenship a reality. There are many ways to connect agency, motivation, student interests, and community needs to academic standards and growth—and it's very possible to do so in a non-partisan way.

"Problem-Based Learning" is one instructional strategy to make that happen. In it, students identify a community- or school-based problem that they would like to solve, or where they can at least have some degree of positive impact.

In our process of implementing this process, we often begin with students doing interviews of their classmates, family members, and neighborhood residents to identify areas of concern after we've done a practice one in class. However, sometimes we forgo this step if it's immediately clear that there is already a priority issue present. As an example, when there were increased immigration raids and students and their families wanted to learn more about their rights, or when we learned our school's neighborhood had the lowest rate of returning US Census surveys and was in danger of losing federal funds.

Next, the class reviews the issue or issues of concern, and explore if any fit the criteria that Larry used when he was a community organizer: Is it specific (or can it be broken down into something specific)? Is it winnable in a reasonable amount of time? For example, stopping immigration raids were not "winnable," but organizing a forum to answer questions about immigrant rights was. If it can't fit that criteria, then it's often a problem that is too large for the class to organize around.

After we narrow things down, students begin to do research on possible solutions and then decide on which one to pursue.

In light of immigration raids, our students organized a community forum with immigration attorneys to answer questions. When it came to the US Census,

---

[20] Stefanou, C. R., Perencevich, K. C., DiCintio, M., & Turner, J. C. (2004). Supporting autonomy in the classroom: ways teachers encourage student decision making and ownership. *Educational Psychologist, 39*(2), 97–110. https://doi.org/10.1207/s15326985ep3902_2

[21] PBS. (n.d.). *Horace Mann* (1796–1859). Only A Teacher: Schoolhouse Pioneers.

students created multilingual information sheets on the importance of completing the surveys and distributed them throughout the neighborhood. When students identified the lack of halal food in the school cafeteria, they organized meetings with food service staff.

All these efforts were easily able to be connected to multiple reading, writing, listening, and speaking academic standards.

Of course, these kinds of activities take time and effort, and there are many valid reasons why teachers might just not have both available.

In those cases, though, there are less intensive ways to support students developing democratic citizenship skills.

One way is to just have students write a letter to the editor of their local paper about an issue of personal concern, or create a related podcast, or TikTok video. In fact, *The New York Times*' The Learning Network has resources, and even contests, for some of those kinds of activities as does NPR through their student podcast contest.

And just plain volunteering should not be forgotten. Volunteering to help many nonprofits may not make huge societal-changing waves, but it does support Civil Society, which in turn supports our democracy. Teachers can help ensure these volunteer efforts connect to the broader idea of democratic citizenship by having students research the role of Civil Society in a democracy today and in the past while they're volunteering with a nonprofit of their choice. Gaining a better understanding of the role of mutual aid in our communities can be a key source of knowledge for them and their families.

These kinds of activities can help provide students with the skills they need to navigate their lives if and when elements of society are not supportive of their agency and, in some cases, actively oppose it.

ACTIONABLE FEEDBACK

We are not talking about the "You're so smart! And such a great writer!" kind of feedback.

As Carol Dweck has documented in her work on a growth mindset, which we'll be discussing at length in other chapters, it's important to provide encouragement that supports the idea that "the harder they work, the smarter they get." That kind of feedback ("This is a great conclusion to your essay—look what happens when you take the time to revise!") supports looking at problems as obstacles to be overcome instead of having a fixed mindset, which views your present situation as destiny and does not prepare you well for coping when things don't go your way.

When it comes to providing critical feedback, we have four guidelines to ensure that it's heard and that it supports student agency:

1. We narrow it down to one-or-two key points, ones that could have a broader and more significant impact (in other words, getting a "bigger bang for our buck").

2. We try to connect our critical feedback to where the student did it successfully elsewhere or earlier ("In this earlier paragraph you did an excellent job of providing supporting details—you just need to do the same here") or, if that's not possible, provide a concrete example from elsewhere to show the student and that they can take with them.

3. Do it verbally—most will not pay attention to your written feedback.[22]

4. Work hard at creating a class culture where feedback is not viewed as an example of failure but, instead, is seen more as a gift.[23]

ENHANCED DISCOVERY LEARNING

This strategy, which we would define as the inductive method discussed in Chapter 7: Strategies for Maximizing Learning, promotes agency by having students construct more of their own understanding instead of giving it to them. A meta-analysis favorably reviewed by education researcher Robert Marzano found that a guided and scaffolded discovery process—which may very well include *some* direct instruction—is superior to lessons primarily relying on either direct instruction or "unassisted discovery" (in other words, lessons with little or no teacher guidance).[24]

HELPING STUDENTS ACCESS PRIOR KNOWLEDGE

One of our guiding principles for teaching is looking at students through the lens of their assets instead of their deficits—they are not blank slates when entering our classrooms.

[22] Meyer, J., Jansen, T., & Fleckenstein, J. (2025). Nonengagement and unsuccessful engagement with feedback in lower secondary education: The role of student characteristics. *Contemporary Educational Psychology, 81.* https://doi.org/10.1016/j.cedpsych.2025.102363

[23] Sparks, S. D. (2023, April 16). Here's how to give feedback that students will actually use. *Education Week.*

[24] Ferlazzo, L. (2011, August 30). Is this the most important research study of the year? Maybe. *Larry Ferlazzo's Website of the Day.*

They bring a great deal of knowledge and experience with them and, in addition to taking advantage of the fact that we tend to more easily learn something new if we can connect it in some way to something we already know, it's important to acknowledge and validate the assets that they bring to the table, so to speak. In addition, it's important for our teaching to learn what they know about particular topics before we teach them.[25,26]

KWL charts are one of our favorite tools for accessing and activating student prior knowledge. Having students write down what they KNOW, then what they WANT to know about, and then to keep track of what they LEARN during our lessons check all those important boxes. Students can periodically share their charts with classmates and with us.

ASSIST STUDENTS TO SEE FOR THEMSELVES HOW MUCH THEY ARE LEARNING

Being successful motivates and increases self-confidence, which is a key element of agency.

Teachers can obviously provide lots of feedback to enhance those feelings of success, but isn't it better, and more reinforcing of agency, if students identify their progress for themselves? Creating opportunities for these "temporal comparisons," where students compare themselves to their past selves instead of to others, can help solidify positive self-concepts they have of themselves.[27]

We can create those kinds of conditions in several ways, including:

- Providing students a list of vocabulary words and/or concepts prior to beginning a unit and asking them to put a checkmark next to the ones they already know. Then, after the unit is done, ask them to do the same. There should be many more checks the second time.

- Have students record themselves reading a passage at the beginning of the school year and then have them record the same passage each quarter so they can see improvement in their reading fluency and prosody.

[25] Center for Advancing Teaching and Learning Through Research. (n.d.) Use students' prior knowledge to build motivation new learning from prior experience. Northeastern. https://learning.northeastern.edu/using-students-prior-knowledge-and-experience-to-enhance-motivation/

[26] Rea, S. (2015, August 13). *New Information Is Easier to Learn When Composed of Familiar Elements*. Carnegie Mellon University.

[27] Wolff, F., Petrak, A., Dicke, T., & Möller, J. (2025). Temporal comparison effects on students' academic self-concepts: An investigation of different comparison periods in the 2I/E model with weighted achievement levels. *Journal of Educational Psychology, 117*(2), 273–291. https://doi.org/10.1037/edu0000894

- Ask students to keep their essays or other writing assignments from throughout the year and then have them revise one-or-two of them in May or June so they can see how their writing has improved.

WAIT TIME

Playing games of classroom gotcha do not facilitate student agency. Setting up students for success, on the other hand, do.

The typical wait time between a teacher's question and their calling on a student to respond is between 0.7 to 1.4 seconds. This is a gotcha environment.[28]

Increasing that time to three seconds can result in better quality and longer student answers.

We typically preface our questions by saying something like "I'm going to ask a question. Please do not shout out the answer. Instead, I'm going to give you a few seconds to think about it and then call on someone to answer." Or, instead of calling on someone to answer, we'll move it into a Think-Pair-Share exercise.

We tend to not ask *lots* of questions. Instead, we prefer fewer ones leading to more thoughtful responses. Consider documenting how often you ask questions and what kinds of questions you ask. You might even want to ask a student to help you keep track of your wait time.

REINFORCE THE DIFFERENCE BETWEEN OPINION AND JUDGMENT

In supporting student agency, we also want to reinforce the idea that though they have power within themselves, they don't necessarily have all the answers, and that agency is enhanced when exercised in community with others.

This can be framed as demonstrating curiosity rather than judgment or, as we again harken back to Larry's community organizing career, it is better to describe it as the difference between opinion and judgment.

Opinion is what you think before asking questions about the topic at hand and talking with others.

Judgment is what you have, and what you show, after asking questions and talking with others.

There are several ways we communicate this difference with students, including when using Write-Pair-Share, always encouraging them to modify their original written responses afterward with new ideas they heard from others; encouraging students to write down an opinion they have about a topic before we begin studying it and then afterwards write about whether their opinion has changed; having them

[28] Busch, B. (n.d.). Boosting participation: Wait times and question types. *InnerDrive*.

share about opinions they've had in the past and changed (preceded by us doing the same) and learning about historical figures who publicly changed their minds about important topics and what influenced them to do so.

USING REACTANCE

Professors David Yeagar and Christopher Bryan developed and studied the concept of reactance. Reactance describes how most of us and, in the case of this book, particularly adolescents, react negatively when we feel others are trying to manipulate us unfairly for their gain.[29]

So, instead of prioritizing teaching students about the unhealthy impacts of eating junk food, or smoking cigarettes, or the dangers of sports betting; instead, emphasize the strategies corporations are using to make them want to eat that junk food or make that bet.

It doesn't mean you have to be silent about those other negative aspects of the behavior, but researchers have found that highlighting this kind of corporate manipulation is much more effective in altering teen behavior.[30]

We've used this strategy in classroom management as well. Sometimes, when one student is regularly provoked by another, we'll explain to them that the other student knows how to get a reaction. "Why do you want him to control you?" is a question we'll ask that is often quite effective.

Understanding and gaining control of reactance can be just one more way students can build a sense of agency.

What Could Go Wrong

With so many ideas on how to cultivate student agency, we could see how some teachers might feel overwhelmed by them all.

Don't be.

If you feel that way, try one idea a month—try it on, see how you and your students feel about it. If it works well, continue doing it. If not, *fuhgeddaboutit* and try another one.

A teacher can be fully committed to student agency and still not use all or most of the strategies we recommend. Our checklist is not the be all/end all on agency.

---

[29] Milkman, K. (2025, May 27). What is reactance and how can it be harnessed for good? *Milkman Delivers*.

[30] Milkman, K. (2024, October 7). Rebel with a cause: With guests Francis Kelly & Christopher Bryan (No. S14:EP5). *Choiceology*. [Podcast].

Another challenge could be that your colleagues might not be as supportive of student agency as you. As in most of the strategies discussed in this book, this lack of support shouldn't substantially impact your application of them in your own classroom, but having them be more widespread would only help everybody.

One simple way to begin the discussion of student agency at your school would be to have colleagues read one of the short pieces on the topic you can access through links in the Technology Connections section and then follow it with a discussion focused on these kinds of questions:

- Where do you have agency in your own life?

- Where might students have agency, if they have it at all, in their lives?

- What might be examples of fake student agency (where it just looks like they have power) and genuine student agency (when they have genuine power)?

Chapter Summary

If we only had a few minutes to chat in the teacher faculty room, here's what we'd want you to remember about student agency:

Technology Connections

You can find many different lesson plans and student hand-outs to help with goal-setting at *The Best Posts On Students Setting Goals* https://larryferlazzo.edublogs .org/2010/05/18/my-best-posts-on-students-setting-goals/.

For more ideas on peer tutoring and peer mentoring, visit *The Best Posts On Helping Students Teach Their Classmates—Help Me Find More* https://larryferlazzo.edublogs .org/2012/04/22/the-best-posts-on-helping-students-teach-their-classmates-help-me-find-more/; *The Best Resources On Peer Tutors* https://larryferlazzo.edublogs .org/2023/02/04/the-best-resources-on-peer-tutors/ and *The Best Resources On The Value & Practice Of Having Older Students Mentoring Younger Ones* https://larryferlazzo .edublogs.org/2013/02/03/the-best-resources-on-the-value-practice-of-having-older-students-mentoring-younger-ones/.

Resources on teaching students the value of self-talk can be found at *The Best Resources On The Value Of Positive "Self-Talk"* https://larryferlazzo.edublogs.org/ 2016/06/30/another-study-finds-that-self-talk-works/.

For lesson ideas on how to teach students about the brain, visit *The Best Resources For Showing Students That They Make Their Brain Stronger By Learning* https://larryfer lazzo.edublogs.org/2011/11/26/the-best-resources-for-showing-students-that-they-make-their-brain-stronger-by-learning/.

And for more ideas on how to reinforce student agency, visit *The Best Resources On Student Agency & How To Encourage It* https://larryferlazzo.edublogs.org/2016/03/06/ the-best-resources-on-student-agency-how-to-encourage-it/.

CHAPTER 3

Differentiated Instruction

What Is It?

"Differentiated instruction" can be a loaded term in the world of education.

To critics, it can mean that teachers are expected to create separate lesson plans for each student in the class and implement them in the moment. Some of the same critics suggest that it can mean a "dumbing" down of the curriculum and standards for many students and that the most capable students are particularly disadvantaged by it.[1]

Personally, we think those objections are generally red herrings in most situations, not at all reflecting how differentiation plays out in the vast majority of classrooms.

We believe, like Carol Ann Tomlinson, one of the foremost thinkers on this topic, that differentiated instruction means that teachers plan for their learners that have the greatest mastery on the curriculum and develop scaffolds so that others can access those same learning opportunities.[2] We think how Aida Walqui and George C. Bunch framed it in the context of teaching English Language Learners applies to everyone: *Amplify, don't simplify*.[3]

Differentiating instruction doesn't mean teachers can't have ways, such as peer tutoring from the previous chapter, engaging and related extra credit projects, for those more advanced students to extend their learning further in their back pocket.

---

[1] Delisle, J. R. (2015, January 6). Differentiation doesn't work. *Education Week*.

[2] Tomlinson, C. A. (2015, January 28). Differentiation does, in fact, work. *Education Week*.

[3] Seger, W. (n.d.). Embracing the Science of Reading and Multilingual Education: The call for a comprehensive approach. *How Amplifying the Curriculum Supports Multilingual Learners*.

As teachers committed to differentiated instruction, we recognize students have different strengths and levels of skills proficiency and background knowledge. The label of "advanced" fluctuates weekly, if not daily.

Obviously, this idea of "teaching up," as Tomlinson puts it, for everyone has some exceptions, primarily for students receiving special education services and whose Individualized Education Program (IEP) calls for content modifications.[4] However, even in those circumstances, teachers might be surprised at how much content can be made accessible to those students if we look at them through the lens of assets and not deficits (see Chapter 6: Emphasizing Students' Assets, Not Deficits).

The "how" of differentiation has traditionally been organized into:

- content
- process
- products
- learning environment.[5]

We'll use these categories to organize the Application section and get more in-depth there.

But first, we'll be sharing lots of practical ideas on how to implement differentiation. We do want to emphasize, though, that we believe it's ultimately more of a *way of thinking* than a grab bag of instructional strategies. It's about, as the old Civil Rights anthem goes, keeping our eyes on the prize—in our case, always remembering what are the key skills or knowledge we want *all* students to learn and always being ready and willing to demonstrate flexibility, compassion, and creativity to maximize the odds of that happening.

Some researchers have identified two approaches to differentiation—"designed" and "interactional."[6] "Designed differentiation" is when teachers proactively plan various strategies in advance, while "interactional differentiation" is when teachers act in the moment.

We have found in our teaching that, more often than not, differentiation of the second kind—resulting in requiring more *thinking* in the moment (but not necessarily more *work* for us)—has made differentiation successful for our students and for us.

[4] Tomlinson, C. A. (2024, October). Making the choice to teach up. *Educational Leadership, 82*(2).

[5] Tomlinson, C. A. (n.d.). What is differentiated instruction? *Reading Rockets: Differentiated Instruction.*

[6] Puzio, K., Colby, G. T., & Algeo-Nichols, D. (2020). Differentiated literacy instruction: Boondoggle or best practice? *Review of Educational Research, 90*(4), 459–498. https://doi.org/10.3102/0034654320933536

One year in Larry's class, students were completing a unit on Natural Disasters by writing an argument essay about which natural disaster they felt would be the worst to face.

As students were writing, Larry noticed that Alex had put his head down on his desk. Larry approached him and asked if he was okay. "I just can't do this, Mr. Ferlazzo," Alex answered. Larry knew that Alex often felt challenged in class, and he also knew he was a big football fan. He said, "Alex, how about instead of writing about the worst natural disaster, you write about which NFL team you think is the best, and use the outline and writing strategies we went over for an argument essay?" "I could do that?" Alex asked, surprised.

When Larry confirmed that he could, Alex then got right to work and, though what he handed in wasn't a perfect essay, it was definitely a passable one that demonstrated he understood the basics of how to construct an argument.

Later that week, Alex's mother came to the school for a meeting with his counselor and sought out Larry in his classroom. She was clearly emotional as she told him that it was the first essay that Alex had ever written and how grateful she was for Larry helping him.

In this situation, Larry kept his eyes on the prize of wanting Alex to learn how to write an argument essay and demonstrate it by writing one. However, he differentiated the product on the spur of the moment, based on what he knew from his relationship with Alex. Larry could have harangued Alex about sticking to the exact details of the assignment, which likely would have gone nowhere.

Instead, by a simple demonstration of flexibility that required absolutely no extra work on his part, Larry got the formative assessment result he needed, Alex got a huge boost in self-confidence that carried him forward through the school year, and Larry developed a rock solid alliance with his mother that came in handy any time in the future that Alex needed some additional encouragement.

Of course, not every demonstration of differentiated instruction will result in this kind of storybook ending.

But you might be surprised by how many will!

Why We Like It

We like differentiated instruction for the simple reason that using it makes us better teachers!

Our students are living, breathing human beings who are unique individuals with different gifts and challenges. Our students may not have different "learning styles" (because that's not really a thing, despite how common the phrase is in education writing), but that doesn't mean we can get away with not thinking about how we can truly engage each student to the best of their, and our, abilities and then act on it.[7]

Supporting Research

Substantial research supports the effectiveness of differentiated instruction. It has been found to significantly increase literacy achievement scores.[8] Other research has found similar gains when used in math classes, along with increased student engagement and motivation.[9] Additional studies found that *all* students, including "English Learners, gifted students, and struggling students" benefitted from differentiated instruction.[10]

It is also true that *some* studies have found that more advanced students *might* not benefit in situations where teachers are not skilled enough in offering differentiated instruction.[11] Of course, a similar case can probably be made for just about any type of instructional strategy—if a teacher doesn't know how to do it well, some of their students are likely not to benefit from it.

We cannot repeat Dylan Wiliam's comment too many times: Everything works somewhere; nothing works everywhere.[12]

The point of this book is to provide tools and ideas to try out and *practice* with—after all, we are *practitioners*! Figure out which of these ideas will work in *your* classroom and help *all* your students!

Application

We'll divide this Application section into the four areas we described earlier that are usually discussed when talking about differentiation: content, process, products, and learning environment. The line between those four areas is often fuzzy—it's often not one or the other. It's the strategy that's important, not under which one it's categorized.

---

[7] Ferlazzo, L. (2017, March 30). The best resources for learning about the issue of "Learning Styles." *Larry Ferlazzo's Website of the Day.*

[8] Puzio, K., Colby, G. T., & Algeo-Nichols, D. (2020).

[9] Subban, P. (2006). Differentiated instruction: A research basis. *International Education Journal, 7*(7), 935–947. Page 943.

[10] Tomlinson, C. A. (n.d.). What is differentiated instruction? differentiated instruction: maximizing the learning of all students. *Iris Center at Peabody College at Vanderbilt.*

[11] Ziernwald, L., Hillmayr, D., & Holzberger, D. (2022). Promoting high-achieving students through differentiated instruction in mixed-ability classrooms—A systematic review. *Journal of Advanced Academics, 33*(4), 540–573. https://doi.org/10.1177/1932202X221112931

[12] Barton, C. (2016, November 3). *Mr Barton's Maths Podcast.* Dylan Wiliam—Author, Researcher, Trainer and Assessment for Learning Expert (No. 16). [Podcast].

It's also important to remember that many differentiation strategies, such as the teacher speaking slowly, providing directions in writing and visually, and modeling examples are not really differentiation strategies at all because they help make content more accessible to everyone!

Do teachers have to use all these differentiation strategies for every lesson or assignment? Of course not!

Teachers are the experts on their classrooms. Use your judgment about what works best for you and your students and what is humanly possible to make sure you don't burn-out.

There is one key pre-requisite that comes before any of these strategies—teachers need to know their students, which is the way they become experts on their classrooms. There's a reason we put the Relationships chapter first in the book! Remember we have lots of recommendations on how to make that happen. We can't overstate its importance.

In addition to learning about students by building relationships with them, we also recommend learning about them through asking their parents/guardians questions like:

- What school lessons or topics have seemed to engage or motivate your child the most?
- When have they seemed most excited about going to school?
- What kinds of school activities do they talk to you the most about?
- What advice would you offer me on how to be the best teacher possible to your child?

Yes, it's likely impossible to find the time to talk to the parents/guardians of 150 students about these questions. However, in some situations, you might be able to get a high return rate by emailing or texting a Google form. And, in other situations, you will probably be able to identify a handful of students in each of your classes with whom you might need assistance to engage, and those few phone calls could result in a gold mine of information.

After all, you may be the expert on your classroom, but a parent/guardian is the expert on their child and will likely be able to articulate things the students themselves are unable to.

CONTENT

Content refers to the knowledge and skills that students are *expected to learn*. As we discussed earlier, the idea of differentiated instruction is not to lower standards so that some students learn the appropriate content and others learn less. Rather, the idea is to be strategic and creative in providing scaffolds so everyone learns the content standards while, at the same time, offering opportunities for those who might be more advanced to go beyond them.

Engineering the Text

Text engineering is a concept and term originally developed by Elsa Billings and Aida Walqui. It refers to making complex text more accessible but without reducing the actual text complexity (in other words, without changing the words).[13] This can be done by enlarging the size of the words, including multilingual word definitions, adding subtitles and images, creating more white space, writing pre-questions before paragraphs, providing audio support if the text is online, etc.

Yes, this requires added teacher time for engineering. However, these engineered texts can be reused each year. In addition, once you've created several texts (or copied from ones created by other teachers), it's possible to upload them to Machine Learning (ML) sites as models and ask them to create similar ones for new texts you upload. Of course, as with all generative Artificial Intelligence (AI)-created materials, teacher proofreading and editing is a must! In our experience, generative AI can create decent first drafts, but they always require revision.

Students can be given the option of choosing the original text or the engineered text to read.

A link in the Technology Connections section will lead you to many examples of engineered text.

Jigsaw

Jigsaw is a strategy with multiple variations but basically involves dividing a broader concept (e.g. biography of a historical figure, the concept of heliocentrism, any lengthy article) into smaller sections. Then, individual students or small groups become "experts" on those smaller sections which they then teach to their classmates. The teaching part is key here, otherwise you run the risk of students not actually engaging with the content.

Differentiation comes into play by assigning more complex smaller sections to advanced learners and lesser complex ones to those students who might need more support. For example, if learning about a historical feature, some students might prepare a presentation on the challenges faced by the person and how they

---

[13] Billings, E. & Walqui, A. (2021). De-mystifying complex texts: What are "complex" texts and how can we ensure ELLS and MLS can access them? (Report No. 3). NYSED Office of Bilingual Education & English as a New Language.

overcame them or what might be the most important elements of their legacy. Others might study the figure's family or their biggest successes.

All students are involved in learning the *same* content. But all of them are involved in teaching something *different*.

A resource in the Technology Connections section will take you to practical ideas on how to use the Jigsaw strategy in your classroom.

Audio Support for Text

Giving students the option of listening to text supports students who might have reading disabilities, like dyslexia, as well as English Language Learners who might have decoding or pronunciation challenges.[14] In addition, just offering the option can enhance students' sense of autonomy and increase motivation (see Chapter 5: Developing Classrooms That Promote Self-Motivation).

For online text, it's easy for students to use headphones or ear buds with a screen reader. When it's a hard copy text, they can take screenshots with their laptop or phone and, from there, use a screen reader. If they're working with a peer tutor, their tutor can read the text aloud to them.

Multilingual Support

If it's a fairly simple text, and you have Intermediate or Advanced English Language Learners in the class, pre-teaching a list of essential vocabulary words with multilingual definitions (easily created through a generative AI tool or Google Translate) can provide adequate multilingual support.

However, if it's a fairly simple English text, and you have ELL Newcomers in class, or it's fairly complex, and you have Newcomers and/or Intermediate ELLs, we'd recommend offering students the option of either taking a screenshot and translating it on their phone or using an online tool on their laptop to do the same thing. Machine translation accuracy for many languages has reached extraordinary levels.

Another option is to encourage students to use one of the tools that will translate text into "parallel text," with English on one side of the screen and their home language on the other. A link in the Technology Connections section will lead you to a list of those tools.

---

[14] Keelor, J. L., Creaghead, N., Horowitz-Kraus, T., & Silbert, N. (2020). Text-to-speech technology: Enhancing reading comprehension for students with reading difficulty. *Assistive Technology Outcomes and Benefits, 14,* 19–35.

It doesn't appear to us that researchers agree on an exact percentage of vocabulary knowledge needed to fully understand a text, but it does seem to be pretty high (over ninety percent).[15] We think teachers should bear that in mind when evaluating what kind of multilingual support their English Language Learner students might need.

Extra Credit

We know some teachers are not fans of extra credit, but we think creating extension activities for students who have a greater appetite for learning works as an excellent differentiation strategy.

Whether it's doing peer tutoring if their work is done early (see Chapter 2: Student Agency, NOT Student Empowerment), having multiple articles related to the topic being studied available for students to read and respond to, offering online sites that utilize adaptive learning technology (see below), or having students work on text used in the "Advanced Learning For All" activity or in literature circles (see below), there is no shortage of potential advanced learning opportunities.

One advanced activity we often offer to students uses a big poster of Bloom's Taxonomy sentence starters that we hang on our classroom wall. We invite students to use them to create their own prompts or assignments using the starters under the higher-level thinking skills categories and complete them.

We also often offer students the opportunity to do extra credit with a partner, which enhances engagement and motivation.

Easier Text or Videos to Acquire Needed Prior Knowledge

As we mentioned earlier, effective differentiation is about making high-level content accessible to all—we want students to be able to access more complex text or other assignments, not make them simpler. But in order to access that work, some students might not have the prior knowledge required to understand that content.

In those situations, providing leveled reading passages covering the same topic but having different Lexile levels is an activity we often use. We don't assign specific students specific levels—each student can decide on their own which they want to use. The same holds true with different kinds of videos.

See the Technology Connections section for a link leading to many sources of these kinds of leveled reading passages. Of course, teachers can also put a text into

---

[15] Conti, G. (2025, February 27). Why the input we give our learners must be 95–98% comprehensible in order to enhance language acquisition—the theory and the research evidence. *The Language Gym*.

a generative AI chatbot and ask it to create multiple versions for different grade levels. Remember to carefully review any product it creates before you share it with students!

Online Adaptive Learning Technology

Online Adaptive Learning basically means that the questions and tasks being asked of the user are adjusted based on the user responses to previous questions and tasks.

Though they are typically not sophisticated enough to work well for creative or higher-order thinking tasks, they are well-suited for grammar, basic reading comprehension, simple writing instruction, and some math learning.

See the Technology Connections section for a link that will lead you to many online adaptive learning tools.

Independent Reading

We have often used independent reading, also known as free voluntary reading, as a "do now/warm-up" activity in our classes. During these first 10 minutes of class, students read a book of their choice from our extensive, multi-level and culturally representative classroom libraries, from home, or a book they have checked-out from the school library. As they quietly read, we are taking attendance and having brief individual conferences with students, often discussing the book they are reading as well as other topics.

Students can choose to read any classroom appropriate book, and if you're worried about what could go wrong, in all of our years of teaching, neither Katie or Larry has had a student bring in a text we needed to ask them not to bring in again. Also, when we know students' interests, we may make recommendations.

We should point out that we try to be flexible about how students want to read during this time. If a student is sleepy, we might encourage them to sit on their desk. Our classrooms open to the outside, so we're supportive of a small number of students bringing chairs outside and sitting where we can monitor them through the classroom windows.

Look at the Technology Connections section for research on this kind of reading and other strategies for implementing it.

Literature Circles

Another strategy we sometimes use to promote reading and differentiated instruction are self-selected literature circles. Any student can create a group of between two and five students to read a book of their choice (sometimes it's one we have multiple copies of in our classroom library, school bookroom or library; we've also been successful posting a Donor's Choose request to purchase multiple copies of a particular book. Sometimes you can find sets on Facebook Buy Nothing or teacher exchange groups in your area).

The groups meet once or twice each week during the warm-up independent reading time and follow a protocol.

1. When you arrive at the library, please check in with the librarian. Make sure the librarian has a seating chart with your names.
2. Each person shares the one or two sentence **summary** they wrote about the chapter or chapters they were to read. Discuss which one you like the best and why.
3. Each person shares the **connection** ("this makes me remember. . . .") they wrote about the chapter or chapters they were to read. Please ask at least one question about each connection.
4. Each person shares the **question** they wrote about the chapter. Discuss what you think the answers might be to each one.
5. Each person shares what their **favorite part** or parts of the chapter was/were, and why they liked it.
6. Each person makes a **prediction**. What do you think will happen next in the story and why? Do you agree?
7. Decide as a group what chapters you will read by the next meeting.
8. Thank the librarian and return to class.

Visuals

Extensive research, and most teachers' experiences, highlight the value of using visuals (pictures, diagrams, infographics, etc.) in different content classes.[16,17,18]

We are not talking about boring PowerPoints or Google Slides with endless bullet points and pretty flowers.

Rather, we are recommending strategic use of images, along with text support, that engage students and "amplify" important content.

[16] Schoenherr, J., Strohmaier, A. R., & Schukajlow, S. (2024). Learning with visualizations helps: A meta-analysis of visualization interventions in mathematics education. *Educational Research Review*, 45.

[17] Bobek, E., & Tversky, B. (2016). Creating visual explanations improves learning. *Cognitive Research: Principles and Implications, 1*(1), 27. https://doi.org/10.1186/s41235-016-0031-6

[18] Colorín Colorado. (n.d.). Using visuals. *Teaching ELLs.*

See the Technology Connections section for more ideas on using visuals in the classroom.

Advanced Learning Open to All

We've generally used this strategy with an advanced textbook, but there's really no reason it can't also be used with a collection of articles, narrative books, or even with a series of prompts for writing essays.

We initiate it by first approaching students in class who seem to be the most self-motivated. We explain to them that we have been impressed by their appetite for learning and want to invite them to participate in an advanced program—for extra credit.

In this activity, we would give them an advanced textbook and meet once or twice each week during the independent reading time. We'd either quietly meet in the back of the classroom, or a student teacher would take them outside. They or I would do some brief teaching about the textbook and then we'd assign them to do some of the subsequent exercises in the book prior to the next meeting of the group.

As time goes on, we invite additional students to join the group, and it's also not unusual for other students to begin asking about the group and eventually asking if they could join—it becomes a "cool" group! It's not unusual for us to get as many as 50% of the class participating after a few months to do this extra work!

PROCESS

Process is used to describe *how* students learn the content. There are many variations we'll discuss here (or have already discussed under "content" since there's not always a firm line between these categories), ranging from some students choosing to work on their own instead of in groups to working on different topics when using the Jigsaw learning strategy.

Formative Assessments

Formative assessments are the "secret weapon" in implementing effective differentiated instruction—in fact, in implementing any kind of effective instruction! You can't really be an effective teacher if you don't know before you teach your lesson what your students know and what they know after you've taught it! And, even during it!

Formative assessments are low-stakes and frequent check-ins to determine where students are in the learning process. They differ from summative assessments, which are typically given at the end of units or semesters, or benchmarks, to measure overall achievement.

The information gained from formative assessments is critical for making adjustments to what we're doing in the classroom. Without it, we are prioritizing our teaching over our students' learning.

Education researcher Robert Marzano has called formative assessment, "one of the more powerful weapons in a teacher's arsenal."[19]

Not only can we use formative assessments to adjust our teaching, but the results can also be used by *students* to adjust their learning.

There are *many* different kinds of formative assessments. Here are a few of our favorites:

- Mini-whiteboards. As far as we're concerned, nothing beats all students having a mini-whiteboard, marker and eraser. We pose a question, ask students to not hold them up until we say to do so, and, voila, you get an immediate "check for understanding."

- Online games like Wayground (formerly Quizizz), Kahoot, Blooket, and many other sites. Teachers can use countless pre-made games on every imaginable topic, use Artificial Intelligence to create more specific ones, or manually create more. Students love playing them and you get immediate results.

Though we often use them right at the end of class, sometimes we fit them in earlier and have students complete a form with these two questions developed by educator Tyler Rabin:[20]

- Looking at the questions you got correct, what concepts are you doing well with currently?

- Looking at the questions you missed, what are some concepts you need to focus on learning next?

We use either of these oral directions:

- Give me a thumbs up, thumbs down, or thumbs in the middle to help know if I've explained things well and you understand it. It's fine to put a thumbs down—that's on me, not you.

- Here's a tiny scrap of paper. Don't put your name on it. Write a one, two or three—one means that you're very clear on _______, two you're in the middle, or three you're not clear at all.

[19] Marzano, R. J. (2006). *Classroom Assessment and Grading That Work*. Association for Supervision and Curriculum Development.

[20] Rabin, T. (2025, May 30). 15 Formative Assessment Hacks to Boost Students' Learning. *Edutopia*.

The Technology Connections includes two links that lead you to scores of other formative assessment strategies.

Voice Typing

Many students, including English Language Learners, may have never mastered keyboarding skills. In those cases, if you are having students type essays on a laptop, voice typing is an easy way to help level the playing field.

Google Docs has an exceptionally accurate voice typing tool, and there are also other online options.

Small Groups or Working Independently

There are several different elements to this topic.

1. Give students an option to either work alone or work in groups or with a partner. Prior to distance learning during the pandemic, we generally had very, very few students who wanted to work on their own. Since that time, though it's still a minority of students, we've found those numbers have substantially increased. We typically respect students' preferences. However, for students who always say they want to work on their own, we sometimes have conversations with them about the value of working in groups periodically and developing those skills, particularly since they'll likely be doing more of that when they pursue higher education opportunities.

2. Think carefully about how many students to have in a group. On this issue, we are big proponents of generally keeping it to pairs. We just find that having to monitor making sure that everyone carries their weight in larger groups is too burdensome for us and the students. However, there are occasions when we have working in partners as a first step that leads to working in a larger group (during Jigsaws, for example).

3. Then there's the issue of *how* to divide into groups. Personally, we have a strong personal preference for student choice. We generally begin the year by explaining that we'll be assigning different partners for the first two months so that students get to know each other and can get a better idea of who they want to work with for most of the year when they can choose their partners. We also strongly encourage students to not *always* choose the same partner.

Of course, the elephant in the room for this part is the question of grouping by ability. We're not big fans of regularly dividing into ability level groups and feel that they tend to worsen achievement gaps instead of reducing them, and the research isn't really compelling that we should be doing it.[21] However, we will often bring together a handful of students who are experiencing similar challenges during an assignment and activity and pull them together for a quick five-minute mini-lesson to provide extra support. Or, ask a student who has mastered a skill or subject more quickly to work with two or three students who need extra support. But these groups are *fluid* and temporary.

There are always exceptions to just about everything in a classroom. When we do the activity previously described in the Advanced Learning Open to All section, that becomes a larger self-selected group. Even though they are doing advanced work, it's open to anyone who wants to do it. It's grouped not by their ability, but by their appetite for learning.

We try to ensure that students have the opportunity to participate in interest-based groups, mixed ability level groups, student-choice groups, and other variations. As Carol Ann Tomlinson explains, "In a sense, the teacher is continually auditioning kids in different settings—and the students get to see how they can contribute in a variety of contexts."[22]

See the Technology Section for a link to resources exploring the question of grouping by ability, as well as a link for resources looking at other issues around small group work.

Graphic Organizers/Sentence Starters/Writing Frames/Writing Structures

Graphic organizers are typically somewhat. . .graphic. They are designed with squares, circles, etc. organized in a way to assist students to understand, think through, and apply different concepts and ideas. We find them particularly essential to help students prepare for writing tasks. After students become familiar with different types of graphic organizers, we often encourage them to start choosing on their own which ones would be most helpful to them for particular tasks and even suggest that they try designing their own, as well as giving them the option to not use one at all.

Sentence starters are what they say they are—a few words to help students get started on writing or speaking. ("I think the main idea of the essay is ________.") They can be particularly helpful in encouraging students to develop experience in using academic language. ("I agree/disagree with __________ because ________.") You can also even include sentence starters *within* graphic organizers.

---

[21] Sparks, S. D. (2018, August 26). Are classroom reading groups the best way to teach reading? Maybe not. *Education Week*.

[22] Rebora, A. (2008, September 10). Making a difference. *Education Week: Teaching*.

Writing frames are expanded sentence starters. They are basically multiple sentences of "fill-in-the-blanks" with the key information or critical thinking concepts left for students to complete.

Writing structures, on the other hand, are more-or-less guidelines or formulas to assist students to plan their writing. One of our favorites is called the ABC Paragraph—ANSWER the question, BACK IT UP with evidence, CONNECT your evidence to your answer (the C could also mean "Make a COMMENT or CONNECTION" depending on your preference).

After initially providing all students with sentence starters, writing frames, and writing structures, we generally just either leave copies available for students to use, or encourage them to keep older ones they can refer to if needed. Our differentiated instruction attitude with these—again, after all students develop familiarity with them—is similar to what you'll see on telephone pole posters and bulletin boards: "Take what you need, leave what you don't."

In the Technology Connections section, you can find links to many graphic organizers, sentence starters, writing frames, and writing structures.

Recommended Sequences or Checklists

We've found that, especially for major projects, some students find a sequence, or a series of clear steps to take to complete the project, very helpful. In fact, based on their anonymous feedback, *most* of them do.

Figure 3.1, Suggested Sequence for Writing Your TOK Essay, is an admittedly long example of one of these guidelines that Larry uses for his International Baccalaureate Theory of Knowledge class. He's always recruited many Intermediate and Advanced English Language Learners for his TOK classes, and this kind of "sequence" guide works as a helpful scaffold to ELLs and to English-proficient students. This sequence sheet helps students organize their work and still leaves all the higher-order thinking up to them.

Suggested Sequence for Writing Your TOK Essay

1. Choose a prompt that is interesting to you (or, at least, not totally boring). Try to pick one that you think the class activities we did have prepared you to write, so you have something to start with.
2. Meet briefly with Mr. Ferlazzo after you have chosen your prompt.
3. Choose an outline to use. The outline for the slideshow is the one preferred by many students, but it's fine if you decide to use one of the other two outlines, also. It's entirely up to you. If you decide to use the slideshow outline, just make a copy of it.

(continued)

4. Copy-and-paste your prompt in the outline. In the outline, first define key words in the prompt. For example, if you use this prompt:

> Within areas of knowledge, how can we differentiate between change and progress? Answer with reference to two areas of knowledge.

. . .then you would want to define the words "change" and "progress."

5. Decide on your thesis statement. In other words, what is your position on the prompt—do you agree, disagree, or are in the middle. For example, if you are using this prompt:

> Can there be knowledge that is independent of culture? Discuss with reference to mathematics and one other area of knowledge.

. . .after you define the key words in the prompt, your thesis statement might or might not be something like this:

> In some areas of knowledge, it is possible to have knowledge that is independent of culture, but in other areas of knowledge, it is not possible.

6. Then, complete your first paragraph by saying which areas of knowledge you will be using in your essay to explore the prompt and support your thesis statement.

7. Now, it is time for you to make your claims (and provide evidence to support them) that support your thesis statement. Here are four ways to develop claims and find support for them:

i. First, review the "What We've Done This Year" slideshow. Look at activities we've done under each area of knowledge and note if there are any applicable to your essay. Remember, it's easy at this point to change the areas of knowledge that you said earlier you were going to use if you find one that is better after reminding yourself of what we did this year.

ii. Second, think about any personal experiences you've had that might support your thesis statement.

iii. Third, review the textbook for ideas.

iv. Fourth, search the Internet for ideas. One way to do this is to rephrase your prompt, type "theories" after it, and press "search." For example, if you were going to use this prompt:

> How do historians and human scientists give knowledge meaning through the telling of stories? Discuss with reference to history and the human sciences.

. . .you could search:

> Story-telling when studying history theories
> Story-telling in human sciences theories

Note that you should cite the textbook and Internet sources as references. If you use quotations in your essay, always restate them in your own words after using the quote. Doing this ensures to you and to me that you understand its meaning.

8. You should then have one or two paragraphs focused on each of your two areas of knowledge (in other words one-or-two on one area of knowledge and another one-or-two on the other one). Each of your paragraphs should follow this format:

(a) Your claim

(b) One or two pieces of evidence and real-life examples supporting your claim

(c) Ending the paragraph restating how your claim, evidence and examples support your thesis statement.

(continued)

9. After you have supported your thesis statement with claims from your two areas of knowledge, you should then have a counterclaim, ideally for one of your claims from each area of knowledge.

A counterclaim does not have to be a statement completely opposing one of your claims. It can just say that there can be an exception—sometimes—to your claim. You are just acknowledging that your claim may not be accurate 100% of the time.

10. End with a short restatement of your thesis statement and why you believe it is accurate.
11. If you have access to ChatGPT, and *if* you want to use it, after you have written your first draft, you can use it to help improve your essay. However, you can only use it in this way.
12. Paste your essay into ChatGPT. Then write, "Identify and correct any grammar or punctuation errors."
13. Then, review its corrections and decide if they make your essay better. If they do, then use them. Don't assume that all of ChatGPT's ideas are good ones. Remember, you want your essay to emphasize your voice, not ChatGPT's voice.
14. If you do use ChatGPT, please list ChatGPT under references, the date you used it, and how you used it.

A TOK essay for IB is written for a specific audience—the IB Examiner, who may spend very limited time reviewing it. This essay outline is designed for that audience, so *some* suggestions for a general essay may not work well for it.

Figure 3.1 TOK Essay Sequence

"Checklists" can also help keep students on track. They can help students plan and self-monitor their progress. Figure 3.2, TOK Exhibition Checklist, is an example of one from Larry's class.

Time Flexibility

Once we explain the parameters of an assignment, we'll often (though not always) just ask our students how long they think it will take for them to complete it. Many times it's a bit of a quick negotiation, and we'll generally agree to a slightly longer time than we might have originally planned.

But the payoff is increased student agency and a greater commitment on their part to get it done in time. For students who complete the assignment quickly, there are always peer tutoring or extra credit options for them to extend their learning.

The Zeigarnik Effect

Bluma Zeigarnik, a Russian psychologist, identified what came to be called the Zeigarnik Effect: Once we start doing something, we tend to want to finish it. What can this teach us about differentiation? When we know a task will be

You will receive 100 points extra credit if you do every one of these steps AND submit this completed form by the due date.

- ☐ I have selected a prompt from the list of 35. Place an X and write the date you submitted it: _________

- ☐ I have decided on which Theme (either Knowledge and the Knower, Knowledge & Technology Theme, Knowledge & Indigenous Societies) I will primarily use for my Exhibition objects and essays. Place an X and write the date you submitted it: _________

- ☐ I have reviewed all the activities we did in Google Classroom on that Theme (see the "What We've Done This Year" slideshow to find the list and then go to the actual activities and the class slideshows for those days). Place an X and write the date you completed your review of those activities: _________

- ☐ I have read the description of the kinds of objects that can be used for the Exhibition that can be found in the Exhibition section from earlier in the year. The specific description can be found at "TOK Exhibition Introduction" and was posted on October 31st, 2023. Place an X and write the date you reviewed that document: _________

- ☐ I have read through the "TOK Exhibition Example from a TOK Teacher" and have read at least three object essays written by Burbank students earlier this year found at "Examples of TOK Exhibitions" or at "Good Student Final Exhibition Examples from 2021/22." Place an X and write the date you reviewed these documents: _________

- ☐ I have identified my three objects, made sure that each has a personal connection with me, and have spoken to Mr. Ferlazzo about each one of them. Place an X and write the date you completed this: _________

- ☐ I have identified which of the activities we did connected to the theme I am using that connect to each of the objects. Place an X and write the date you completed this: _________

- ☐ I have written about how each object connects to the theme and explained how it helps answer the prompt. Place an X and write the date you have completed this: _________

- ☐ I have done research to identify potential other important points to include in my responses to the prompt: Place an X and write the date you have completed this: _________

- ☐ I have laid out my Exhibition according to the guidelines and confirmed that it meets the word count requirement. Place an X and write the date you have completed this: _________

- ☐ I have submitted the Exhibition by the deadline. Place an X and write the date you have completed this: _________

Figure 3.2 TOK Exhibition Checklist

challenging for some students, we can present a variety of ways to get started: a menu of questions to answer, the option to create a drawing or visual representation of a concept, the option to begin the assignment working with a partner, etc. We can also encourage students to get started by just answering the first question or the easiest one. This is also where sentence starters and writing frames can come in handy.

Multilingual Support

For reading, we discussed in the Content section how and when students can consider using Google Translate, other machine translation tools, or sites that will create "parallel text." For writing, as we'll discuss in *Chapter 4: Tech Has Its Place, But Also Has To Be Kept In Its Place*, we've come around to what some might consider a somewhat controversial position—we think English Language Learners should, in many cases, be allowed to write in their home languages and then convert it to English with translation tools, especially in content classes. After years of teaching, we've come to see that if we truly want to see accurate representations of their knowledge and understanding, why wouldn't we want them to produce writing in this way?

Preview-View-Review is another long-used differentiated instruction method to help make content accessible to English Language Learners. The idea is that the lesson is briefly previewed in the students' home language, the lesson is then conducted in English, and then it's briefly reviewed in the students' home language. Obviously, logistically it can be challenging to implement this method, especially in a large class and/or if the teacher doesn't actually speak students' home languages.

In those cases, an easy work around is to find online text or video resources on the topic in the students' languages and share them ahead of time, which students can use in both the "preview" and "review" sections. You can find a link in the Technology Connections section that will lead you to many of those resources and, of course, you can always just use generative AI and machine translation to easily create your own. Again, as a reminder, be sure to carefully review any product before it goes in front of students.

ELL teacher Sable Schwab has created an excellent short and sweet Preview-View-Review guide that offers many other helpful ideas for teachers who don't speak their students' home languages, and you can see that in Figure 3.3 Preview, View, & Review.

Finally, another way to support ELLs during the learning process is to connect them to a buddy who will sit near them and help them understand the content. This arrangement, which must be agreed to by both the ELL and their potential buddy, can be helpful to both. (We've previously discussed how research shows both the tutor and the person being tutored can benefit.) In an ideal world, the buddy can speak the ELL's home language but, if they don't, we've found that some guidance from the teacher works fine, too (see the Technology Connections section to access those resources).

Step	Description	Guiding Questions
Preview 10%	Foreshadow the target concept allowing L1 support	• What keywords do students need to know to understand the concept? Do these words connect to the L1? • Are there videos or readings about the target concept in the L1 I can have students take notes on before the lesson? • What background knowledge is needed to understand the target concept? How can I activate it? • What supports do I need from the ELL department to preview this concept?
View 80%	Instruction completely in English with supports (Students can access translation technology if necessary, but they are ultimately expected to engage in English.)	• Can I use visuals or real objects to describe this concept? • Is there a graphic organizer that matches the target concept? • Is there a way for students to learn the concept with a hands-on approach? • Is there room for collaborative learning? • What teaching methods would a Special Education teacher use to teach these concepts to students with IEPs? • Who is a strong native English-speaking student I can pair with my ELL who can model answers during turn-and-talks? • What sentence starters can I provide to get students talking in a more academic way during turn-and-talks? • Can I put this through ChatGPT or Magic AI to level this text and/or create other supports that could work for other students as well? • What do I need from the ELL department to support the view portion of the lesson?
Review 10%	Have students summarize the concept in their own way, including in their L1 or even informal student language	• How can I get students to summarize their learning in their own ways (L1, pictures, etc.)? • What do I need from the ELL department to support the review portion of the lesson?

Figure 3.3 Preview, View, & Review

Source: Reproduced with permission of Sable Schwab

Pre-Teaching Vocabulary (Frontloading)

Though research is somewhat mixed about the value of pre-teaching key vocabulary prior to a lesson, we have often found it to be helpful (though our instruction should also include teaching on how students can identify the meaning of unknown words through context clues).[23,24]

As part of a differentiated instruction protocol, we don't just plan to explicitly teach the word's meaning. Instead, we always begin by asking students to first write down what they think it means, and more often than not they can teach their classmates rather than us doing so.

Closed Captioning for Video/Modifying Speed

When showing a video to the whole class, turning on closed-captions is a must—oftentimes the acoustics in our classrooms are terrible, as are the speakers connected to our computers. But even if we had a perfect sound system, making them visible can also be particularly helpful to English Language Learners, and researchers have found they assist in comprehension for non-ELLs, too.[25]

And people on videos tend to speak so fast! Slowing them down by 25% can assist everybody.

Of course, if students are watching the videos individually on their laptops, it's important for teachers to make sure they know how and why they should do the same on their own.

Using Visuals

We discussed the importance of using visuals in the Content section, and a similar case can be made for Process. We would encourage teachers to always think about how they can incorporate visuals to support text that students are reading, including possibly taking advantage of how generative Artificial Intelligence tools are more and more able to accurately develop illustrative diagrams and infographics from texts. But—and say it with us—be sure to review any visuals you use generative AI to create. Your relationship with students can take a hit if you put inaccurate information in front of them.

[23] Kerr, P. (2020, October 9). Questions about pre-teaching vocabulary (PTV). *Adaptive Learning in ELT*.

[24] Pellicer-Sánchez, A., Conklin, K., & Vilkaitė-Lozdienė, L. (2021). The effect of pre-reading instruction on vocabulary learning: An investigation of l1 and l2 readers' eye movements. *Language Learning, 71*(1), 162–203. https://doi.org/10.1111/lang.12430

[25] Benefits of Captions. (n.d.). Utah State University: Accessibility. www.usu.edu/accessibility/captions/benefits

Bookmarks with "Hints"

Bookmarks with hints or clues that students can use as actual bookmarks or just tape in their folders or notebooks can be a helpful tool for differentiated instruction. Those that need them will use them (though, obviously, some will forget), and those who don't can ignore them. They could be reminders of grammar rules, math formulas, active reading strategies, multilingual translations of key words, etc.

Searching something like "academic clue bookmarks to give to students" on the Internet will lead you to countless examples to choose from that you can download or you can make your own.

Reteach

Decades ago, Larry was helping translate for a former colleague who was meeting with a parent of a student who was struggling in his colleague's class. Larry's colleague explained that he was often available for after-school tutoring. The student's mother exclaimed in frustration, "My son tells me the problem is that when you tutor him, you explain things the exact same way you did the first time when he didn't understand it!" It was a learning experience for Larry and his colleague.

As we mentioned earlier, we'll often bring together small groups of students who are sharing the same struggles together for a brief mini-lesson, and often instead of us teaching it, we'll ask another student to lead it. And sometimes we realized we just did a bad job teaching something the first time around and do it again to the entire class.

The key, though, is remembering what that parent said—if students didn't get it the first time we taught it, it's unlikely most will get it if we just repeat the same lesson. In many ways, doing so is similar to what some people do when a person they're speaking with doesn't know English—they just say the same words louder!

So, yes, reteaching is a differentiation strategy. But be thinking about how you can communicate the lesson in a different way. If you didn't use visuals the first time around, use them now. If you didn't model something then, model something now. If you didn't use a student example, see if you can use one now.

Connecting to Prior Knowledge

We discussed the importance of connecting new concepts to prior knowledge in the previous chapter, and it's worth repeating again here. When asking students what they might already know about a certain topic, be sure to clearly provide "expansive" definitions. In other words, if you're teaching a lesson about Mardi Gras, don't just ask students what they know about Mardi Gras. Instead, ask them what they know about community celebrations and what happens in them.

PRODUCTS

By products, we and others mean *how students demonstrate that they have learned* the expected content. The story we shared about Alex earlier in this chapter is an example of this kind of differentiation—Larry gave Alex the opportunity to demonstrate his understanding of how to write an argument essay by writing about football instead of natural disasters.

Students can complete the same types of mental tasks while producing different end products. Education researcher Douglas Reeves describes this as "not uniformity of work, but similarity of proficiency."[26] The idea is that students can gain proficiency even when completing different types of assignments or a different number of assignments (one big project versus five smaller assignments). This can happen, for example, in our classrooms when students need to demonstrate they understand how to use reading strategies while reading different books. Some students might be reading 300-page books while others read a series of much shorter texts. As long as the level of text is challenging to them and students are using similar reading strategies to increase comprehension and drive analysis, then the length/genre/topic of the book doesn't need to be uniform.

Different Options for Culminating Projects

In Chapter 5: Developing Classrooms That Promote Self-Motivation, we'll discuss further the value of choice in creating the conditions for student autonomy for engagement and motivation, but it also has a clear role in differentiation and, specifically in the area of "products."

When some educators talk about the role of choice in this area of differentiation, they describe it as having differing tiers of academic rigor.

We have a different perspective. Though we obviously make modifications in product expectations if students have IEP's that call for them, we have found that, as mentioned before, as long as we "keep our eyes on the prize" of the most important standards that we want our students to learn, we can adequately differentiate in the *ways* that they can show understanding.

We can offer multiple prompts to choose from, options of creating videos, slideshows, essays, museum exhibits, answering prompts with objects and explaining how those objects do just that, making an infographic, an academic poster similar to ones presented at academic conferences, etc.

We're not big users of rubrics, though when we use them, we either make them as "improvement rubrics" (see Chapter 6: Emphasizing Students' Assets, Not

---

[26] Reeves, D. R. (2011, December 13). From differentiated instruction to differentiated assessment. *ASCD Whole Child.*

Deficits) or ones we co-create with students. Researchers suggest it's much more effective to show students multiple examples of past projects at various levels of proficiency.[27] We like to share culminating projects from different units (not the units students are presently doing to avoid plagiarism or copying) and explain what grades each received. Then, students say why they think each project received those grades—in effect, developing a rubric through inductive learning (see Chapter 7: Strategies for Maximizing Learning.)

There are countless examples of these kinds of differentiated "choice boards," also known as "learning menus" online. There's a link in the Technology Connections section to some we've curated.

Figure 3.4 shows a simple Choice final that Larry has done with his ELL Newcomer students.

Show how well you know English through writing, reading, speaking and listening.

For Writing (choose one): You may write two versions—one without using Google Translate and one using Google Translate. Your grade will be based on whichever one is higher:

- Write a dialog.
- Write a short story different from what you wrote about earlier.
- Write about a memory (autobiographical incident).
- Write a paragraph about your family.
- Write a letter to a friend or family member saying what you appreciate about them.
- Write a letter to Mr. Ferlazzo or to your pen pal saying what your hopes for the future are and why.

For Reading:

- Choose a book. You will go to Voice Typing on the Google Doc in Google Classroom under "Reading Exam." You will read for at least one minute into the Google Doc (reading for longer is great!). You can practice with your peer tutor for a few minutes before you do the Exam.

For Speaking:

- Go to Voice Typing on the Google Doc in Google Classroom under "Speaking Exam." You will speak for as long as you can—try to talk for at least one minute (speaking for longer is great!). You can write up to ten words on an index card to help you remember what you are going to say. Your peer tutor will count the words. You can practice with your peer tutor for a few minutes before you do the Exam.

For Listening:

- Go to Brainpop. Then go to Brainpop, Jr. Choose any video you want. Watch it two times. Then take the Easy Quiz. Be sure to click "Submit to Teacher." Then take the Hard Quiz. Then click "Submit to Teacher." You can watch more videos and take more quizzes for extra credit.

Figure 3.4 Choice Board for ELL Newcomers

---

[27] Lemov, D. (2015, August 10). Dylan Wiliam advises: Forget the rubric: Use work samples instead. *Doug Lemov's Field Notes.*

Multilingual Support for Assessments

As we've previously mentioned, for many content classes we recommend that English Language Learners be allowed to use machine translation tools for reading and writing to complete the same work as everyone else in class. For Newcomer and Intermediate classes where it's important for them to develop a basic skill level of English literacy, then offer word banks, sentence starters, and writing frames as differentiation options.

Student-Created Test Questions

First, teach students about the difference between "right there" (literal) questions and "think about" (interpretative) questions (or thin/thick or $1/$10 questions; there are lots of ways to think about different types of questions). Literal ones have the answers in the text, and the answers to interpretative ones are not obvious, but require them to infer by reading between the lines.

Next, have students write several of both types of questions based on the text the class is reading, like a chapter in a Social Studies book.

The teacher then can post a large selection of both types of questions in Google Classroom, a class bulletin board, or on a student hand-out.

Then, students can be asked to answer a certain number of both types of questions as an assessment.

This assessment is similar to the idea we mentioned earlier under "Different Options for Culminating Projects" of offering multiple prompts for students to choose from. The difference here is that these are *student-created* prompts, and, because of that, they provide the added benefit of enhancing student agency.

Educator Joe Schwartz has some particularly interesting ideas on how to use this strategy in a mathematics classroom, and you can find a link to his ideas in the Technology Connections section. To us non-math teachers, he appears to basically give students data and then have them write two types of questions which he calls thin/thick which their classmates then answer.

Extra Credit for More Advanced Projects

We find it pretty energizing and not too time-consuming to think about extension projects for our most motivated and advanced learners. We previously mentioned some of these ideas in the Content section.

Usually, it's a matter of developing connections between what we know of students' interests and the content we are studying, having brief conversations with them, and coming to an agreement. If nothing seems to click, they can always choose to finish the "regular" culminating project early and tutor a classmate.

LEARNING ENVIRONMENT

Learning environment typically refers to "the way the classroom works and feels."[28] This can range from the classroom "culture" that has been created to its actual physical layout.

Seating Arrangements

We typically let students sit where they want to sit on the first day and ask them to stay there until we learn everyone's names. After that time, they're free to move elsewhere—if they want to sit where someone else is sitting, then they have to negotiate with the other person and apply no pressure to them. We also caution students that we retain the full right to move where people sit based on behavior and, if that happens, will try (no guarantees offered) to give them two options to choose from at that point.

In the context of differentiation, we will sometimes have conversations with students about sitting next to specific classmates, whether it's for being a "buddy" with an ELL or for being an ongoing "peer tutor" for a struggling student. We'll also support students with vision issues by seating them near the front and encourage a student who might be easily distracted to sit away from the windows. Obviously, we'll also make accommodations for disabled students to enhance accessibility (i.e. an area for a student in a wheelchair should be in an area where they can easily reach the door).

Anchor Charts/Word Walls

Anchor Charts and Word Walls are basically the "Bookmarks With Hints" we discussed earlier—just bigger versions of them taped or pinned to the walls. Though they can be fully teacher-created (you can find tons of them online), it's obviously better if students can be co-creators.

Whether it's having students write and draw their definitions of the pre-taught vocabulary they learned for a unit, multi-lingual translations of key concepts, or important mathematical formulas, these regularly changing supports—as long as they are large, easily viewed, and visibly pleasing—can function as key supports for differentiation.

Supportive Class Culture/SEL

Building a classroom culture that supports risk-taking, where students know classmates have their backs, acknowledges we're all in this together, and actively

---

[28] Mccrea, P. (2024, March 14). The power of routines. *Evidence Snacks.*

promotes mutual respect can be the key to successful differentiation and student learning proficiency.

We are big fans of many of Facing History's community building activities, which can be done at the beginning of the school year or at any time for a class reset.[29]

One way to encourage all students to consistently work at their best is to praise effort and not intelligence. Carol Dweck has published research on the benefits of praising students' effort versus their intelligence. She recommends teaching children the difference between a "growth mindset" (the belief that intelligence can be developed through effort and practice) and a "fixed mindset" (the belief that intelligence is innate). We'll be discussing this concept further in Chapter 9: Providing Effective Student Feedback.

One way to develop students' growth mindset is to encourage them to take risks and learn from mistakes. Some students are afraid of making mistakes and being ridiculed for it. We want to turn that attitude on its head, helping them learn that, as Dweck says, we should instead "celebrate mistakes."[30]

Options to Move

We don't know about you, but sitting for much of an entire school day would be tough on us, and we're sure it's tough on many students because they've told us through surveys and conversations.

We try to create opportunities for our students to move. For example, in Larry's TOK class, after the warm-up students count off and move into different groups to share what they wrote. If we see a student who is clearly sleepy or tired, we'll tell them to go outside and get a drink of water and/or give them the option to stand in the back instead of sitting at a desk. We hold the line at students who want to lay down on the floor or on two desk chairs but, other than that, we try to be as flexible as possible so we can remove as many barriers to learning that are within our control.

Class Routines

Routines are sequences of actions we do with a certain amount of automaticity. We all have them in our personal lives—how we prepare in the mornings, what we do prior to going to bed in the evenings, how we warm-up before doing an athletic activity. These kinds of routines provide a sense of familiarity, comfort, and safety—we don't have to think about them, which creates increased mental

[29] Activities for the First Days of School. (2023, August 9). *Facing History & Ourselves.*

[30] Ferlazzo, L. (2011, December 6). "We should celebrate mistakes." *Larry Ferlazzo's Website of the Day.*

bandwidth to think about other, more important things or to even just not think about anything for a while, which is also important for our mental health.

Class routines serve similar functions for our students—and for us. Students should know the warm-up routines, what they should find in Google Classroom each day, and how Jigsaw activities are generally organized. These routines free up students' mental bandwidth so they can focus more on the learning instead of the organizing, as well as enhancing classroom community since "everyone's on the same page."[31]

We're not suggesting that we should do the same thing every day. What we are suggesting is that we should do some things the same way every day, we should do certain regular activities using the same process, *and* we should periodically mix it up with new and unusual lessons, too.

Different students will value class routines with different levels of importance, and, because of that, they can be important foundations for successful differentiated instruction.

What Could Go Wrong

It would be easy to feel overwhelmed by all the options for differentiated instruction in this chapter. But remember you don't have to do them all. In fact, you don't even have to do most of them.

Try out a few of them—one at a time. If one strategy doesn't work the first time, don't give up on it. Try it a few times, and if it doesn't seem to work for you or your class, put it on the shelf and try another. You've got the whole school year—and future years—to see what works!

Don't be inflexible if you have a student facing exceptional challenges. As we've mentioned, except for students with IEP's requiring modifications of learning content and expectations, we focus on getting all students to achieve proficiency.

However, most teachers have had, as we have had, some students whose challenges are greater than most, and who may need extra initial support to develop self-confidence, skills, and motivation first, before they are willing or able to work to reach those more advanced goals. In those cases, we make modifications for them, too, as a step towards moving forward. We are candid in our conversations in these situations and explain that we are offering these changes to help students be successful. We might create a simpler prompt, or reduce essay requirements, in an effort to create the conditions for students who need to feel successful to be successful. We seldom, if ever, hear any pushback from other students ("Why does he get to do that, when I have to do this?") because they usually "get it."

---

[31] McCrea, P. (2024).

Chapter Summary

If we only had a few minutes to chat in the teacher faculty room, here's what we'd want you to remember about differentiated instruction:

Technology Connections

Find many examples of engineered text at *The Best Strategies For "Engineering" Text So That It's More Accessible To ELLs* https://larryferlazzo.edublogs.org/2022/02/16/the-best-strategies-for-engineering-text-so-that-its-more-accessible-to-ells/.

Learn how to implement the Jigsaw instructional strategy at *The Best Resources For Learning About The Jigsaw Instructional Strategy* https://larryferlazzo.edublogs.org/2023/05/03/the-best-resources-for-learning-about-the-jigsaw-instructional-strategy/.

You can find tools that will translate and convert text into "parallel text" at *The Best Tools That Show "Parallel Text"—Same Sentences Translated Into Different Languages Side-By-Side* https://larryferlazzo.edublogs.org/2019/12/31/the-best-tools-that-show-parallel-text-same-sentences-translated-into-different-languages-side-by-side/

Find sources of multi-level texts on similar topics at *The Best Places To Get The "Same" Text Written For Different "Levels"* https://larryferlazzo.edublogs.org/2014/11/16/the-best-places-to-get-the-same-text-written-for-different-levels/.

Go to *The Best Free Online Tools Using Adaptive Learning* https://larryferlazzo.edublogs .org/2023/01/01/the-best-free-online-tools-using-adaptive-learning/ for recommended online adaptive learning sites.

Check out *The Best Resources Documenting The Effectiveness of Free Voluntary Reading* https://larryferlazzo.edublogs.org/2011/02/26/the-best-resources-documenting-the-effectiveness-of-free-voluntary-reading/ for ideas on implementing independent reading.

Find resources, and learn ideas, about using visuals *at The Best Ways To Use Photos In Lessons* https://larryferlazzo.edublogs.org/2010/06/27/the-best-ways-to-use-photos-in-lessons/.

For more formative assessment ideas, go to *The Best Resources For Learning About Formative Assessment* https://larryferlazzo.edublogs.org/2010/08/22/the-best-resources-for-learning-about-formative-assessment/ and *to The Best—& Quickest—Ways To "Check For Understanding"* https://larryferlazzo.edublogs.org/2024/04/07/the-best-quickest-ways-to-check-for-understanding/.

For additional information on ability-group, see *The Best Resources For Learning About Ability Grouping & Tracking—Help Me Find More* https://larryferlazzo.edublogs .org/2013/03/20/the-best-resources-for-learning-about-ability-grouping-tracking-help-me-find-more/. And for more ideas on using small groups in the classroom, see *The Best Posts On The Basics Of Small Groups In The Classroom* https://larryferlazzo .edublogs.org/2011/09/18/my-best-posts-on-the-basics-of-small-groups-in-the-classroom/.

You can find examples of many graphic organizers at *The Best List Of Mindmapping, Flow Chart Tools, & Graphic Organizers* https://larryferlazzo.edublogs.org/2009/02/09/not-the-best-but-a-list-of-mindmapping-flow-chart-tools-graphic-organizers/.

Lots of different sentence starters, writing frames and writing structures can be found at *The Best Scaffolded Writing Frames For Students* https://larryferlazzo.edublogs .org/2016/12/01/the-best-scaffolded-writing-frames-for-students/.

For pre-made multilingual resources to support content instruction, visit *The Best Multilingual & Bilingual Sites For Math, Social Studies, & Science* https://larryferlazzo .edublogs.org/2008/10/03/the-best-multilingual-bilingual-sites-for-math-social-studies-science/.

Guidance for peer tutors and "buddies" working with English Language Learners can be found at *The Best Resources To Help Prepare Tutors & Volunteers In ELL Classes— And, Boy, Do I Need Suggestions!* https://larryferlazzo.edublogs.org/2021/08/29/the-best-resources-to-help-prepare-tutors-volunteers-in-ell-classes-and-boy-do-i-need-suggestions/.

You can find many examples of "Choice Boards" and "Learning Menus" at *The Best Posts & Articles About Providing Students With Choices* https://larryferlazzo .edublogs.org/2010/12/21/the-best-posts-articles-about-providing-students-with-choices/.

Educator Joe Schwartz offers some particularly interesting ideas on how to use student-created questions in a math classroom at *Exit 10A: The D Word* https:// exit10a.blogspot.com/2018/09/the-d-word.html?spref=tw

CHAPTER 4

Tech Has Its Place, but Also Has to Be Kept in Its Place

What Is It?

Tech is everywhere—where it should be, and where it shouldn't be.

This chapter is *not* meant to provide an in-depth analysis of all aspects of technology in the classroom.

Instead, we'll just share a few things:

- Why and how we minimize the use of tech in our classroom
- Discuss the few instances where we do use it in helpful ways
- How we handle student cellphone use
- Our thinking and our practices regarding Artificial Intelligence

Why We Like It

We like some aspects of ed tech, particularly how it can help English Language Learners at home where there may be few or no other speakers of English, and how it can be easily used for translation in the classroom and at home to make English content more accessible to them.

In addition, we love how online games can reinforce learning and provide important formative assessment opportunities.

Finally, we love ed tech where it can help us teachers make our materials more accessible to students and save us time in the process!

In other situations, particularly with student cellphone and student Artificial Intelligence use, we lean more towards figuring out strategies to minimize their harm.

Supporting Research

There is extensive research about how tech can support English Language Learners and English-proficient students *in* the classroom.[1] *However*, based on our experience—and extensive research[2,3,4,5]—many, though not all of those benefits (e.g. the translation support we described in Chapter 3: Differentiated Instruction) can be provided as effectively (or more so) by having peer tutors in the classroom—plus the peer tutors themselves also benefit academically. Given those findings, we're not really sure why schools wouldn't use peer tutors, especially in secondary schools where it should be fairly easy logistically to schedule them into classes. See the Technology Connections section for more information on peer tutors.

But, if you don't have peer tutors, the first reference in this section will lead you to extensive research showing how ELLs can benefit from technology, especially in speaking and listening.[6] Use of tech by ELLs can also lead to more improved writing skills.[7]

Surprisingly, there is little research available on ELLs' use of tech *outside* of the classroom to learn English at home. Nevertheless, we think this is a good example of "if it looks like a duck, swims like a duck, and quacks like a duck, then it must be a duck." In other words, if research finds that ed tech can be helpful to ELLs *in* the classroom, then it's likely to be helpful to them *outside* of it, too. We discuss what this looks like for us later in this chapter.

Though we have not had many students with moderate developmental or physical disabilities in our classrooms, the research is clear that tech can be helpful to those

[1] Ferlazzo, L. (2011, February 23). The best places to find research on technology & language teaching/learning. *Larry Ferlazzo's Website of the Day.*

[2] Chang, A., Mauer, E., Wanzek, J., et al. (2025). Examining the academic effects of cross-age tutoring: A meta-analysis. *Educational Psychology Review, 37*(1), 19. https://doi.org/10.1007/s10648-025-09997-z

[3] Terada, Y. (2023, January 13). A research-backed tool kit of what works—and doesn't work—in education. *Edutopia.*

[4] Sparks, S. D. (2015, March 31). "Middle" students find success tutoring peers, in NYC study. *Education Week.*

[5] Dietrichson, J., Filges, T., Seerup, J. K., et al. (2021). Targeted school-based interventions for improving reading and mathematics for students with or at risk of academic difficulties in Grades K-6: A systematic review. *Campbell Systematic Reviews, 17*(2), e1152. https://doi.org/10.1002/cl2.1152

[6] Harper, D., Bowles, A. R., Amer, L., et al. (2021). Improving outcomes for English learners through technology: A randomized controlled trial. *AERA Open.* https://doi.org/10.1177/23328584211025528

[7] Seyyedrezaei, M. S., Amiryousefi, M., Gimeno-Sanz, A., & Tavakoli, M. (2024). A meta-analysis of the relative effectiveness of technology-enhanced language learning on ESL/EFL writing performance: Retrospect and prospect. *Computer Assisted Language Learning, 37*(7), 1771–1805. https://doi.org/10.1080/09588221.2022.2118782

with reading, writing, visual, and organizational challenges.[8] However, in keeping with our rule of not writing about experiences we have not had and strategies we have not actually tried in the classroom, we won't be discussing these ideas in this chapter.

Research on classroom ed tech use for English-proficient students has been decidedly mixed[9,10,11] though, like with ELLs, there has been some positive feedback for homework use.

In terms of student cellphone use, we don't even feel like we have to cite any research on its negative impact on the classroom—studies are ubiquitous.

It's difficult to accurately point to extensive credible research on Machine Learning, also known as Artificial Intelligence, in the classroom because, as education researcher Benjamin Riley has pointed out, so many studies have been found to be "shady."[12] Education technologist Wess Trabelsi uses a different term with a similar perspective: they "can't be trusted"[13] because of "overblown conclusions" among other criticisms. But Trabelsi suggests that the best studies find that overreliance on generative AI, that is AI that generates text or images based on input from a user, is not helpful to learning, but that it has *potential* to help if used as a "supplement" to non-tech classroom methods.

We definitely concur with those findings as they relate to out-of-classroom support for ELLs and have heard from many Special Education teachers that AI can help learning disabled students in and outside of the classroom.

As far as using generative AI to positively "supplement" instruction for other students, we're not yet convinced. However, in this chapter we'll describe how we're making the best of what we consider to be a bad situation.

Application

WHY AND HOW WE MINIMIZE THE USE OF TECH IN OUR CLASSROOM

We mentioned earlier how, in our English Language Learner classes, we hardly ever use tech (outside of online games for formative assessments and Google translate if

---

[8] Garnier, P. (2025). The contribution of technology according to special education teachers working with students with moderate intellectual and developmental disabilities. *International Journal of Developmental Disabilities, 1–9*. https://doi.org/10.1080/20473869.2025.2473421

[9] Grose, J. (2024, March 27). Screens are everywhere in schools. Do they actually help kids learn? *The New York Times*.

[10] Kolb, L. (2024, September 5). 7 Research findings about technology and education. *Edutopia*.

[11] Will technology transform education for the better? (J-PAL Evidence Review). (2019*). Abdul Latif Jameel Poverty Action Lab*.

[12] Riley, B. (2025, May 20). Something rotten in AI research. *Cognitive Resonance*.

[13] Trabelsi, W. (2025, March 7). The Good, the Bad, and the Ugly Science of AI in Education. *AI ∩ K12 = Wess*.

tutors don't understand the ELL student's home language) *in* the classroom because the use of peer tutors, which are usually one-to-one or one-to-two, fulfills the similar purposes more effectively.

However, tech is still a key part of our instructional process with ELLs. Typically, there are no other members of our students' households who know English, so that's where tech comes in.

We ask students to work online at least one-half-hour each night. Though several of the sites we provide them to work on offer us reports on how the student did, the prime motivational and accountability strategy is having regular conversations with students' caregivers, and that seems to be fairly effective.

We regularly encourage students to do this kind of homework by explaining that, though they are likely to be able to graduate high school just with the English they learn and practice at school, because they are beginning to learn English late in their adolescences, learning and practicing more English at home will be essential to their success in college. Since most of our students have high professional aspirations, this kind of rationale seems to strike a chord for them.

See the Technology Connections section for links to some of the sites we have ELL students use at home.

Our thinking about tech use in our classes that have predominantly English proficient students has taken some turns over the years. Prior to 2020, like many teachers, we seldom used it in class (apart from having ELLs use their phones for Google Translate and other students using them occasionally for research), except when we were lucky enough to get space in one of the school's computer labs.

Then came the COVID pandemic, and *everything* was online during distance learning. We generally continued that practice in our non-ELL classes after we returned to physical schooling—students were comfortable with it, and it was so much easier for us teachers with not having to spend hours in the copy room churning out paper copies for all our students, and grading was a breeze!

Then, more recently, we and many other educators became more concerned with the amount of student screentime during the day (not including phones—that's for a different section of this chapter). We also began hearing from some of our students that they were experiencing "screen fatigue."

Though Katie has come to similar conclusions, we're going to use the story of Larry's IB Theory of Knowledge (TOK) classes to share his experiences, which we believe reflect those of many other teachers.

Larry's TOK classes have always gone relatively well—his students always gave him and his classes the highest marks in anonymous evaluations and TOK students who were IB Diploma candidates did fine in the IB-evaluated assessments. And, since distance learning ended, practically everything was done online—daily Google Slides presentations, online assignments, all online readings (though students were always given the option of submitting work with pen-and-paper, an alternative hardly ever used by anyone).

But, then, in the middle of Larry's final school year, he began to have second thoughts about what he was doing in his TOK classes.

The quality of work being done by about 60-or-70% of students—who he would characterize as the most motivated and engaged—was excellent (most of them were IB Diploma candidates). None of those 60% seemed to be doing any (or, if they were, very little) of copying and pasting text online to the many slideshows we did; from what he could tell, few of them were spending much time on non-class related websites on their open Chromebooks; and most of their talking in class appeared to be about joint assignments they were doing. (Hardly anyone at all in the class was using Large-Language Model Machine Learning (Artificial Intelligence) apps, but we'll talk more about that later in this chapter.)

All that was the kind of atmosphere he saw in almost his *entire* TOK class pre-COVID, when most text was on paper, and, instead of slideshows, students were regularly working together to create posters for class presentations.

That last year, however, it appeared to Larry that 30-or-40% of his class (practically none of whom were IB Diploma candidates) seemed considerably less engaged—doing a lot of copy-and-pasting, spending substantial time on non-class-related websites, and definitely not using most of their time talking about assignments.

That doesn't mean that Larry believed 30 or 40% of his students weren't learning at least the basics of the material or concepts in the curriculum—through participating in the almost constant rotating presentations and the required personal reflections on them, he was convinced that most had learned the ideas on the surface level, at least.

He wasn't sure if this potential problem had been present every year since we came back from distance learning, and he had just begun noticing it. Or, perhaps, it wasn't an issue when classes first returned from distance learning because students were so happy to be back, and it just became worse recently.

His observations that year reminded him of an experiment he did many years ago where one year he taught two ELL US History classes covering the same content—but one class was taught entirely in the computer lab and the other in his classroom using no tech at all. The results of content assessments (which, admittedly, were pretty surface level ones) were similar. However, when students completed surveys on how engaged they felt in the class and how much it made them want to learn more about history, the students in the non-tech class were dramatically more positive.

Our question and concern is wondering if tech tends to work more for the students who we sometimes call almost "teacher-proof"—they are going to work towards success no matter what—and leaves others who tend to experience more challenges (we want to emphasize that intelligence is NOT one of them) behind?

We can't say with certainty our lesser-tech strategy is definitively better than high-tech use. But, given that research on the effectiveness of ed tech in the classroom is indeed mixed, as we shared earlier, we would encourage teachers to consider our reflections and do what you think is best for you and your students.

Interestingly, in anonymous surveys, 60% of Larry's students (the same percentage, more-or-less, of students he felt were fully engaged in class) liked using the tech in class, though there's no way of accurately telling if it was the *same* 60%.

If Larry hadn't retired at the end of that year, he would have reverted his TOK class to pre-COVID pen-paper-poster days in future years, a move that Katie is applying more of in her classes now.

WHERE AND WHEN DO WE USE ED TECH?

It's not entirely accurate to say we don't use *any* ed tech with students in our ELL classes. We do use online games for formative assessments, with students either using their laptops or, more commonly, their cellphones to play them (of course, we also often play learning games that don't require tech). And we do the same in all of our other classes, too.

There are three other areas where we do use ed tech and feel that it enhances our teaching.

One, in our ELL classes, visually graphing student progress (or, less frequently, lack of progress) in in-class formative assessments and in online game results can have an incredibly powerful impact on students. Showing their progress visually seems to really "pack a punch," and they often take pictures of them to share with parents.

Secondly, using generative AI to modify teaching materials can make them much more accessible to students, and we'll discuss that later in this chapter.

Thirdly, since it's not unusual for us to need to write well over twenty student recommendations for college or scholarships each year, we will explain later in this chapter how we use generative AI ethically to help us write them, resulting in better letters for our students and saved time for us.

HANDLING STUDENT CELLPHONE USE

As just about every teacher has experienced, student cellphones in the post pandemic period became huge problems in many classrooms—ours included.

Improvements didn't really begin in our classrooms until all teachers in our respective schools agreed to universally enforce a no cellphone rule in the classroom, unless officially authorized by the teacher (e.g. for translation, playing online learning games, etc.).

Here is how we each implemented these bans in our classrooms. Of course, if you are in a school that uses pouches for phones, making them inaccessible to students for the entire school day, you may want to skip this part.

In Larry's classroom, as long as it isn't abused, he allows students to use their phones for "family, work or school." However, prior to using their phone for one of those purposes, students must tell him (this may happen two-or-three times in a typical class and are typically very unobtrusive). If students are using their phone for something else, or don't tell him they are taking their phone out for one of the three authorized uses, he gives them a warning (this may happen three times during a class). If they take it out again, Larry gives them a small paper bag and a piece of tape (this may happen once every two weeks). They then have to tape it up and put it in their backpack (this eliminates any potential power struggle of the student needing to give it to the teacher and, in fact, turns it into a low-key humorous interaction).

One of the key reasons Larry thinks this policy works so well in his classes is because it applies to him, too. He needs to tell students he is going to take his phone out for school or family. If he neglects to tell them before he takes it out or, if students catch him using it for other reasons (like scrolling the news), he has to buy treats for the entire class the following day. Larry makes sure each of his classes "catches him" once early in the school year to communicate this message of mutual accountability.

In Katie's class, she uses a "phone box." As she is greeting students at the door, they are invited to place their phones in the box for that period. Because most teachers at Katie's school follow this same practice, it becomes a routine and most of the students don't have an issue following this procedure. If a student or parent doesn't feel comfortable with this practice, the student is expected to keep their phone in their backpack.

Practically speaking, we find that phones are not an issue for 80% of our students. Many of the other 20%, however, almost appear obsessed with them.

We're not saying either of our ways is the best strategy for *your* classroom. We are saying, though, that recognizing occasional exceptions to rules and having a policy of some sort of mutual accountability are likely to be two important elements of any successful cellphone policy—or, in fact, any policy for anything!

GENERATIVE ARTIFICIAL INTELLIGENCE AND EDUCATION

We're dividing this section into two parts. In part one, we discuss how we handle Generative AI in our classrooms now. In part two, we discuss how we use Generative AI in education now, but not necessarily directly with students.

PART ONE: HOW WE HANDLE GENERATIVE AI IN OUR CLASSROOMS NOW

In our ELL classrooms, apart from the generative AI inherent in translation programs, we've already explained that we use little tech and, instead, maximize the use of peer tutors. And, as we explained earlier, we encourage our ELL students to use various AI tools at home to study English.

Our non-ELL classrooms are different stories. Figures 4.1 and 4.2 share the guidance Larry provides his IB Theory of Knowledge students *after* they do a two-or-three week unit on generative AI, its future, and the ethics of its use. The Figures are lengthy and specific to Larry's class. Their key points are that students need to document their use of generative AI and explain why they are using its suggestions.

A link in the Technology Connections sections will lead you to the actual generative AI unit that Larry taught in his classes, along with other resources that might be useful to you when you're teaching your students about generative AI. The first time Larry did that unit, he then had students work in groups to write class guidelines for generative AI use. Because of time constraints, he didn't use it the second year but, if he continued to teach, he would probably make it a higher priority (Katie does the same in her classes.) A link in the Technology Connections section will lead you to some of those student-created guidelines.

For most of the year, required student writing will be on the paragraph level, and **I ask and expect that you do not use Artificial Intelligence tools during those assignments.** An exception will be when we do a unit on Artificial Intelligence during our Knowledge & Technology Unit, and you will primarily be using AI tools during that time.

Exhibitions

During the first semester, you will be writing what are called TOK "Exhibitions," a series of three-hundred-word short essays explaining how objects that you choose answer a prompt. I ask and expect that you will not use AI tools until the very last part of your writing process, if you use them at all. In these short essays, you will have to connect the objects to your personal experience and to what we have read and discussed in class, so AI really won't be helpful to you in composing the essay. You will, however, have access to many examples and other materials to support you.

There will be three times prior to the final three Exhibitions when you will be writing ones as culminating projects finishing up different units. You may use Artificial Intelligence in the following way each time you have to write an Exhibition.

Also note that you will be able to receive similar feedback and support directly from Mr. Ferlazzo during this essay-writing process without using ChatGPT.

If the Exhibition you write without ChatGPT's changes would get at least a B, and incorporating ChatGPT's changes would increase it to an A, you will receive a final grade of an A. If your pre-ChatGPT work is at a C or D level, the grade you receive will not be raised if ChatGPT improves it.

(continued)

After you have completed your Exhibitions, it is acceptable for you to submit them to ChatGPT or another chatbot using these two prompts in this way (this is optional, however—you are not required to use AI):

1. "Please correct any punctuation, grammar or capitalization errors in the following essay: [paste your essay here]."

2. Then, copy and paste your original Exhibition. In the same document, paste the ChatGPT version. Then, below it, paste your final version that includes any of ChatGPT's corrections that you choose to keep. Label each version. Just because ChatGPT suggests it does not make it better! There will be no grade penalty if you use ChatGPT in this way.

3. If you use ChatGPT in this way, please also write below your essay two things you learned from ChatGPT's corrections about punctuation, grammar or capitalization.

4. After you use ChatGPT in this way, you may then paste your new version, including whatever ChatGPT grammar corrections you have chosen to keep, into ChatGPT along with this prompt: "Please make light improvements in the following essay through word choice and sentence structure: [paste your essay here]"

5. Then, follow a similar format: Copy and paste your original "new version." In the same document, paste the ChatGPT version. Then, below it, paste your final version that includes any of ChatGPT's corrections that you choose to keep. There will be no grade penalty if you use ChatGPT in this way.

6. If you use ChatGPT in this way, please also write below your essay two things you learned from ChatGPT's corrections about word choice and sentence structure.

So, if you use ChatGPT in both of these allowed ways, you will be submitting three versions of your Exhibitions:

- Your pre-AI original, along with the AI version that has corrected it for grammar and punctuation, along with your reflections on those changes.

- Then, if you ask AI to provide light feedback on word choice and sentence structure, you will submit that as well, along with your reflections on its feedback that you might have included.

In a reference, you will need to explain how you used AI in the writing.

TOK Essay

Our final project of the year will be writing a 1200-1600 word essay. It will be acceptable to use AI in developing and writing that essay—if you follow a process that we will carefully review in the spring.

Summary

There will be three periods when using Artificial Intelligence in this class will be acceptable:

- During a two-to-three-week period when we study a unit on Artificial Intelligence.

- During the various times when we are working on Exhibitions, which will total approximately five-or-six weeks.

- During the time when you are working on your Final TOK essay, which will be about four weeks.

Apart from these three periods, my expectation is that students in this class will not use Artificial Intelligence tools for any TOK work—UNLESS we do a special assignment that is specifically related to AI.

Figure 4.1 TOK Class Guidelines for Use of AI In Writing

As with the Exhibition, if the essay you write without ChatGPT's changes would get at least a B, and incorporating ChatGPT's changes would increase it to an A, you will receive a final grade of an A. If your pre-ChatGPT work is at a C or D level, the grade you receive will not be raised if ChatGPT improves it.

Do note that you will be able to receive similar feedback and support directly from Mr. Ferlazzo during this essay-writing process.

If you are going to use ChatGPT to help you write your essay, here are the steps that I would like you to take. If you choose to use ChatGPT, you don't necessarily have to use all the options listed. Just please keep in mind that the key is, like we did with the Exhibitions, submitting your pre-ChatGPT version, along with your post ChatGPT work, with your reflections about what changes you made and why.

1. Use it to improve the grammar, punctuation, and sentence structure in your draft. First, paste this prompt into ChatGPT, followed by pasting your draft essay into it (Note that the expectation is that you have written *at least* 1,000 words—more is even better—on your own before you submit it to ChatGPT): *Please make grammar, punctuation, and sentence structure improvements to the following essay. After each paragraph, explain why you made those changes and how they improve the essay.*

It is possible that, in response to this prompt, ChatGPT may just type out an essay with its changes and not include the reasons behind the corrections. Or, it will offer benefits that don't make sense. Remember that ChatGPT is designed to always help—it will always give you something, even if it's not true. If that's the case, then paste this prompt into it: *Can you type each paragraph and after each one explain the changes that you made in it?*

You will also need to get its corrected version without its explanations, so you can then type this prompt: *Please type a version with all the corrections but not including your explanations.*

Then, in a document titled "Draft Essay Corrected for Grammar and Punctuation":

1. Paste your original draft.
2. The ChatGPT paragraph-by-paragraph version with its corrections and explanations.
3. The corrected ChatGPT version without its explanations. This should also include any changes that you have made to it because you don't like or agree with its corrections. Do not assume that all of its modifications are correct. In particular, please make any changes that you don't believe reflect your "voice," especially modifying any brand new sentences it appears to have inserted into the essay.
4. A few sentences you write at the bottom sharing at least two points you have learned from ChatGPT's modifications that you can apply to your future writing.

2. You may use it to improve the content of your essay. First, paste the version of your essay that has been previously corrected by ChatGPT for grammar, punctuation and sentence structure after you paste this prompt into it: *The following essay has been written to respond to this prompt: [paste the prompt]. Please provide additional examples and evidence to strengthen this essay. After each paragraph, explain why you made those changes and how they improve the essay.*

Again, it is possible that, in response to this prompt, ChatGPT may just type out an essay with its changes and not include the reasons behind the corrections. If that's the case, then paste this prompt into it: *Can you type each paragraph and after each one explain the changes that you made in it?*

Then, in a document titled "Draft Essay Including Content Suggestions from ChatGPT":

1. Paste your draft essay that has been corrected by ChatGPT for grammar, punctuation, and sentence structure
2. The ChatGPT paragraph-by-paragraph version with its content corrections and explanations

(continued)

3. After each paragraph, and after each of ChatGPT's explanations, a short commentary from you (in a different color) saying if you agree or disagree with the changes and, if so, why

4. A few sentences you write at the bottom of the document sharing any lesson you have learned from ChatGPT's modifications that you can apply to your future writing

3. Upload your essay and the rubric, along with this prompt: *I am uploading my essay and the rubric that will be used to assess it. In giving me feedback based on the rubric, behave like a considerate teacher who wants me to learn without just giving me the answers.*

You can do this at any stage of your writing. Whenever you do it, though, include it as part of your submission with the essay you wrote prior to using this prompt, ChatGPT's response, and which of their recommendations you decided to use and why.

NOTE: If you quote from ChatGPT, cite it like you would any other reference. There does not yet seem to be agreement on how to cite use of ChatGPT in other ways, yet. So, for now, if you use ChatGPT in the way outlined in this guidance, you can say "ChatGPT was used for editing assistance with teacher guidance and supervision."

Figure 4.2 AI Guidelines for TOK Essays

Providing clear guidance on generative AI use at the beginning of the school year is critical! You'll notice that the written guidance in the Figures offers ways students can use generative AI. You'll also notice that students have to share their work pre-AI use, their work post-AI use, and share reflections about how and why they think generative AI made their work better. Larry also makes one of the key requirements in these assignments that students need to refer specifically to activities and lessons they did *in* class.

As you can see from the two figures, permissible use of generative AI in Larry's class is a somewhat burdensome process. Because of that, few students choose to use it in those ways. However, we are convinced that the fact that he does create a space and a process for students to ethically use it reduces the chances that students will choose to use generative AI inappropriately. And the lack of unethical generative AI use in his classes seems to bear that out. You'll also note that Larry makes it clear that *he* is available to provide similar feedback to the kind they will likely get from generative AI, and unlike an AI app, he knows their strengths and weaknesses, how to provide personalized feedback, and what's needed to be successful in his class.

Though inappropriate generative AI use in our classes has been rare, it has happened a few times a year. Based on anonymous student surveys we periodically do, it doesn't appear that it's happening more often than that.

As a proactive precaution, at the beginning of each year we do have students complete a writing assessment, which is a response to a prompt. Generative AI is blocked by our district's Internet content filter, so we are comfortable having students do it on their laptops if they prefer but, as always, we offer a handwritten alternative (if AI tools were not blocked, we would require everyone to do it written by hand). This writing gives us a "baseline" that we can use as a point of comparison in the future if we have concerns that generative AI may have been used inappropriately in future assignments.

The few times we have suspicions during the year about student generative AI use, we take several actions. The accuracy of generative AI detection tools is *very* questionable, especially for English Language Learners.[14,15] Because of those issues, we first put the writing through *four* different free generative AI detectors. If all four rate the vast majority of writing as AI-generated, we then visit the student's Google Doc version history to see if, at some point, a large amount of text was copied-and-pasted.

If our suspicions appear confirmed, we arrange to have a private individual meeting with the student. We explain that, as we learned in our generative AI unit, generative AI text detectors can be faulty, so their results aren't conclusive, and we share what they said about the student's writing. Every time we have said that, the student immediately admitted to using generative AI. If they hadn't, we would have then explained what we found in their Google Docs version history but, as we mentioned, we have never had to go that far.

Our attitude about the student's use of generative AI is inquiry, not judgment.

We then explain we want to hear *their* voice, not the voice of a machine. We go on to say we love having them in class; we know they are very sharp students who have great futures ahead of them.

Then, we do what many people have done to us in many areas of our lives—we offer them a second chance, with no penalty.

Some may say we are too lenient. But, come on, these are kids, and many may feel under substantial stress. This quote is often attributed to Robin Williams, though many others have said something similar: *Everyone you meet is fighting a battle you know nothing about.* And they are also dealing with an industry that is relentlessly trying to convince them to use its technology.

We would be less lenient if it happened a second time, but we've never had to face that situation.

So, to summarize how we handle generative AI in the classroom:

1. Teach a unit about generative AI, its ethics (and lack of them), its environmental costs, the manipulative strategies of the companies pushing it, the negative consequences of its use to developing writing and critical thinking skills, *and* its potential benefits.

2. If there's time, after the unit is complete, have students create draft guidelines for generative AI use in class.

---

[14] MIT Management STS Teaching and Learning Technologies. (n.d.). AI detectors don't work. Here's what to do instead. *Teach & Learn.*

[15] Woelfel, K. (2023, December 18). Brief – Late Applications: Disproportionate effects of generative AI-detectors on English learners. *Center for Democracy & Technology.*

3. Get a "baseline" of student writing that we can use for comparison in the future.

4. Provide clear guidelines early about its use.

5. Allow students to submit their work on specific assignments before they used AI and afterward, with their explanations and reflections about how they think AI might have improved their product and what they learned from the experience. Offer specific prompts they can use, including, if there is a rubric, having them get critical feedback from a generative AI app.

6. Make it clear to students that we will make time to provide ongoing support and feedback to students on their assignments, and that our comments will likely be better than what they can get from any generative AI app.

We are not at all sure that these guidelines will hold up in future years or are even the best to use right now.

Larry's generative AI unit includes assignments students do with AI, and we very occasionally have incorporated generative AI in other class assignments as experiments. We do this because we also feel responsible to help our students become more familiar with a technology that has the possibility of transforming our society. Of course, since our district's Internet content filters block generative AI sites, these activities are logistically challenging because students have to use their cellphones to connect to them.

Speaking truthfully, apart from students using the generative AI use guidelines in Figures 4.1 and 4.2 (which can actually be applied to just about any other assigned task, as well) the only generative AI-assisted assignment that we have done with English-proficient students where AI use seems to have genuinely added to student learning was when we had students use a generative AI app to write essays, and then student groups did a detailed critique of them (as we've mentioned, we think generative AI can offer substantial benefits to English Language Learners—see the Technology Connections section for ideas).

Practically all of our other assignments are done in class, so we generally don't have to worry about "AI-proofing" them (or making them "AI-resistant"). However, if we were teaching other classes, and we did have to be concerned about that potential problem, here are some strategies we *might* use:

- As Larry does in his generative AI guidance, require students to discuss activities that were done in class.

- Continue our reliance on small student groups doing research and creating posters that they present to the entire class, or sometimes in a "speed dating" style.

- Have students write about personal experiences, including significant events or difficult decisions and how they changed their lives or what they learned from them.

- We like educator Chanea Bond's strategy of having students complete graphic organizers by hand in class to prepare for any writing project.[16]
- There can always be the policy of requiring all writing done in class by hand.

See the Technology Connections section for links to other ideas for class generative AI guidance, for ideas on how to create assignments that might be more "AI-proof" than others, and yes, for some ideas on how to use generative AI deliberately in certain lessons.

We still feel joy in our teaching, but we're sad that AI has robbed us of those special moments.

We're sorry to have to end this section on a down note, but we are very resentful of generative AI in one particular way. In the past, when we would see an exceptional piece of student writing, we would immediately experience joy. Now, however, instead of our first experience being one of joy, we, instead, often immediately think to ourselves, "Did this student use AI to write this?"

PART TWO: HOW WE USE GENERATIVE AI IN EDUCATION NOW, BUT NOT NECESSARILY DIRECTLY WITH STUDENTS

We've discussed in other chapters how we use generative AI to create differentiated materials for students—always double-checking it for accuracy.

Another way we use it is to help with the twenty-or-more student recommendations we write each year for college entrance and scholarships. We use a three-part process. Part one is having students complete Figure 4.3 Letter of Recommendation Request Form. Part two is uploading several previous letters of recommendation we've written to ChatGPT, a generative AI app, so it learns our "style." Then we tell ChatGPT that we are going to upload the student form and dictate our thoughts and experiences with the student (an idea we borrowed from education Brett Vogelsinger[17]), and we want it to combine the form contents and our comments into a letter of recommendation using our writing style. We then make revisions to it and have an excellent letter—much better than our previous ones—to support our student. We, of course, let them know ahead of time that we will be using generative AI to help us write the letter, but that the letters will be in *our* voice. If we were just doing a few each year, we would still have students use the form, but we wouldn't need to ask for generative AI's help. In the past, both of us have had to spend countless uncompensated hours writing these twenty-to-thirty recommendation letters each year. Like most teachers, we have never said no!

[16] @HeyMrsBond. (2023, December 20). The only way I've found to successfully curb the unauthorized use of AI in my classroom this semester is to devote time in class to outlining written assignments using graphic organizers. https://x.com/heymrsbond/status/1737467281553109350

[17] Vogelsinger, B. (2025, June 24). What does it mean to "use" AI? *The Important Work.*

Your name ____

The better you answer these questions, the better the letter of recommendation I can write for you!

1. What do you think might be your professional career field and why do you want to pursue it?

2. What do you think are your strengths as a student and as a person?

3. What are the biggest challenges you have faced in your life and how have you dealt with them?

4. What extracurricular activities (at school or outside of school) have you participated in and why have you participated in them?

5. What accomplishment are you most proud of and why are you proud of it?

6. What is the hardest thing you have ever done and why did you do it?

7. What is the biggest mistake you have ever made and what did you learn from it?

8. What actions have you taken to help others in or outside of school? Please try to be as specific as possible.

9. Is there anything else that you think I should know that would help me write a letter of recommendation for you?

Figure 4.3   Letter of Recommendation Request Form

A third way we love to use AI is utilizing the AI features in online tools like Wayground (formerly Quizizz) and Blooket to create formative assessment games for all our students and bilingual flashcards for our ELLs. It makes fewer errors for these kinds of simple activities and saves us *a lot* of time when creating review exercises. Of course, we carefully review any content they create for us to confirm there are no mistakes.

A recent Gallup poll said that teachers who were regular users of AI saved 5.9 hours per week, though these data need to be carefully considered as teachers may be over-estimating the time and benefits of AI.[18] That's certainly higher than it saves us, but we'll take one-or-two hours that we can then use to spend in better ways with our students or with our families.

---

[18] Malek Ash, A. (2025, June 24). Three in 10 teachers use AI weekly, saving six weeks a year. *Gallup Education News*.

What Could Go Wrong

More can go wrong here than in just about any topic covered in this book!

If your colleagues aren't enforcing a student cellphone policy and you're the "bad teacher," then you're in a terrible situation. We still think the policies we use are the best strategies to use, but it's going to be tough.

Companies are going to keep on pressuring schools to use AI and, as usual, most districts will be years behind the curve in providing professional development and support to teachers. If you follow our strategy of minimizing use of tech in class and having the kind of generative AI policies we recommend (and involve students in creating those policies), we think you might be able to minimize its harm, but who knows?

The bottom line is so much is so new, we're not even sure what specific ways it can all go south, much less offer ideas on how to deal with those challenges.

The links in Larry's blog, though, are continually updated, so we'd recommend you check them regularly.

Chapter Summary

If we only had a few minutes to chat in the teacher faculty room, here's what we'd want you to remember about technology:

Technology Connections

For more information on peer tutors, see *The Best Resources On Peer Tutors* https://larryferlazzo.edublogs.org/2023/02/04/the-best-resources-on-peer-tutors/.

For a list of sites we have our English Language Learners use at home, visit *The Role Of Tech IN My ELL Classroom? Not Much, But That's Not The Whole Story* https://larryferlazzo.edublogs.org/2024/09/15/the-role-of-tech-in-my-ell-classroom-not-much-but-thats-not-the-whole-story/.

For helpful resources on teaching your students about *Artificial Intelligence, visit A Beginning List Of The Best Resources For Teaching About Artificial Intelligence* https://larryferlazzo.edublogs.org/2023/03/16/a-beginning-list-of-the-best-resources-for-teaching-about-artificial-intelligence/.

See samples of student-created guidelines for AI use at *Student-Created Examples Of Guidelines For Using Artificial Intelligence* https://larryferlazzo.edublogs.org/2023/06/23/student-created-examples-of-guidelines-for-using-artificial-intelligence/.

For other ideas of classroom AI guidance, visit *A Beginning List Of Different Types Of Guidance Educators Are Giving Students About AI Use In Their Classes* https://larryferlazzo.edublogs.org/2025/02/04/a-beginning-list-of-different-types-of-guidance-educators-are-giving-students-about-ai-use-in-their-classes/.

For ideas on how we use AI with English Language Learners, visit *The Best Posts About Using Artificial Intelligence With ELLs* https://larryferlazzo.edublogs.org/2023/06/04/the-best-posts-about-using-artificial-intelligence-with-ells/.

Check out ideas assignments that offer more challenges for students to do with AI at *I Asked Artificial Intelligence To Recommend Student Writing Prompts That Can't Be Easily Helped By AI—Here Are 14 Of Them* https://larryferlazzo.edublogs.org/2023/06/08/i-asked-artificial-intelligence-to-recommend-student-writing-prompts-that-cant-be-easily-helped-by-ai-here-are-14-of-them/. Despite its title, in addition to ChatGPT's ideas, suggestions from many other teachers are included.

Ways to incorporate AI in beneficial ways to students can be found at *The "Best" Ideas For Using ChatGPT, Bard, & Other Forms Of AI With Students* https://larryferlazzo.edublogs.org/2023/05/14/the-best-ideas-for-using-chatgpt-bard-other-forms-of-ai-with-students/.

CHAPTER 5

Developing Classrooms That Promote Self-Motivation

What Is It?

A sure way to burn out as a teacher is feeling that it's your responsibility to constantly motivate students to learn every day.

Not only is it a recipe for burn out, but it's also a recipe for failure.

If there's one thing we have learned—and Larry, in particular, has learned so much that he's written four books just on student motivation—is that we might be able to occasionally motivate a student to do something over the short-term, but if we're serious about anything happening over the long-term, then we have to create conditions that support students motivating themselves.

Self-Determination Theory is probably the most widely known theory on human motivation, and we think it presents the best structure for understanding how to create those critical conditions.[1] It was originally developed by professors Edward Deci and Richard Ryan and highlights three key elements critical for creating the conditions that help support everyone, including students, to motivate themselves—autonomy, competence, and relatedness. Many researchers also either

---

[1] Weir, K. (2025, March 2). Self-determination theory: A quarter century of human motivation research. *Breakthrough Psychological Science.*

include "relevance" within the "autonomy" category or explicitly add it as a fourth criteria[2,3]:

1. **Autonomy:** Students feel like they have a degree of control over what needs to happen and how it can be done.

2. **Competence:** Students feel like they have the ability to be successful in doing it.

3. **Relatedness:** Students feel that doing the activity helps them feel more connected to others and feel cared about by people they respect.

4. **Relevance:** The work must be seen by students as interesting and valuable to them and useful to their present lives and/or hopes and dreams for the future. "Relevance" can apply to topics or activities of "interest" to them, even if they may not necessarily be considered "helpful" or "useful." For example, Larry found an article he recently read about door-to-door salespeople "interesting," but nothing in it is particularly "useful" to him.

Not every lesson has to include *all* four elements, but it shouldn't be too difficult to include at least one of them in most lessons.

This kind of intrinsic motivation—where the energy to work and take actions comes from within us—contrasts with extrinsic motivation—where that kind of energy is moved in response to outside rewards and punishments. Research, and our own experiences, suggests that these kinds of extrinsic "motivators" may prompt immediate action, but they also tend to undermine intrinsic motivation over the long term; as well as reducing creativity.[4,5,6,7,8]

The world, and our classrooms, are not always an either/or situation. We are huge believers in the power of intrinsic motivation, yet situations arise fairly commonly when we use extrinsic strategies. We've already discussed the use of extra credit in previous chapters. We've all had experiences where if a student doesn't want

[2] Assor, A., Kaplan, H., & Roth, G. (2002). Choice is good, but relevance is excellent: Autonomy-enhancing and suppressing teacher behaviours predicting students' engagement in schoolwork. *British Journal of Educational Psychology, 72*(2), 261–278. https://doi.org/10.1348/000709902158883

[3] Center on Education Policy. (2012). *What Is Motivation and Why Does It Matter?* The George Washington University.

[4] Dean, J. (2023, February 17). What is motivation? *PsyBlog.*

[5] Deci, E. L., Koestner, R., & Ryan, R. (2024, November 4). Research bite #2: Extrinsic rewards and intrinsic motivation in education. *Tips for Teachers.*

[6] Terada, Y. (2019, July 25). Extrinsic motivation: It might be even worse than you thought. *Edutopia.*

[7] Kanowitz, S. (2017, August 2). They offered to pay people to go to the gym. Guess what happened? *The Washington Post.*

[8] Turgeon, H. (2018, August 21). Which is better, rewards or punishments? Neither. *The New York Times.*

to put their phone away, we threaten to call the hall monitor, who will take their phone for the entire rest of the day. And what are grades if not an extrinsic hammer?

Of course, sometimes we, and our students, can have intrinsic and extrinsic motivations simultaneously. We have written our books because the writing and thinking process behind doing so has made us better teachers *and* we like receiving royalty payments. Our students may very well enjoy learning what we're teaching *and* are appreciative of our calling their parents/guardians and telling them their child is doing great in class.

Some researchers suggest that "motivation transformations" are possible, by jump starting students with extrinsic motivation and then they move themselves towards intrinsic motivation by developing an enjoyment of learning. Interestingly, these same researchers write that, "this idea is still theoretical, and there is not much empirical evidence to support it."[9] This is likely yet another example of some academic researchers living in a bubble since many parents, grandparents, and educators, including us, have had occasional success with making this kind of change happen, though it's successful—in our experience, at least—only a very small percentage of time. Larry had success supporting one of his granddaughters becoming an avid reader after he created a reading board game, and another after instituting a point system for an "out of control" class we discuss in Chapter 8: Classroom Climate and Culture.

This chapter will share our experiences, and recommendations, on how to prioritize the former and more sparingly use the latter.

The real question is what do we teachers tend to do more of, which is the strategy we try to go to first and what do students hear from us more about? Is it us using the strategies we discuss in the Application section of this chapter? Or are we viewed by our students as primarily wielding the power of rewards and punishments in order to obtain compliance?

Why We Like It

What teacher wants to take on the full responsibility of having to motivate 150 or more students every single day in a school year?

Not only is that exhausting, but we're only with them one hour out of twenty-four! We're not going to be there the other sixteen hours when they're not sleeping to encourage, cajole, prompt, push, and cheer them on.

We feel that it's absolutely necessary for educators—and education researchers—to make the issue of student motivation a much higher priority than it often is in policy and practitioner discussions. So much research and energy is spent on

---

[9] Bardach, L., & Murayama, K. (2025). The role of rewards in motivation—Beyond dichotomies. *Learning and Instruction, 96.* https://doi.org/10.1016/j.learninstruc.2024.102056

identifying "effective" instructional strategies. However, it doesn't matter if it's effective if students won't do it![10]

Brazilian educator Paulo Freire wrote:

> The teacher is of course an artist, but being an artist does not mean that he or she can make the profile, can shape the students. What the educator does in teaching is to make it possible for the students to become themselves.[11]

If we're truly serious about supporting the long-term success of our students and supporting the long-term staying power of teachers, it seems to us that leading with strategies that create the conditions where student intrinsic motivation can thrive is one of the most effective ways we can "make it possible for the students to become themselves."

Supporting Research

Self-Determination Theory, its primary elements, and the undermining effects of extrinsic motivation—specifically studied in the education context—have all been supported by many different researchers.[12]

It's obviously not the only theory about motivation in the world, but it's certainly one of the most well-accepted and respected.[13]

Though most researchers don't tend to rank Self-Determination Theory's elements in comparison to each other, some believe that a sense of competence is most important for students to want to learn, while others suggest that relatedness is the biggest motivating factor.[14,15,16]

---

[10] Ferlazzo, L. (2014, July 26). It doesn't matter if it's "effective" if students won't do it. *Larry Ferlazzo's Website of the Day*.

[11] Horton, M., & Freire, P. (1990). *We Make the Road by Walking: Conversations on Education and Social Change*. (B. Bell, J. Gaventa, & J. M. Peters, Eds.). Temple University Press. Page 181.

[12] Howard, J. L., Bureau, J., Guay, F., et al. (2021). Student motivation and associated outcomes: A meta-analysis from self-determination theory. *Perspectives on Psychological Science, 16*(6), 1300–1323. https://doi.org/10.1177/1745691620966789

[13] Knispel, S. (2017, June 14). What really motivates us. *University of Rochester Marketing and Communications Society & Culture*.

[14] Barshay, J. (2021, September 27). What almost 150 studies say about how to motivate students. *The Hechinger Report's Proof Point*.

[15] Yu, S., & Levesque-Bristol, C. (2020). A cross-classified path analysis of the self-determination theory model on the situational, individual and classroom levels in college education. *Contemporary Educational Psychology, 61*.

[16] Xie, K., Vongkulluksn, V. W., Cheng, S.-L., & Jiang, Z. (2022). Examining high-school students' motivation change through a person-centered approach. *Journal of Educational Psychology, 114*(1), 89–107.

In addition to all the research, Self-Determination Theory just makes sense to us and reflects what we have learned in our personal and professional lives.

Application

Many of the strategies we discuss in other chapters, particularly the ones on building relationships and developing student agency, also contribute to creating the conditions for student self-motivation.

We'll also be discussing the role of providing student feedback in motivation in Chapter 9: Providing Effective Student Feedback.

Here are some other ideas, divided into the four key elements we described earlier as needed to support student intrinsic motivation:

AUTONOMY

Choices

We discussed the value of offering student choices in Chapter 2: Student Agency, NOT Student Empowerment, and it's also an important component of supporting student self-motivation.

Whether it's periodically giving students the option of choosing their partners for group work (with clear behavioral guidelines), providing options for essay prompts, giving various alternatives for how they might present culminating projects (video, essay, podcast, slideshow presentation, etc.), or letting students choose their books for independent reading time—opportunities abound for building student autonomy through choice.

Other more ambitious areas for student choice can be having small groups choose the "problems" they want to focus on in a Problem-Based Learning assignment (also discussed in Chapter 2: Student Agency, NOT Student Empowerment) or, again in small groups, choosing objectives for a Project-Based Learning activity. These kinds of research tasks typically lead to a concrete . . . project (poster, slideshow, report) accompanied by a presentation, often, though not always, to an audience of classmates *and* others. For example, our students have done Project-Based Learning lessons on different career choices

> *Just giving students options does not automatically mean that it promotes student autonomy, however. The choices need to be personally meaningful to students, adequate support needs to be provided so that they feel like they can be successful in completing them, and, ideally, students have a strong voice in determining who they can work with if the assignments are done in groups (recognizing that the teacher must enforce behavioral standards).*[17]

[17] Parker, F., Novak, J., & Bartell, T. (2017, September 25). To engage students, give them meaningful choices in the classroom. *Kappan*.

after first researching and determining the criteria for a "good" career. In the "Teaching Others" section of the Student Agency Chapter, the end-of-year assignment where groups can teach the class about a topic of their choice (subject to teacher approval) is another example of Project-Based Learning.

Choice Boards, also known as Learning Menus, are another way to offer student choices. These offer multiple equally academically rigorous assignments with similar learning objectives. See the Technology Connections section for a link to see examples, or just search for the countless ones available online.

Student Voice

Researchers have found that students tend to have increased academic achievement if they feel that their teachers and schools are responsive to their ideas and suggestions.[18]

We discussed one way to do this in the Agency chapter—using a weekly Google Form survey and doing anonymous class evaluations—making sure you acknowledge/respond to what students say! We also shared other ideas in that chapter to support student voice, including listening to how much time they think they need to complete assignments, developing "student leadership teams," and supporting community engagement.

Another strategy for supporting student voice is using "Connection" or "Community-Building" Circles. Though some teachers use them as regular activities, we've tended to only use them as a structured way to invite student voice in response to significant events that have negatively affected many of them—the police killing of an African-American man holding a cellphone in his family's backyard near our school, fear of family members being deported, the death of a classmate. A link in the Technology Connections section will lead to resources offering specific guidance for organizing these circles, but a simple summary of them is that the class sits in a circle, a guiding question is presented, and a "talking piece" is shared around (only the person holding it can speak).

We do like another strategy for elevating student voice that other teachers we respect have done, though we have not. It's assisting students to create an online school newspaper or to contribute to one that is already existing. Neither of our schools have had one, and we haven't had it in us to start one. But the advantages of it to promote student voice are obvious.

---

[18] Blad, E. (2022, June 16). Really listening to students has an academic payoff, new research finds. *Education Week.*

COMPETENCE

Progress Principle

Harvard professor Teresa Amabile tracked thousands of diary entries from hundreds of workers and discovered that their making small progress on meaningful projects appeared to be the key element in their feeling more motivation. She labeled this finding "The Progress Principle."[19]

We've applied this finding to the classroom by adapting an idea by author Daniel Pink. He calls it a "Progress Ritual" and encourages people at the end of the day to write down three "small wins."[20,21]

We don't do it daily, but we do it as often as we can and definitely at least once a week, usually on a Friday. We ask students to write down three things they learned or accomplished in school during the previous week or previous 24 hours, and then we have students share what they wrote in a "speed-dating" style.

Positive Reinforcement

What a teacher says and how they say it can have a big impact on students' confidence levels. We'll discuss "teacher talk" more in Chapter 9: Providing Effective Student Feedback.

Here, we'd like to highlight a couple of points. One thing that's important to note when supporting a growth mindset and encouraging students to feel more confident in taking risks is to provide positive commentary on students' actions instead of labeling "the kind of person we think they are." In other words, praising Maria for "clearly putting a lot of thought and time into the draft essay on this new prompt" is more likely to reinforce a sense of competence instead of calling her a "smart student." If we do the latter, Maria may feel worse about herself when she makes mistakes or doesn't do as good work when trying new things in the future, and therefore may be less likely to take those risks because it may put her self-image as a "smart student" in question. We are applying Carol Dweck's growth mindset paradigm by praising her *actions,* which are completely within Maria's control, and not some amorphous label about her intelligence.[22]

[19] Amabile, T., & Kramer, S. (2011, May). The power of small wins. *Harvard Business Review*.

[20] @DanielPink. (2025, July 26). Try it tonight. Write down three small wins from your day. Reply here with one of them. Let's celebrate progress. X. https://x.com/DanielPink/status/1949099674897719634

[21] Ferlazzo, L. (2010, May 17). The best posts & articles on "motivating" students. *Larry Ferlazzo's Website of the Day*.

[22] Dweck, C. S. (2008). The perils and promises of praise. *Best of Educational Leadership 2007–2008,* 65, 34–39.

Secondly, teachers can support students not only by *what* they say, but in the *tone* of voice they use when they say it. Researchers, and our own experience, has found that students tend to respond better and feel more supported when teachers speak in a quieter voice, more slowly, and more softly than in the opposite way.[23]

Mental Imagery

Visualizing success, particularly visualizing overcoming obstacles to success, can be an effective way to support students' sense of competence and help with motivation.[24,25]

Larry has used it often with both his English Language Learner classes and with his classes primarily composed of English-proficient students. Students are asked to silently enter his classroom where the lights dimmed and he's playing meditative music. Once at their desk, they're asked to close their eyes. Larry will then lead students through a short visualization exercise ("You've entered a restaurant and are going to order your meal in English" or "You're getting ready to begin writing your essay but you don't know how to start").

Participation is optional—there is no penalty if students just want to sit there quietly. However, through his surveys, he's found almost everyone reports taking part in them. Prior to the first mental imagery exercise, he does a lesson sharing research about it, and videos, particularly of famous athletes, talking about how much it helps them improve.

An added benefit, not to be discounted, is that Larry finds it can be a huge classroom management help to get everyone quieted down and focused, especially for classes that come right after lunch or after Physical Education.

Larry is not a trained education researcher, but his surveys of students have regularly shown that students participating in visual imagery consistently outperform those who do not.[26] Students like doing it, too! In fact, it's not uncommon for students themselves to both suggest scenarios for visualization *and* volunteer to lead them.

[23] Paulmann, S., & Weinstein, N. (2023). Teachers' motivational prosody: A pre-registered experimental test of children's reactions to tone of voice used by teachers. *British Journal of Educational Psychology, 93*(2), 437–452. https://doi.org/10.1111/bjep.12567

[24] Lane, A. M., Totterdell, P., MacDonald, I., et al. (2016). Brief online training enhances competitive performance: Findings of the BBC lab UK Psychological Skills Intervention Study. *Frontiers in Psychology, 7*. https://doi.org/10.3389/fpsyg.2016.00413

[25] Ferlazzo, L. (2021, September 28). Intriguing info on how Michael Phelps uses visualization & how I'll use it with students. *Larry Ferlazzo's Website of the Day*.

[26] Ferlazzo, L. (2010, February 28). More results from students visualizing success. *Larry Ferlazzo's Website of the Day*.

See the Technology Connections for videos and other resources on mental imagery, including lesson ideas for introducing the concept to students.

Scaffolding

A scaffold in the classroom, like a scaffold outside a building under construction, is a *temporary* support put in place to facilitate success. The idea is that at some point after students have used the scaffolds, they won't need them anymore and will feel confident about doing the work on their own. The word was first applied to education by researchers David Wood, Jerome S. Bruner, Gail Ross in 1976[27] and many educators since that time then have found that it can be used effectively for student learning.[28,29] Of course, many teachers also used them prior to 1976 and just didn't call them "scaffolds."[30]

Chapter 3: Differentiated Instruction is filled to the brim with scaffolding ideas like sentence starters, writing frames, engineered text, pre-teaching vocabulary, and the use of visuals, just to name a few of the ones we described there.

Some educators try to distinguish between *differentiation* and *scaffolding*, suggesting that differentiation often describes differences in the tasks that students have to complete, and scaffolding refers to steps they need to take to complete the task.[31] We respect our fellow educators but, as far as we're concerned, this is a case of "You say tomato and I say tomato"—we don't think it matters what you call them in the classroom.

If you are looking for even more scaffolds than the ones we described in Chapter 3—and there are, indeed, many—go to a link in the Technology Connections section.

Letters to Students

Larry tries to write short letters—more like notes—to his students at least once a year. Each letter shares something he appreciates about them, what they did well, and what he hopes they would be able to do in the final months of the school year to tie in with what he knows about the dreams they have for themselves.

[27] Wood, D., Bruner, J. S., & Ross, G. (1976). The role of tutoring in problem solving. *Journal of Child Psychology and Psychiatry, 17*(2), 89–100. https://doi.org/10.1111/j.1469-7610.1976.tb00381.x

[28] Fisher, D., Frey, N., & Almarode, J. (2023, May 5). Scaffolding success. *Language Magazine*.

[29] Aubin, G. (2022, September 22). Scaffolding - more than just a worksheet. *Education Endowment Foundation Blog*.

[30] Gaffney, J. S., & Rodgers, E. (2018). Scaffolding research: Taking stock at the four-decade mark. *International Journal of Educational Research, 90*, 175–176. https://doi.org/10.1016/j.ijer.2018.04.001

[31] Hess, K. (2024, February 21). How to be strategic with scaffolding strategies. *MiddleWeb: All About the Middle Grades*.

For example, in one he wrote:

> I really appreciate how you've turned things around this semester and have become a serious learner. Even when there are plenty of opportunities to get distracted, you've been doing a good job at staying focused. You've said you want to be more of a leader, and I know that in the last three months of the school year you can do that by helping other students more in small groups.

His students are always surprised when they enter class and see envelopes with their names on them sitting on their desks. And they almost always have some visible positive impact on student attitudes and, from what they say in their weekly "Check-Ins" (see Chapter 1: Relationships, Relationships, Relationships), enhance their sense of self-confidence.

AGENCY

So many of this book's chapters are interconnected! Just about every strategy we suggested in Chapter 2: Student Agency, NOT Student Empowerment *also* supports students developing a sense of their own competence!

Writing About Values

Several years ago, Larry learned about a research finding that doing a simple 15-minute writing activity three to five times during a school year at important transitional times, like the beginning and end of the year, or right before a final exam, could result in long-lasting academic benefits, especially to students experiencing academic challenges.[32]

The researchers concluded that having students write about values that are important to them develops resiliency and reminds them that "their entire self-worth was not riding on a single test result" and increases their sense of competence.

Larry often used this exercise in his classes, and was always pleased with the positive impact the actual writing and the class sharing afterward seemed to have on his students.

Unlike a fair number of studies on academic interventions, this one has more recently been duplicated in larger scales and has continued to be found effective.[33]

[32] Carey, B. (2009, April 16). Task to aid self-esteem lifts grades for some. *The New York Times*.

[33] Ferlazzo, L. (2018, September 9). New research finds that simple writing exercise about personal values can have a big impact. *Larry Ferlazzo's Website of the Day*.

Here is our summary of the three-part exercise the researchers did and, with little change, Larry used (though Larry never did it more than three times during the school year).[34]

Researchers had students write three-to-five times during one school year about their values.

The first two times, students were given this list of values:

- athletic ability
- being good at art
- being smart or getting good grades
- creativity
- independence
- living in the moment
- membership in a social group (such as your community, racial group, or school club)
- music
- politics
- relationships with friends or family
- religious values
- sense of humor.

The first time, they were asked to circle one; the second time, they were asked to circle the two or three on the list that were most important to them.

Next, they were asked to think about times when those two or three values (the first time, they just wrote about the one they circled) were most important to them and then to write a few sentences about why they were important to them.

Finally, students were asked to write if they agreed or disagreed with these statements (there were six levels of agreement/disagreement that students could check):

- "These values have influenced my life"
- "In general, I try to live up to these values"
- "These values are an important part of who I am."

In the third, fourth, and/or fifth times, researchers made minor changes such as giving a different list of values or asking students to write about which values might be most important during a certain time period, like Winter Break.

---

[34] Cohen, G. L., Garcia, J., Purdie-Vaughns, V., et al. (2009). Recursive processes in self-affirmation: Intervening to close the minority achievement gap. *Science*, 324(5925), 400–403.

RELATEDNESS

Encourage Sense of Belonging

A sense of belonging generally means that students feel "accepted, included, and supported at school."[35] It's a key part of creating the conditions for intrinsic motivation to thrive, and having a sense of belonging in school has been found to enhance student engagement and increase academic achievement. Many of the practices discussed in Chapter 1: Relationships, Relationships, Relationships and in Chapter 2: Student Agency, NOT Student Empowerment have also been found to support students' sense of belonging. Supporting students' identity and connecting with their families as partners in learning, which are discussed in in Chapter 10: Cultural Responsiveness, Not Cultural Tokenism, can do the same.[36]

It's important to note that students of color have historically been found to feel less of a connection to school than white students and that students who identify as LGBTQ + have similar feelings, which suggests that teachers should prioritize some of the practices we recommend in Chapter 10.[37,38]

In addition to those many suggestions, we also try to build those connections through specific community building activities, like:

Daily Dedications: We borrowed educator Harry Seton's idea of having our students create and present a slide at the beginning of each month dedicating their day of learning to someone important to them—real or fictional—and why.[39] We do one "round" of these each year. It's a great opportunity for students to learn about each other, and students regularly tell us how their family members cried when they saw that their child highlighted *them.*

Baby Pictures: We do a similar round of students presenting images of themselves as babies, along with stories and/or descriptions of their babyhood from family members. It's priceless!

Academic Warm-Ups Including Personal Comments: More often than not, the "Warm-Ups" or "Do Nows" that our students immediately work on when they enter our classrooms contain two parts. One is an academic prompt or

---

[35] IES Regional Educational Laboratory Midwest. (2025). *The importance of student sense of belonging.*

[36] Healey, K., & Stroman, C. (2021). Structures for belonging: A synthesis of research on belonging-supportive learning environments. *Student Experience Research Network.* Pages 2 and 12.

[37] Seton, H. (2021, January 8). A daily ritual that builds trust and community among students. *Edutopia.*

[38] Seton, H. (2021, January 8). A daily ritual that builds trust and community among students. *Edutopia.*

[39] Seton, H. (2021, January 8). A daily ritual that builds trust and community among students. *Edutopia.*

task related to what we are studying at the time. The second part is usually a personal question ("Who's your favorite singer and why?" "What's your favorite ice cream?"). Having students share both provides another opportunity for connection and finding commonalities.

Being Kind

Small gestures of kindness in the workplace can go a long way toward enhancing belonging and motivation in the workplace, and there's no reason to think that this same research can't be applied to the classroom.[40] One way Larry does this is by bringing fruit to put in a basket on his desk several days each week that students can take—and which many students contribute to, as well. Katie has a small celebratory bag of tiny gifts she gives to each of her students on their birthdays.

These acts of kindness can be contagious, and student fruit contributions are just one example. Another example happened in Larry's class one year. Sometimes, as a classroom management tool, he offers to give a student who is having behavioral challenges a sticky note. He tells them to leave it on their desk and write a mark after they have been focused on their work for ten minutes. Then they'll get extra credit for every mark they have at the end of class. It often, though not always, works quite well.

One day he asked "Ralph," who was experiencing many challenges and affecting the entire class—to take a sticky note, but he was very resistant. "Roberto" heard their discussion, came over, and said "Mr. Ferlazzo, I need my sticky note, too." Larry was surprised, since Roberto didn't have any need for it, but gave it to him. Once Ralph saw that Roberto was getting one, too, he was fine taking one.

A few minutes later, I asked Roberto why he felt he needed a sticky note. He replied, "I don't, Mr. Ferlazzo. But I figured that it would make Ralph feel better about using one."

Now that's an example of student belonging.

Small Group Learning

Clearly, creating opportunities for students to learn together in small groups is an obvious way to promote relatedness. We have discussed small group learning in several previous chapters, particularly in Chapter 3: Differentiated Instruction.

We would just like to re-emphasize the importance of having high expectations for small group work, keeping the group numbers small, and providing student choice for group members—after the teacher has spent the first couple of months ensuring that all students have gotten some chances to work with each other.

---

[40] Penn State. (2019, September 10). A little kindness goes a long way for worker performance and health. *ScienceDaily*.

RELEVANCE

Linking Lessons to Personal Goals

Regularly asking students to identify how what they are learning might be able to help them in their lives or future careers has been found to increase motivation and academic achievement.[41]

There are two ways to facilitate this kind of self-generation of relevance. One is being more direct in asking students to connect a specific lesson to their lives, and the other is having them choose any school content and describe how it is relevant to them.

We do the former pretty simply—periodically, we just ask students to write a short paragraph explaining how they think what they learned that day in our class or in the recent unit can be helpful to them in their lives. After they write about this kind of learning transfer, we have them share through a "speed-dating" system. Many get even more ideas after they hear from their classmates.

The second version—where students can choose any school content and describe its relevance—we use for a more extended lesson. Character Lab created a specific "Build Connections" lesson that we like a lot and is freely available online.[42] Using a scaffolded student form (we have republished it in Figure 5.1, and you can find completed examples at a link in the Technology Connections section), students make one list of their interests and goals, then right next to it a list of topics they have learned about in class. They are then asked to make lines connecting as many of the two different lists as possible. Finally, they choose one from each column and explain in a short paragraph how they are connected. Again, students share in a "speed-dating" style.

As opposed to students self-generating how class content is connected to their lives, *direct communication* simply means teachers explaining how it's relevant. Some researchers have found that, though this method might be effective with students who perceive themselves as well-skilled academically, it may actually be de-motivating for others for various reasons.[43] Some contributing factors could be because it may be viewed as a condescending message and/or they may want to reassert autonomy.[44,45]

[41] Boryga, A. (2024, September 17). To motivate teens, ask them "who's your future self?" *Edutopia.*

[42] Character Lab. (n.d.). *Build connections for classrooms.* Available from https://characterlab.org/activities/build-connections-for-classrooms/

[43] Hulleman, C. S., Godes, O., Hendricks, B. L., & Harackiewicz, J. M. (2010). Enhancing interest and performance with a utility value intervention. *Journal of Educational Psychology, 102*(4), 880–895. https://doi.org/10.1037/a0019506

[44] Denworth, L. (2021, May 1). Adolescent brains are wired to want status and respect: That's an opportunity for teachers and parents. *Scientific American.*

[45] Yeager, D. S., Henderson, M. D., Paunesku, D., et al. (2014). Boring but important: A self-transcendent purpose for learning fosters academic self-regulation. *Journal of Personality and Social Psychology, 107*(4), 559–580. https://doi.org/10.1037/a0037637

BUILD CONNECTIONS

Connect school topics to personal interests in your daily life.

Name ______________________

① What are your interests, hobbies, and personal goals?

② What topics have you learned about in class recently?

③ Brainstorm connections. Draw lines between any interests in column ① and topics in column ② that you think are connected.

④ Develop a connection by filling in this sentence:

______________________ and ______________________
interest from ①   *topic from ②*

are connected because ______________________

⑤ Think more about your connection by filling in this sentence:

______________________ could be important to
topic from ④

my life because ______________________

Figure 5.1 Form for Building Connections For Classroom Lesson From Character Lab.

Source: Reproduced from Character Lab / CC BY-ND 4.0

Other research, however, suggests that teachers pointing out connections is better than not discussing them at all, especially if those connections are more near term (the math we're learning will help you figure out how to get the best car loan) than far term (the math we're learning will help you purchase a house).[46]

In Chapter 2: Student Agency, NOT Student Empowerment, we discussed the value of a student goal-setting process that focused on "process goals" rather than their ultimate goals. This kind of prioritization is important, but it doesn't mean we should completely ignore discussing ultimate/long-term goals. Having students identify their longer-term goals, and then having them identify process goals—or steps they can take—to achieve them can be an important strategy for identifying the relevance to them of what is happening in the classroom.

[46] Sparks, S. D. (2013, July 10). "Active" student engagement goes beyond class behavior, study finds. *Education Week.*

For example, "Luis," one of Larry's English Language Learner students, showed no interest in learning English. He said he was planning to return to Mexico and join the military. Larry asked if he was planning on being a private or if he wanted to be an officer. Luis replied that he wanted to be an officer. Larry then asked him where he thought they sent their best officers for training. Comprehension dawned on Luis' face—the United States, he answered.

Though he did not become super-engaged after that interaction, Luis certainly showed *much* more interest than before in class.

Piquing Curiosity

Piquing students' curiosity, sometimes called the "curiosity gap," can make content relevant because students are eager to scratch that itch.[47]

We'll discuss Inductive Learning, one of our favorite teaching strategies, more in Chapter 7: Strategies for Maximizing Learning, but that instructional strategy puts students in the role of a detective using clues to solve the case—in effect, creating a curiosity gap to fill.

And, boy oh boy, reactance lessons, which we discussed in Chapter 2: Student Agency, NOT Student Empowerment, can spark a curiosity gap on steroids. The levels of student outrage increase after they learn each new way corporations try to manipulate them to bet, smoke, or buy junk food!

In fact, just about any potential controversial topic—and which school subject *doesn't* have a long list of topics that could fit under that description—could serve a similar purpose, though you probably want to take care, talk to your administrator, and consider the political situation of your local school community before deciding on which ones to introduce to the class—no one benefits from your getting fired!

Connecting Lessons to Student Interests

Instead of pushing students to connect what *you* want to teach, another option is to consider what *they* want you to teach.

Putting this into action could range from inviting students to bring in texts (written or otherwise) that they like—music lyrics, TikTok videos, comics, TV shows, fan fiction, and, yes, books—that the class could use for analysis (requiring, of course, that their language be classroom appropriate) to teachers taking into consideration what they know of their students' interests into their lesson planning.[48]

---

[47] Dean, J. (2025, November 8). How to use the curiosity gap to motivate change. *PsyBlog*.

[48] Berwick, C. (2025, June 4). From superheroes to Taylor Swift: Using students' passions to ignite learning. *Edutopia*.

For example, if you have many football fans in class, there's no reason why in January you couldn't use Super Bowl ads as a centerpiece of a unit on argument and persuasion.

See the Technology Connections section for more ideas for making these kinds of connections.

What Could Go Wrong

Don't feel like every lesson has to contain all four elements of Self-Determination Theory! Do try to ensure that each of your lessons has at least one of them, though. As you get more and more comfortable and familiar with all the elements, you'll find that you naturally start including more of them in all your lessons.

Chapter Summary

If we only had a few minutes to chat in the teacher faculty room, here's what we'd want you to remember about motivation:

Technology Connections

You can find many examples of Choice Boards and Learning Menus, along with other suggestions about offering student choices, at *The Best Posts & Articles About Providing Students With Choices* https://larryferlazzo.edublogs.org/2010/12/21/the-best-posts-articles-about-providing-students-with-choices/.

Learn more about how to organize *Community Building Circles at The Best Resources For Organizing "Connection" or "Community Building" Circles* https://larryferlazzo.edublogs.org/2025/08/09/the-best-resources-for-organizing-connection-or-community-building-circles/.

Find resources on mental imagery at *Best Posts On Helping Students "Visualize Success"* https://larryferlazzo.edublogs.org/2010/12/23/my-best-posts-on-helping-students-visualize-success/.

Explore many different types of scaffolding at *The Best Resources On Providing Scaffolds To Students* https://larryferlazzo.edublogs.org/2017/01/05/the-best-resources-on-providing-scaffolds-to-students/.

You can access the *Building Connections lesson plan from Character Lab here: Build Connections For Classrooms* https://characterlab.org/activities/build-connections-for-classrooms/.

Find more ideas about how to connect student interests to lesson plans *at The Best Ideas For Helping Students Connect Lessons To Their Interests & The World* https://larryferlazzo.edublogs.org/2017/12/09/the-best-ideas-for-helping-students-connect-lessons-to-their-interests-the-world/.

CHAPTER 6

Emphasizing Students' Assets, Not Deficits

What Is It?

Asset-based instruction can simply be described as emphasizing what our students know and can do, rather than what they don't know and can't do. Or, as Ms. Howard explained in an episode of *Abbott Elementary*, "Talk about what they do have, not what they don't." Asset-based instruction is sometimes also referred to as Asset-Based Pedagogy.[1] It is closely connected to Culturally Responsive Teaching, which is discussed in Chapter 10 as well as Strength-Based Education.[2]

This chapter isn't about ignoring deficits. Rather, it's about using assets with a positive mindset and attitude to address deficits; it's about validating the many gifts our students bring to the classroom (no one, after all, comes to us as a "blank slate") and leveraging them in ways similar to how Dr. Rudine Sims Bishop described the roles of books: "mirrors" to reflect their own lives, "windows" to observe the worlds of others, and "sliding glass doors" so they can actually transport themselves into those worlds.[3]

Researchers in child development suggest that all children have some "islands of competence," and we teachers need to identify what they are and assist them to use those islands as foundations for growth.[4]

---

[1] Kwok, A., Waddington, J., Davis, J., et al. (2023). *Beginning teachers & strategies for asset-based pedagogy.* (Ed Working Paper: 23–732). Retrieved from Annenberg Institute at Brown University. https://doi.org/10.26300/S6CK-7V61

[2] Lopez, S. J., & Louis, M. C. (2009). The principles of strengths-based education. *Journal of College and Character, 10*(4), 2. https://doi.org/10.2202/1940-1639.1041

[3] Reading Rockets. (2015, January 30). *Rudine Sims Bishop's mirrors, windows and sliding glass doors.* [YouTube]. https://www.youtube.com/watch?v=_AAu58SNSyc

[4] Shaw, R. (2025, May 12). The wrong way to motivate your kid. *The Atlantic.*

By focusing on our students' assets, teachers become, as education journalist Jo Napolitano described, "talent scouts rather than deficit detectors."[5]

By prioritizing our students' assets, we can better apply Dr. Carol Dweck's idea of "The Power of Yet."[6] There may very well be many things our students don't know and can't do—yet. But we can use the many things they do know and can do to help get them there.

Keeping students' assets central to our pedagogy can also help us resist the pull of a deficit lens that can distract us from many of the institutional and systemic reasons why our students and their families may face challenges that show up in the classroom and beyond. It can be easier to blame our students' families for not caring because they didn't show up to "Back To School Night" than to reflect on economic policies that require them both to work two jobs in order to survive, or to get frustrated with a student's lack of attention in class because they're afraid they or their family members might get deported instead of questioning the way US immigration is enforced.

Through an asset-based lens, we teachers can be more aware of those institutional barriers and pursue strength-based instructional strategies such as, in those two cases, having projects involving students asking their parents/guardians questions about their lives, and/or having students study the history of US immigration and how their own stories might compare to those who came here in the past.

Why We Like It

What is a better prescription for a fulfilled life-long teaching career than an orientation toward looking at our students through the lens of their assets instead of hanging out in all too many teacher lounges where complaining about students can be a common pastime?

A colleague of Gandhi told Larry decades ago in explaining Gandhi's success: "He looked at every challenge as an opportunity, not as a pain in the butt."[7]

Think about the people you like to spend time with—do they tend to be those with a deficit mindset, regularly pointing out the faults in others and explaining why ideas won't work? Or, is it more energizing to be with those who tend to have a more positive attitude (though not those with "toxic positivity") who promote positivity no matter what and those who have Mahatma Gandhi's attitude around challenges?

---

[5] Napolitano, J. (2024, October 15). University of Wisconsin-Madison 2024 WIDA Conference. *Opening keynote.*

[6] Dweck, C. (2014, September 12). *The power of yet.* [TEDxNorrköping].

[7] Psychology Today Staff. (n.d.). Toxic positivity. *Psychology Today.*

Supporting Research

Research has found that highlighting assets, especially for students with lower socioeconomic backgrounds, can result in increased academic persistence.[8] In addition, studies have found it particularly beneficial for English Language Learners.[9]

Some research also indicates that applying aspects of Asset Based instruction in the classroom can mitigate a major challenge faced by teachers and students of color—a tendency of teachers to have low-expectations of students' ability, which can turn into a self-fulling prophecy.[10]

Research finds that we tend to learn something new more effectively if we can connect it to something we already know.[11,12] The more we teachers can highlight our students' assets, the greater pool of prior knowledge there is for us to encourage them to activate.

Finally, researchers have unsurprisingly found that people tend to be in better moods when focusing on their assets instead of their deficits.[13] As far as we're concerned, we're for anything that can help us teach the standards *and* help our students be in a positive mood about doing it!

One of several studies that Harvard professor Raj Chetty is well-known for is his so-called "Lost Einsteins" research.[14,15] In it, he concludes that there could be millions of "lost Einsteins" who just didn't achieve as great success because they just grew up in different neighborhoods with access to different opportunities. Assuming his conclusions are accurate, and there is little reason to believe otherwise, what better way for teachers to begin finding and supporting these "lost Einsteins" than by building on their assets?

[8] Hernandez, I. A., Silverman, D. M., & Destin, M. (2021). From deficit to benefit: Highlighting lower-SES students' background-specific strengths reinforces their academic persistence. *Journal of Experimental Social Psychology*, 92. https://doi.org/10.1016/j.jesp.2020.104080

[9] Peyton, H. (2022, March 24). Asset-based teaching strategies for Elementary English Learners. [Thesis.] Concordia University, St. Paul.

[10] López, F. A. (2017). Altering the trajectory of the self-fulfilling prophecy: Asset-based pedagogy and classroom dynamics. *Journal of Teacher Education, 68*(2), 193–212. https://doi.org/10.1177/0022487116685751

[11] Busch, B. (n.d.). How much does prior knowledge help? *InnerDrive*.

[12] Mohammed, S. (n.d.). *Prior knowledge—mental hooks for learning: IgnitED Research Insight*. The Learning Accelerator.

[13] Reynolds, E. (2022, February 16). Psychological interventions focused on our strengths may improve mood faster than those focused on weaknesses. *The British Psychological Society*.

[14] Ferlazzo, L. (2017, December 4). The best reports on the new "lost Einsteins" study. *Larry Ferlazzo's Website of the Day*.

[15] Semuels, A. (2017, December 4). America's lost Einsteins. *The Atlantic*.

Application

FUNDS OF KNOWLEDGE

We've previously discussed the importance of student prior knowledge and activating it to help enable them to learn new knowledge. Funds of Knowledge, a concept developed by Professor Luis Moll, refers specifically to the prior knowledge developed by students and their families through the "social and emotional experiences" of their lives.[16]

One way to think about the differences between the two is that "prior knowledge" emphasizes the things/concepts that students have learned from everywhere and anywhere—previous classes, YouTube, books they've read, etc. "Funds of knowledge" refers to what they've learned from specific culturally-connected sources—their families and neighbors' professions, cultural practices, religious lives, community life, home languages traditions, etc. In other words, Funds of Knowledge refers to much of what our students have learned outside of school.

The first step in using students' Funds of Knowledge is learning from them and their families what their Funds of Knowledge are! One way to do this is by making home visits to families. Our local teachers' union helped found the Parent Teacher Home Visit Project (https://pthvp.org/) in 1998, which now works with districts throughout the United States. Teachers in our district have the option to be trained and paid stipends to visit students' families. Larry has made many visits over the years, and Funds of Knowledge related projects that have happened as a result include parents who made Hmong flutes presenting to classes as part of music lessons and parents and students creating community gardens on school grounds.

We recognize it's often hard to find the time to make these kinds of visits—Larry was only able to make them once his children were older. Another, perhaps more realistic, way to identify these Funds of Knowledge is through a student survey that includes simple questions asking about family traditions, values, outings, favorite television shows and movies, traditional meals, etc. See a link in the Technology Connections section to several versions that are freely downloadable online.

Asking students to have conversations with family members as part of homework assignments is another potential strategy. You can find a link to many ideas for this kind of homework in the Technology Connections section.

Once you identify these Funds, it's time to consider ways to incorporate them in lessons. In addition to the ways we've already mentioned where Larry used the information he gained in his home visits, we've also incorporated Funds of Knowledge in these ways:

- Our ELL students, after learning the elements of feudalism and its supposed ending in the Middle Ages, asked their family members if they had experienced

---

[16] Illinois State University. (2020). Key concepts & principles. *Funds of Knowledge*.

any of its elements during their lifetimes. Once their surveys were complete, they wrote a class letter to the textbook's authors questioning their blanket statement that it had ended hundreds of years ago (they never responded!).

- Students created career presentations about the jobs their family members held and then used that process as a model for them to explore additional careers they might be interested in pursuing.

- Students made posters and slideshows about their home cultures, leading to "speed-dating" presentations.

- As part of learning about the US Civil War, students interviewed their family members about what they knew about civil wars in their home countries.

- As part of a science lesson, Hmong students used bamboo to build small models of their homes in Laos and popsicle sticks to model typical American construction. They then put thermometers in the different homes, which were left out in the sun all day. Guess which ones were considerably cooler than the other?

- Muslim students led lessons about Islam and, specifically Ramadan, when the class is studying world religions. In fact, they identified errors in the textbook we were using!

Researchers have found that students in classes utilizing their Funds of Knowledge have increased engagement, enhanced self-confidence, and improved learning attitudes.[17]

ASSET STORIES

Doctoral student Ivan Hernandez did research and found that if he asked students from a lower socioeconomic background to write about their "assets," it increased their level of academic persistence. These are some of the questions he asked his students as prompts for their writing:[18]

- What about you has been overlooked or undervalued?

- What strengths have you gained from your unique life experiences?

- How can you use these abilities to help you achieve your goals—and help the world?[19]

[17] Volman, M., & 'T Gilde, J. (2021). The effects of using students' funds of knowledge on educational outcomes in the social and personal domain. *Learning, Culture and Social Interaction*. https://doi.org/10.1016/j.lcsi.2020.100472

[18] Hernandez, I. A., Silverman, D. M., & Destin, M. (2021). From deficit to benefit: Highlighting lower-SES students' background-specific strengths reinforces their academic persistence. *Journal of Experimental Social Psychology*. https://doi.org/10.1016/j.jesp.2020.104080

[19] Hernandez, I. (2021, December 8). Experiences are assets: Teachers can help marginalized students recognize their strengths. *Education Week*.

Larry tried this idea out in his classroom, and it turned out to be an incredibly moving classroom experience as students shared some impressive stories. It forced a number of classmates—and Larry—to look differently at each other, and definitely enhanced his classes' sense of community.

We've used a more simplified version of this idea with ELL Newcomer students and English-proficient students. We call it a "What I'm Good At" presentation. Students prepare four slides (or they might use a poster), each using the sentence starter "I'm good at. . . . ." and illustrated with an image. We do our own models. Students then share them in a speed-dating style.

ASSETS OF ELLS

Many, if not all, of the assets we discuss here also apply to children with disabilities. We focused on ELLs because that's where our expertise is. We hope you see this section as an example of how to think about the assets of students who are often labeled based on perceived deficits.

As most teachers who have had ELLs in their classes know (and, according to recent research, that's the case for 45% of educators in US public schools), they have as much intelligence, if not more than our English-proficient students, and research backs up this claim.[20,21] In addition, researchers have found that they tend to have superior problem-solving skills and an increased sense of self-reliance as compared to non-ELL students.[22,23] They just don't know English—yet—though many ELL students speak multiple other languages.

In fact, studies have also found that having ELLs in class benefits English-proficient students, too, not least of all because it forces teachers to work harder at making their content accessible, which benefits everyone, as well as the fact that many tend to be highly motivated to learn, and that attitude can have positive effects on their peers.[24,25]

[20] Office of English Language Acquisition. (2023, June). *Educators of English Learners: Availability, Projected Need, and Teacher Preparation.* United States Department of Education.

[21] Villegas, L. (2025, January 22). Three studies shine a light on positive English learner outcomes. *New America.*

[22] Ijadi-Maghsoodi, R., Koushkaki, S. R., Klomhaus, A., et al. (2025). Resilience and traumatic stress among Latinx English language learners: A cross-sectional study of students from an urban school district. *BMC Public Health*, 25(1), 2458.

[23] Gándara, P. (2015). The implications of deeper learning for adolescent immigrants and English Language Learners. *Jobs for the Future.*

[24] Ferlazzo, L. (2024, October 30). A look back: Research redux: The presence of immigrant students helps everybody. *Larry Ferlazzo's Website of the Day.*

[25] Ferlazzo, L. (2024, October 9). New study reinforces past findings: The presence of ELLs can help everybody. *Larry Ferlazzo's Website of the Day.*

So, apart from those obvious assets that ELLs bring to our classes, how can teachers highlight and build upon their gifts?

Here are a few ideas:

- Look for opportunities to teach and use cognates—words that are somewhat alike in both the student's home language and in English. Thirty-to-forty percent of English words have a Spanish-language cognate, and it's easy to find lists of them online.

- Affirm "translanguaging," which is used to describe ways students can use their home languages to develop their English skills. Using cognates is one way, and there are many others—using the Preview/View/Review instructional strategy discussed in Chapter 3: Differentiated Instruction, having small groups of students who speak the same home language work together on assignments to help each other, and having all students write weekly letters to their parents in their home languages about what they learned that week.

- When ELLs make spelling or grammar mistakes in English, keep in mind educator Dan Meyer's comment: "Make yourself more interested in the sense that your students are *making* rather than the sense they *aren't* making. Celebrate and build on that sense."[26] Their "mistakes" are often likely to be applying the rules of their home languages, or applying the rules of English without remembering its many illogical exceptions. Use these "errors" as opportunities to acknowledge and teach, not to chastise.

- Periodically have ELLs teach you and their classmates words and expressions in their home languages.

IMPROVEMENT RUBRICS

Rubrics used in the classroom often focus on what's missing, especially in the "lower" categories. However, just as teachers can make similar points using more asset-based words when we talk with students, we can do the same in written rubrics.

An improvement rubric emphasizes what students have done well in their essays or projects, with suggestions to make them better. Of course, the teacher has to provide additional instruction and support on how to make those improvements.

This kind of rubric is in contrast to ones that often lead with criticisms.

You can see two examples of improvement rubrics in the Figures. Figure 6.1 is one we have students use to assess themselves near the end of the year. We have them

---

[26] Meyer, D. (2018, July 26). My month teaching summer school & the curse of content knowledge. *Dy/Dan*.

ESSAY 1	ESSAY 2
I opened my essay with an attention grabber (a hook).	I opened my essay with an attention grabber (a hook).
1 2 3 4	1 2 3 4
I used a thesis statement saying the main idea of the essay.	I used a thesis statement saying the main idea of the essay.
1 2 3 4	1 2 3 4
I wrote a list in the introduction paragraph saying what topics I would cover in the essay.	I wrote a list in the introduction paragraph saying what topics I would cover in the essay.
1 2 3 4	1 2 3 4
I organized my essay into paragraphs.	I organized my essay into paragraphs.
1 2 3 4	1 2 3 4
I used topic sentences in all my paragraphs.	I used topic sentences in all my paragraphs.
1 2 3 4	1 2 3 4
I used the correct verb tenses (past or present).	I used the correct verb tenses (past or present).
1 2 3 4	1 2 3 4
Punctuation was correct throughout the essay, including in dialogues.	Punctuation was correct throughout the essay, including in dialogues.
1 2 3 4	1 2 3 4
I wrote a conclusion in which I summarized my main points and left the reader with something to think about.	I wrote a conclusion in which I summarized my main points and left the reader with something to think about.
1 2 3 4	1 2 3 4

Figure 6.1 End of Year Improvement Rubric

Source: Adapted from Larry Ferlazzo (2011)

review two essays they wrote in the preceding months, assess them with this rubric, and then choose one to rewrite. Figure 6.2 is one created by two of our talented colleagues Lara Hoekstra and Nicole Scrivner. It's a CER-OR rubric, which stands for:

- Claim
- Evidence
- Reasoning
- Opposing Viewpoint
- Rebuttal

	1	2	3	4
Makes a **Claim**	Has a sentence that relates to the prompt. Might have "yes" or "no."	Uses language of the prompt as a frame for the claim. Might have "I agree/disagree" without explanation.	Has a clear and relevant claim with explanation.	Has a clear, relevant, unique claim that is thoughtfully explained.
Evidence to illustrate claim	Attempts to use evidence.	Has relevant evidence to back up the claim, but the evidence is stuck in the middle of the paragraph.	Sets up relevant evidence with the signal phrase.	Relevant and insightful evidence is efficiently introduced.
Reasoning Explains what the evidence means and why it matters	Follows evidence with an attempt to explain the evidence.	Attempts to explain what the evidence means and may try to explain why it matters or connects to the claim.	Explains what the evidence means and how the evidence supports the claim with more than one sentence.	Has a solid explanation of evidence, and insightful commentary on what the evidence means in relevance to the claim.
Opposing Viewpoints Explains what the other side believes	Mentions what the other side might believe.	Attempts to explain an opposing viewpoint.	Has a logical explanation of the opposing viewpoint. Word choice is inclusive in acknowledging the other side.	Has a logical and insightful explanation of the opposing viewpoint. Word choice is inclusive in acknowledging the other side.
Rebuttal/ Counterclaims Responds to the opposing viewpoint— the clapback	Mentions a response to the opposing viewpoint.	Has a rebuttal to the opposing viewpoint.	Logical rebuttal responding to opposing viewpoints.	Insightful and logical rebuttal to opposing viewpoints.

Figure 6.2 CER-OR Improvement Rubric

Source: Created by Lara Hoeksta and Nichole Scrivner. Used with their permission

WALL OF FAME

Periodically ask students to identify a piece of their work they consider to be excellent (you can suggest ones, too) to be taped on a "Wall of Fame" where it can be exhibited.

Wall or window space can be challenging in a secondary classroom with five different classes during the day. In those cases, they can be taped to easel paper and a student's class job can be to put them up at the beginning of each class and roll them down at the end. Or, you can leave each class's Wall of Fame up for a week and just rotate them. Consider giving students a few minutes now and then to explore the works on The Wall and provide them with small pieces of paper and a sentence starter like "I liked (name of student) essay/drawing/paragraph/graphic organizer/reflection because ___________________________" and then share what they wrote with their classmate. Provide examples of what to say first and, if you think some students might not receive any compliments, you can write notes for them or privately arrange with some trusted students to write them.

A digital format for these kinds of Walls of Fame, along with student feedback, is also an option.

TEACHER EXPECTATIONS

There has been substantial research on the role of teacher expectations on student achievement, and studies have found that they have tended to have an outsized negative impact on students of color since, more often than not, many educators, particularly those who are white, have lower expectations for them.[27,28,29]

Strategies teachers can use to focus on the assets and potential of students and to be aware of our biases and prejudices include:

- Being aware of it![30] It is not-too-hard, including for us, to take what may look like the "path of least resistance" and have lower expectations and "be easier" on certain students—and justify it in the name of "differentiation." As we explained, though, in Chapter 3: Differentiated Instruction, 9 times out of 10, "teaching up" is the better way.

[27] Gupta, N., & Sampat, S. (2021, July 29). How teacher expectations empower student learning. *Brookings' Center for Universal Education*.

[28] Brown, E. (2016, March 31). White teachers and black teachers have different expectations for black students. *The Washington Post*.

[29] Umansky, I., & Dumont, H. (2019, December 3). Do teachers have biased academic perceptions of their English learner students? *Brown Center Chalkboard at Brookings*.

[30] Gupta & Sampat, 2021.

- Communicate optimism! Going overboard can be damaging to students, so we shouldn't be expecting all of our students to be winning Nobel Prizes in the future.[31] But we can clearly exude a positive attitude about what we think they're capable of achieving *and* provide **sufficient support** so that they can be successful in achieving it.

- For assignments, as we've discussed in previous chapters, provide clear models of what good work looks like and what it doesn't look like.

- Provide specific praise and positive reinforcement.

- Give timely feedback and lead with strengths.

- Self-reflect if you are communicating high expectations *and* check how truly self-aware you are by having students periodically do quick anonymous surveys asking some version of this question: "Do you feel like (name of teacher) feels that you can be successful?" or, as a study on this topic did, ask students to agree or disagree with this statement "Your teacher thinks all students can be successful."[32]

- Finally, just follow the Golden Rule—treat *all* your students the way you would want to be treated!

LEAD WITH STRENGTHS IN FEEDBACK

When you provide feedback to students on their work, always try to begin with a positive comment about something they did well.

We'll discuss more specifics about providing student feedback in Chapter 9: Providing Effective Student Feedback, but please, please, please remember this point!

COMMUNITY ASSETS LESSON

Each year, we've done one of our favorite lessons. First, students make a list of the qualities they feel are important for a good neighborhood—the kind of area they would like to live in. Students typically write things like *good mass transit, restaurants and stores that have food I like, doctors and hospitals are nearby, affordable housing,* etc.

Then, students turn what they've written into a checklist. We go on one field trip and walk around the school's neighborhood (which might not be considered attractive by *some*), and students check off what elements they see. Next, we go to the most exclusive area in town with our clipboards and do the same thing (one year a

---

[31] Murayama, K., Pekrun, R., Suzuki, M., et al. (2016). Don't aim too high for your kids: Parental overaspiration undermines students' learning in mathematics. *Journal of Personality and Social Psychology, 111*(5), 766–779. https://doi.org/10.1037/pspp0000079

[32] Gershenson, S. (2022). *The Power of Expectations in District and Charter Schools.* Thomas B. Fordham Institute.

resident actually called the police on us!). Finally, students write an argument essay explaining which neighborhood they think is better, and 90% of the time it's the one surrounding our school—*their* present community.

This lesson explicitly highlights the assets of our students' community, and they like doing the activity as much as we do.

We did this lesson during pandemic related distance learning by using Google Maps Street View. If your district makes going on field trips extraordinarily difficult, like some do, this digital version is also an option.

GROWTH MINDSET

Having a growth mindset means that no one is born with fixed intelligence or fixed abilities and, instead, the vast majority of both are developed through effort and learning.[33] By helping our students understand what a growth mindset is, it helps them reframe challenges as opportunities to learn. As students develop this attitude, they are more likely to have faith in themselves to improve and learn.

There are various ways to introduce the growth mindset concept to students. We've sometimes shown a short video of Professor Carol Dweck, who developed the idea, to a class, or had students read a short article about it (many are available online). In our English Language Learner classes, we've sometimes just shown clips like Yoda's "Do. . .or do not. There is no try" or one from the *Meet the Robinsons* cartoon with their signature line, "Keep moving forward!"

We then share with students an example of a Growth Mindset story. Here's one from Larry:

> I have shown a growth mindset here at school. Last year, I taught a very bad lesson on writing a story. Students didn't really know what I was talking about, and I didn't provide them enough support. I was very disappointed in myself. I could have just moved on to the next lesson and forgotten about my mistake. Instead, that night I spent time thinking about what I did wrong and what I could do better. I made a new lesson. The next day, I apologized to the class, and I taught students how to write a story in a much better way. Everybody learned how to write a story. I felt better because I learned from my mistake and did a better job.

Next, we provide them with Figure 6.3 Growth Mindset Paragraph Frame they can use to write their own Growth Mindset story. Students then write their stories and share them speed-dating style.

---

[33] Center for Teaching and Learning. (n.d.). *Growth mindset*. Available from: Teaching and Learninghttps://ctl.stanford.edu/students/growth-mindset

Name:	
	My Growth Mindset Story
Topic Sentence:	I have shown a growth mindset at (school, home, playing sports, etc.)
The Problem:	
How the problem affected me and made me feel:	
What action I took to show a growth mindset:	
How showing a growth mindset made me feel:	
Now, put it all together into one paragraph:	

Figure 6.3   Growth Mindset Paragraph Frame

Source: Reproduced from Larry Ferlazzo, 2023 / with permission of Taylor & Francis

We regularly refer back to this lesson during the year, both in class discussion and in individual student conversations.

What Could Go Wrong

Don't think that prioritizing students' assets means that you can't offer strong critique. They are not mutually exclusive, and we talk about it in Chapter 9: Providing Effective Student Feedback.

You don't have to keep all your frustrations bottled up! We teachers are human, and we all sometimes give in to deficit thinking. Do everything possible to avoid doing so in front of students and, if you don't, you can always offer a sincere apology. Try to limit venting to family and very close friends, and *never* do it in writing.

Chapter Summary

If we only had a few minutes to chat in the teacher faculty room, here's what we'd want you to remember about student assets:

Technology Connections

Find links to different versions of Funds Of Knowledge surveys you can use with students at *The Best "Funds Of Knowledge" Surveys Available Online* https://larryferlazzo.edublogs.org/2025/09/14/the-best-funds-of-knowledge-surveys-available-online/

Find ideas for how to integrate families into student homework assignments at *The Best Student Projects That Need Family Engagement* https://engagingparentsinschool.edublogs.org/2014/02/09/the-best-student-projects-that-need-family-engagement-contribute-your-lessons/.

CHAPTER 7

Strategies for Maximizing Learning

What Is It?

The instructional strategies listed in this chapter are ones we try to keep in mind for most of our lessons.

It is *not* one of those awful checklists that a fair number of teacher credential programs make their students create for lesson plans they're supposed to teach. We are not suggesting that you, nor are we saying that we, incorporate every strategy listed in this chapter, plus all the other ideas we describe in this book, all the time.

Rather, these are the key instructional strategies we try to use often and if you asked our students, they would say that they're commonly used in our teaching.

Why We Like It

We like the strategies in this chapter because they work—for us and for our students. We like using them, and students tend to like participating in them, and it seems like they learn from them.

As you can tell from all the chapters in this book, and from all our previous books, we are big proponents of "learning by doing," advocated by John Dewey, and you'll find that the strategies we share here and keep in our "toolbox" for regular use reflect that pedagogical philosophy.[1]

---

[1] Pedagogy for Change. (n.d.). *John Dewey*. Great Pedagogical Thinkers.

Supporting Research

Since we'll be reviewing so many different instructional strategies, we'll be briefly discussing the research behind each one when we talk about them in the Applications section.

Application

GOAL OF LESSON

We've always found that the best way to plan a lesson is to start by figuring out what you want students to take away from it and then plan backwards. Though this kind of "backward planning" is common in many areas of life (it was a key strategy Larry used in his community organizing career); it was popularized in the education field by researchers Grant Wiggins and Jay McTighe in 1998 by their book *Understanding by Design* and often described since then as "backward design."[2]

Personally, we just think it's logical or practical—whatever you want to call it. We just take a minute (or longer) to think through what we want to get out of a lesson before we start planning it. Proponents of "backward design" also say that the next step after you figure out your goal is to create an assessment of that learning before you plan what is actually going to happen in the lesson. Sometimes we do that, sometimes we don't. Oftentimes we're not sure what assessment makes the most sense until after we determine what is going to happen in the lesson.

The research supporting backward design appears to primarily focus on post-secondary education but, really, it seems applicable in the K-12 environment, too.[3,4]

WARM-UP

A "warm-up," also known as a "do-now," is an activity that students can begin to work on as soon as they enter the classroom. It should require no verbal explanation from the teacher (except on the very first days of school). We either write it on the front whiteboard or display it on a projected slide. We have a monthly warm-up

---

[2] Gonzalez, J. (2020, June 21). *Backward Design: The Basics*. Cult of Pedagogy.

[3] Teaching & Learning Resource Center. (n.d.). *Using Backward Design to Plan Your Course*. The Ohio State University.

[4] Stapleton-Corcoran, E. (2023, January 25). *Backwards Design*. Center for the Advancement of Teaching Excellence (CATE).

sheet—either online or on paper—where students write the date and, then, beneath it, their response to the warm-up. We also periodically have students use that same sheet to write other comments in response to activities that day and then collect and review the warm-up sheet at the end of each month.

Larry likes to have a three-part warm-up:

1. A question related to the lesson that day, perhaps a quotation to which students write a response.

2. A personal question that can help students to get to know each other (What's your favorite movie and why? What has been the best thing that has ever happened to you?).

3. A "retrieval practice" activity (see below).

It usually takes between four and seven minutes for students to complete the Warm-up in Larry's class. He then has students quickly "count-off" and has small groups share their answers with each other (students are required to write in their warm-up at least one response they heard from someone else and the name of the student who said it) and then Larry calls on a few to share with the entire class.

The entire activity typically takes twelve-or-so minutes.

Of course, not every one of his warm-ups follows this routine. He doesn't do them at all on "short days"—one day each week is a shortened school day because teachers meet for collaborative planning time. Other days the lesson will require more time, so the warm-up only has one of the three points or none at all. Or perhaps students won't break into small groups and he'll just call on a few to share with the entire class.

See the Technology Connections section for a link to lots of other good warm-up ideas.

We think it's less important that you follow Larry's routine and more important that you have some kind of a routine for a warm-up activity.

RETRIEVAL PRACTICE

Retrieval practice is the practice of remembering something that you've learned previously without any reminders or clues being immediately available to you. In other words, the information you're remembering is not in front of you on a piece of paper. Flashcards and quizzes are the most common examples of retrieval practice, but there are many other types, as well. Retrieval practice will then make that information more easily available to you in the future when you need it. It increases the likelihood that the knowledge you have acquired will be moved into long-term memory.

There is so much research available finding its effectiveness as a learning strategy that there is little dispute about its overall effectiveness.[5,6]

In the context of Warm-Ups, instead of just having one retrieval question, another option is to have three—the first question related to something related to yesterday's lesson, the second connected to a lesson from last week, and the third about something students learned last month.

Another way we've occasionally used it in Warm-Ups is through a retrieval grid, originally developed by Kate Jones. Figure 7.1 shows one example from educator Andrew Watson. It contains questions about *Macbeth,* and searching for retrieval grids online will yield a zillion results. Basically, they offer a series of questions in three categories—knowledge learned from three different periods. Some use from yesterday, last week, and two weeks ago, while others use

Answer enough questions to Earn 15 points

What do the soldiers carry toward Dunsinane? Why?	"____ is ____ and ____ is _____. Hover through the fog and filthy air."	Why do the two murderers suspect the 3rd?	Name Duncan's two sons.
Why does it matter that the play's last 4 lines rhyme?	Complete this line: "Macbeth shall never vanquished be until. . ."	What is the "damned spot" Lady Macbeth tries to wash out?	Like famous Roman military leader, Macduff was. . .
Why is Macduff unhappy at the end of act IV?	Name two unexpected gusts at Macbeth's Act III banquet.	Complete this line: "Stars, hide your fires./ Let not light see my . . ."	The witches promise Banquo that. . .

2 weeks ago 3 Points
Last week 2 Points
This week 1 Point

Figure 7.1   Macbeth Retrieval Grid

Note: Please note the three different shades for the boxes (white, light gray, dark gray).

Source: Created by Andrew Watson, https://translatethebrain.com/, Used with permission

[5] Adesope, O. O., Trevisan, D. A., & Sundararajan, N. (2017). Rethinking the use of tests: A meta-analysis of practice testing. *Review of Educational Research, 87*(3), 659–701. https://doi.org/10.3102/0034654316689306

[6] Agarwal, P. K., Nunes, L. D., & Blunt, J. R. (2021). Retrieval practice consistently benefits student learning: A systematic review of applied research in schools and classrooms. *Educational Psychology Review, 33*(4), 1409–1453. https://doi.org/10.1007/s10648-021-09595-9

from yesterday, last week, and last month. The greater the time period, the more earned points. Obviously, they can be used during other class times, too, but we've just used them as Warm-Ups.

Andrew also raises an important point about them—that it's possible that these grids, at times, might overwhelm a student's working memory. One way to deal with that concern could be to reduce the number of questions they contain.

The other ways we've used Retrieval Practice during class have included:

- Brain Dumps. When we give formal tests, we often add a final sheet and invite students to write down anything else they can remember that they learned about the topic. It's not unusual for us to gain a better sense of what students actually learned through that activity than through their answers to the test questions.

- Periodic low-stakes or no-stakes quizzes—perhaps using mini-whiteboards, which are one of our favorite teaching/learning tools, and are great for formative assessments. Of course, regular tests work, too. Some suggest that in order for it to formally be "retrieval practice," the assessments need to be low-stakes, but we're not convinced that element needs to be a requirement in order for it to be an effective learning activity.

- Think/Pair/Share. This is just a minor tweak of a common strategy. We ask students some retrieval practice questions and then have them share responses with a partner.

- Flashcards. We primarily use these in our ELL Newcomer classes, though we would imagine they would also come in handy in specific other classes, like in Science. We think they work best when students create physical cards of their own and practice with them. However, online tools like Wayground (formerly Quizizz) also have excellent tools for making virtual ones in seconds, which can also be turned into games.

These are only the ways we've primarily used Retrieval Practice. A link in the Technology Connections section will lead you to many other examples.

HOOK

Just as writing teachers have taught students since forever about the importance of using some kind of "hook" to initially grab their readers' attention, a similar argument can be made for applying the same idea at the beginning of a lesson.

Does this mean that teachers need to have one every day? No! But it definitely can't hurt, and only help, if it's done now and then, at least.

One "hook" strategy for a lesson is using novelty—something that students might find unusual, either for its content or its delivery. Researchers suggest that novelty might even be a new element to add to Self-Determination Theory as a key and effective way to support student intrinsic motivation.[7]

Some ways we have used novelty (sometime right after a Warm-Up, sometimes instead of one) have included:

- Had students enter the classroom to rousing music from the US Civil War before we began to learn about it.

- Offered students pieces of hardtack we had baked using a Civil War recipe, again as part of our learning about the war.

- Shown a video, without providing any prior context, of the famous "Daisy" political advertisement for Lyndon Johnson that starts with a little girl picking petals off of a daisy and ends in a nuclear explosion. The video kicked-off a unit on the use of emotion in advertising.

- Students entered the classroom to find pieces of candy on everyone's desk with a notice on the front whiteboard saying if they didn't eat it for fifteen minutes they would get a second one. This activity was an introduction to learning about the infamous Marshmallow Test on self-control.

- Larry told his class the tragic story of his great uncle, who was lobotomized as part of an unethical experiment a hundred years earlier, as an introduction to a unit on ethical and unethical scientific experimentation.

- Students entered to see images of several pieces of unusual art (including a banana glued to a wall) along with the question: "Which of these do you think are art and why?"

- In Chapter 5: Developing Classrooms That Promote Self-Motivation where students can motivate themselves, we shared how we periodically ask students to write about how they can apply what they learned to their lives outside of school or in other classes. Sometimes, instead of waiting until the end of the lesson to talk to them about doing that activity, we'll tell them in advance at the beginning of the lesson that we want them to be thinking about it since they'll be making those connections later.

- Making Warm-Up questions into Essential Questions, developed by Jay McTighe and Grant Wiggins, that are especially designed to provoke

[7] Stoa, R., & Chu, T. L. (Alan). (2023). An argument for implementing and testing novelty in the classroom. *Scholarship of Teaching and Learning in Psychology, 9*(1), 88–95. https://doi.org/10.1037/stl0000223

deeper thinking.[8] For example, some that we have used to introduce units have been:

- Why do people move to a new place?
- What does the word "freedom" mean to you?
- Is math invented or discovered?

Pre-questions like these—and other kinds of introductory ones—have been found to help students create a "mental model" that can help them learn more effectively.[9] You get the idea.

INSTRUCTION

Written and Oral Directions

Writing down short instructions for students on a whiteboard or document camera, as well as explaining them verbally, is another way to maximize learning. These kinds of multiple stimulations can enhance memory.[10] Even when students still forget what to do, teachers can then just point to the instructions instead of repeating them again. . .and again. . .and again.

However, if there will be several steps that students will need to do, it might be better to keep them hidden and uncover them one at a time. Doing so can avoid confusion and students trying to jump ahead without completing the necessary initial steps.

In addition, after we've provided instructions, we sometimes have students turn to a partner and explain the directions to each other.

Of course, it is still likely that a teacher will still receive a, "What are we supposed to do?" question from at least one student. It just goes with the territory! But getting one of those questions is still better than receiving multiple ones.

Activating and Connecting to Prior Knowledge

As we've previously discussed, researchers have found that it is easier to develop new knowledge if we can connect it to something we already know.[11] If you can link it to

---

[8] McTighe, J., & Wiggins, G. P. (2013). *Essential Questions: Opening Doors to Student Understanding.* ASCD.

[9] Motz, B. A., Chinni, A., De Leeuw, J. R., et al. (2025). ManyClasses 2: The effects of prequestions on media interactions and learning. *Journal of Educational Psychology.* https://doi.org/10.1037/edu0000978

[10] Willis, J. (2007). Review of research: Brain-based teaching strategies for improving students' memory, learning, and test-taking success. *Childhood Education, 83*(5), 310–315.

[11] Van Kesteren, M. T. R., Rijpkema, M., Ruiter, D. J., et al. (2014). Building on prior knowledge: Schema-dependent encoding processes relate to academic performance. *Journal of Cognitive Neuroscience, 26*(10), 2250–2261. https://doi.org/10.1162/jocn_a_00630

existing knowledge, then you don't have to start from scratch and build some kind of framework in our minds to make sense of something new.

There are many ways to help students begin to make those connections. The ones we use most often are:

- KWL Charts. Have students create three columns on a sheet of paper or on a document and title them "What I Think I Know," "What I Want to Know," and "What I Have Learned." Give students the topic of the lesson and have them start off by completing the first three columns, and then share with classmates. Later, they can begin to add to the third column. There are many variations of these charts. We're old fuddy duddies and still stick to KWL, but feel free to explore all the other versions online and decide which you like the best.

- We either tell students the topic of the lesson and ask them how it might be connected to something we did previously, or we just tell them the connections directly.

- As we've discussed earlier, pre-teach important vocabulary connected to the upcoming lesson, but first identify if some students already know some of the terms so *they* can actually do the pre-teaching.

- In Chapter 3: Differentiated Instruction, we talked about the Preview/View/Review instructional strategy to use with English Language Learners. Providing ELLs with background knowledge in their home language about an upcoming lesson can be helpful to everyone.

The Technology Connections section provides a link leading to many other ways to help students activate and connect to prior knowledge.

Inductive Teaching

When inductive methods are used in teaching and learning, students are presented with examples and are challenged to identify patterns in them. The brain is designed to see the world through a lens of seeking and generating patterns; it is how we make sense of the world and create meaning. A challenge to teachers is to guide this natural impulse into the areas of problem solving and critical thinking. As Renate and Geoffrey Caine state, "although we choose much of what students are to learn, we should rather than attempt to impose patterns, present the information in a way that allows brains to extract patterns."[12] When we provide students pattern-seeking opportunities, they can increase brain cell activity and enhance memory and learning.[13]

[12] Caine, R. N., & Caine, G. (1990). Understanding a brain-based approach to learning and teaching. *Educational Leadership*.
[13] Willis, 2007.

Inductive teaching uses a progression of going from the specific to the general. This instructional strategy contrasts with deductive teaching and learning in which the teacher presents the rule or concept and then reinforces it with examples. In other words, it applies a sequence of going from the general to the specific.

Inductive teaching is basically a matter of guiding students to identify patterns and explain the reasoning behind those patterns. Students function as detectives. Interestingly, the ability to recognize patterns has been identified by many large employers as an important skill they are seeking in job applicants.[14]

Substantial research has shown that inductive teaching methods can be more effective than other instructional methods typically used in the classroom in multiple areas, including in learning grammar and math.[15,16] Research also suggests that having students organize their learning materials (which is what happens in inductive teaching) results in far better knowledge retention.[17] Studies have also found that it tends to be superior to other methods in promoting students' ability to transfer learning to other situations.[18]

Inductive teaching can mean students categorizing teacher-created data sets, which can be texts or just about anything else. Larry taught a science class once to ELLs where students were learning about the density of water, and they were testing out a variety of objects to see if they would float or not.

A text data set in Geography class could be about a country and have twenty short snippets of information that could be placed in the categories of geography, economics, culture, and population. We would have students cut up and separate the short paragraphs, glue them on a large paper under the categories, and highlight the evidence they believe supports their decision to put it there. From there, students could be tasked with researching and adding more information under each category, summarizing what they found, and turning it into a research paper. Or, sometimes we just ask students to choose what they think are the most important points in each category and justify their response.

We've used similar data sets to teach *many* topics, including:

- the elements of an essay (Hooks, Introductions, Thesis Statements, Topic Sentences, Supporting Details, Conclusions)
- President John F. Kennedy's life (Family, Accomplishments, Challenges)

---

[14] Wilson, E. (2015, June 10). 5 skills employers want that you won't see in a job ad. *Fortune*.

[15] Shirav, A., & Nagai, E. (2022). The effects of deductive and inductive grammar instructions in communicative teaching. *English Language Teaching, 15*(6), 102. https://doi.org/10.5539/elt.v15n6p102

[16] Purnawasi, M. (2024). The effectiveness of inductive teaching in mathematics. [thesis] West Texas A&M University.

[17] Stafford, T. (2011, October 24). *Make Study More Effective, the Easy Way*. Mind Hacks.

[18] Sparks, S. D. (2015, June 18). Can sorting teach students to make better connections among subjects? *Education Week*.

- types of Government with quotes from different political leaders (Democracy, Fascism, Communism, Monarchy)
- the seasons of the year to Newcomer English Language Learners (Summer, Fall, Winter, Spring)

Sometimes we provide the categories and sometimes we ask students to choose their own. Students can work alone or with a partner.

Figure 7.2 International New Year's Traditions Data Set is a simple one we use for Intermediate English Language Learners, but it does provide a general sense of what these text data sets can look like. For English-proficient students, each item can be a few sentences long.

We've also had students create data sets for their classmates to use on different topics of interest.

Concept attainment, originally developed by Jerome Bruner and his associates, is another example of inductive learning and teaching.[19] In Concept Attainment, a teacher shows a list of "good" and "bad" examples, and students have to work together to identify why the items are listed under each one.

Among many other topics, we've used it to teach the qualities of a good claim, the correct uses of have and has, and the difference between a good and bad "hook" to begin an essay.

Categories: Food, Names of New Year, Times of New Year, How New Year Is Celebrated

1. Many cultures celebrate New Year's Day on January 1st.
2. The Chinese New Year is also called the Lunar New Year.
3. There is always a big celebration in Times Square in New York City on New Year's Eve.
4. The Persian New Year is called Nauruz.
5. Khabse are cookies that are only made on Losar, the Tibetan New Year.
6. Rosh Hashanah is the name of the Jewish New Year.
7. Losar is the name of the Tibetan New Year.
8. Seven foods starting with the letter *s* are served on the Persian New Year.
9. Apples and honey are served on Rosh Hashanah.
10. The Vietnamese New Year is usually on the same day as the Chinese New Year.
11. The Islamic New Year is also known as the Hijri New Year.
12. In Vietnam the new year usually begins in February.
13. A shofar (ram's horn) is blown during Rosh Hashanah.

Figure 7.2 International New Year's Traditions Data Set

[19] *Concept attainment.* (n.d.). [Document]. Retrieved from https://www.csun.edu/sites/default/files/Holle-Concept-Attainment.pdf

Figure 7.3 Concept Attainment Example on Adjective and Periods is an example of one we have used with English Language Learner Newcomers. At first, everything would be covered except for the yes and no titles. Then, the teacher would explain that they are going to give various examples, and students will identify why certain ones are under yes and others are under no. After the first yes and no examples are shown, students are asked to think about them, and share with a partner why they think one is a yes and one is a no. If no student can identify the reasons behind the yeses and the no's, the next examples are uncovered, and the process continues until the end.

If you use student writing as an example, which we often do (with student permission, but without identifying whose names are connected to which examples though students tend to call out their own examples, including the "no" ones), Concept Attainment can be turned into an affirming and fun error correction game.

There are many other ways to use Inductive Teaching in the classroom. A link in the Technology Connections section will lead to explanations of them.

Simulations

Researchers have found that simulations can provide superior learning opportunities for students in many ways, including through promoting critical thinking and greater understanding of content than more traditional teaching methods.[20] Though useful in all classes, they are particularly effective in language learning classes.[21]

Yes	No
He has a brown shirt.	She has a t-shirt pink.
She has a small dog.	The eagle has eyes big.
She has blue eyes.	He has hair black.

Figure 7.3 Concept Attainment Example on Adjective and Periods

[20] Caniglia, J. (2019). *Simulations as a Teaching Strategy*. Kent State University Center for Teaching and Learning.

[21] Zvarych, I., Tonkonoh, I., Bopko, I., et al. (2024). The effectiveness of using simulation in learning a foreign language. *Forum for Linguistic Studies*, 5(3), 1916.

They are mainstays in our English Language Learner classrooms through role-playing real-life scenarios that our students will encounter in their day-to-day lives. You just can't beat simulations for conversation practice!

Online simulations are often used in science classes, economics classes may use stock market games, and there are many history-related ones. We're very wary of using those based in history, though, because many can "tokenize" the roles of marginalized people.[22] Instead of role-playing a person escaping from being enslaved or being a refugee fleeing genocide, we think having students read or listen to people who actually experienced those horrors is a better instructional strategy.

In our classes composed primarily of English-proficient students, there are a few ways we've used simulations. One is through the role of what we call Critical Thinking Dialogues as a precursor to writing an Argument essay about a topic we've been studying. We also try to inject a bit of levity into them—only if it's appropriate—and students first practice in small groups and then perform in front of the class. Figure 7.4 Critical Thinking Dialogue Ethnic Studies is an example of one.

Practicing for job interviews is another simulation we've often used in class.

See a link in the Technology Connections section for more simulation ideas.

Student One: Have you taken an Ethnic Studies class yet? Do you know what it is about?

Student Two: Yes, I have/No I have not.

Student Three: It teaches about how different groups have contributed to make the United States what it is today and talks about the challenges they have faced, including racism.

Student One: That sounds interesting. I've heard that some people don't like it. They say it makes people not like each other, and makes them feel less like a part of this country. What do you think?

Student Two: I think it is a (good/bad) idea because ______________________________. What do you think?

Student One: I think it is a (good/bad) idea because ______________________. What do you think, ______________________?

Student Three: I think it is a (good/bad) idea because ______________________.

Student One: It does sound more interesting than what Mr. Ferlazzo's teaches us.

Student Two: You should be nice to Mr. Ferlazzo. He tries his best.

Student Three: Yes, just because he is old and makes lots of mistakes, we should be nice to him.

Figure 7.4 Critical Thinking Dialogue Ethnic Studies

[22] Gonzalez, J. (2019, July 7). Think twice before doing another historical simulation [Podcast]. *Cult of Pedagogy.*

Collaboration Versus Cooperation

Though collaborative learning and cooperative learning are considered the same thing by a great many educators, we think they are, in fact, two different things.

The problem, however, is that if you type in the query, "What is the difference between collaborative and cooperative learning?" into an online search box, you'll get many different responses, including quite a few that are contradictory.

The most persuasive interpretations of their meaning—to us, at least—suggest that collaboration means student discussions are designed to help individuals improve their own work. In other words, it might mean students reading/analyzing a passage on their own, discussing what they wrote in a group and then revising their final product. Or it might mean students writing an essay on their own, talking about it with partners, and then making changes—a peer review. Or, when using the Jigsaw method of instruction (see Chapter 3: Differentiated Instruction), students can work individually on their own presentation, share it with others who have the same content to teach, improve their own work based on feedback and what they saw from others, and then actually make an *individual* presentation.

Cooperative learning, on the other hand, can mean just giving responsibility to a small group and having them work together to create a final product.

Research suggests that collaborative learning can be a more effective learning strategy, but we think both have their place in the classroom. In the world as we'd like it to be, we would have all the time in the world and more consistently do collaborative activities.[23] However, in the world as it is, time is more limited, so we probably do more cooperative learning activities.

See a link in the Technology Connections section for more precise instructions on doing a Jigsaw activity collaboratively or cooperatively.

Wait Time

We've previously discussed the importance of "Wait Time." As a reminder to ourselves, and to our students, we often preface a question we ask the class by saying "I'm going to ask a question. Please don't call out the answer. I want you to think for a few seconds about it, and then I'm going to call on someone (or, then I'll ask you to share with a partner)."

---

[23] Ferlazzo, L. (2021, November 26). A look back: New study finds a specific form of "collaboration" gets the best results. *Larry Ferlazzo's Website of the Day*.

Cold Calling

A discussion on Wait Time leads naturally to thinking about what to do when that time ends. Cold Calling refers to the practice of not having students raise their hands to respond to a question but, instead, the teacher calls on students to provide their answer.

Researchers, and anecdotes,[24] suggest that cold calling done in a supportive way can encourage class participation but that cold calling done with a "gotcha" attitude can create an atmosphere of intimidation and anxiousness.[25]

So, how can teachers make cold calling work for everyone? Here are some ideas:

- As we discussed in the previous section, increase wait time so students can gather their thoughts.

- Call on students *after* they have shared their answers in a Think-Pair-Share activity (or after students have shared answers on mini-whiteboards), so they have already practiced what they are going to say.

- Offer students a lifeline like in the game show *Who Wants To Be A Millionaire* so that students can metaphorically "Phone-A-Friend" in the class for help answering the question.

- If students are doing an activity and you know that you will shortly be doing some cold-calling, privately let students know ahead of time that you will be calling on them. This strategy can be particularly helpful to students you know tend to be anxious or to English Language Learners who might be particularly nervous about speaking up in class.

Teacher Talk

Some researchers have found that in many classrooms teachers are talking over 80% of the time, though studies have found that students tend to be the least engaged when their teachers are doing just that.[26] There seems to more-or-less be consensus on what the ratio *should* be in English Language Learner classes—70% student

---

[24] Gooblar, D. (2019, September 4). What Elizabeth Warren can teach us about teaching. *The Chronicle of Higher Education*.

[25] Terada, Y. (2023, April). Does cold calling work? Here's what the research says. *Edutopia*.

[26] Gewertz, C. (2020, January 3). How much should teachers talk in the classroom? Much less, some say. *Education Week*.

talk 30% teacher talk, though we can't find a commonly agreed on ratio for English-proficient classes.[27,28]

However, it seems to us that over 80% is *way, way* too much, especially if that's when students are more likely to be less engaged! Personally, since we both also teach ELL classes, we think the 70/30 ratio works well for all classes, with most class time devoted to individual, partner, and small group work.

We've previously discussed teacher tone, and we'll talk more in Chapter 8: Classroom Climate and Culture about what *words* to use when we're talking. It doesn't matter what percentage of teacher talk is happening in class if that talk is negative, anxiety-producing, and intimidating!

You can also find a link in the Technology Connections section for more resources on "Teacher Talk."

Movement

Sitting at a classroom desk for an hour can be deadly.[29,30] The one time Larry had to do it when he brought his class over to listen to a teacher, he fell asleep!

We're not big practitioners of what some call "brain breaks" or taking up class with specific movement activities. We are, however, big proponents of creating multiple opportunities for students to move during class. These could be:

- "Numbered off" groups meet in different sections of the room to share their Warm-Up responses.
- Think-Pair-Share, and the sharing can be with someone who has the same color socks, or with someone you haven't spoken with during the week, or any other kind of connection.
- Frequent partner/small group work where students can move to any location in the room they prefer, or outside as long as we can see them through the window.

[27] Kostadinovska-Stojchevska, B., & Popovikj, I. (2019). Teacher talking time vs. Student talking time: Moving from teacher-centered classroom to learner-centered classroom. *The International Journal of Applied Language Studies and Culture*, 2(2), 25–31.

[28] Hafeez Malik, A., Rashid, A., & Ali Raza Abbasi, S. (2023). Exploring the impact of excessive teacher talk time on participation and learning of English Language Learners. *VFAST Transactions on Education and Social Sciences, 11*(2), 46–55.

[29] Current research is telling us that there are positive correlations between movement/physical activity, learning and achievement. (n.d.). *Movement and Learning.*

[30] Studies Weekly. (2023, April 17). Incorporating movement into classroom learning. *Studies Weekly.*

- As long as full class instruction isn't taking place, students can get up to throw something away, or to get tissue, or classroom supplies without asking for permission.

- Regular sharing of work through "speed-dating," with every other row moving down one desk.

We often specifically encourage movement—even if students are going to share with someone right next to them, we insist they stand up and move a bit. Our mantra is that movement increases blood flow to the brain.[31]

Relevance

We discussed the importance of relevance in Chapter 5: Developing Classrooms That Promote Self-Motivation. When planning a lesson, and during the lesson itself, we are always looking for opportunities to connect the content to students' interests, hopes, and dreams and would recommend that you do the same.

Fun

William Glasser identifies having fun as one of the five basic psychological needs that all humans need.[32] Certainly, at its best, learning something new that is personally relevant to the learner and gained through an engaging lesson plan can be fun.

We discussed the importance of a teacher's sense of humor in Chapter 1: Relationships, Relationships, Relationships. Class games are obviously another potential source of fun, and we discuss later in this chapter how we often end our classes with games and how they can double as formative assessments.

We have also had success in "framing" different learning activities as "fun," even though they might not necessarily appear that way at first to some students. Introducing inductive learning, clozes (fill-in-the-blank passages), and sequencing activities all as puzzles are examples of this kind of reframing that we believe to be accurate and that seem to often have our desired effect.

Visuals

Many studies have shown that memory and learning can be enhanced by using photos and other imagery.[33] These kinds of engaging visuals should not be confused,

[31] Greene, D. (n.d.). *Research Shows Walking Increases Blood Flow in the Brain*. New Mexico Highlands University.

[32] Choice theory: 5 basic human needs. (n.d.). *William Glasser Institute UK*.

[33] Ulusoy, E. (2019, November 23). Importance of visuals in class discussions. *Spring 2020: Critical Conversations and the Academy*.

however, with the "visual" of projected text-ridden slides that teachers just verbally repeat!

Images can be used to increase vocabulary comprehension by connecting them with new words. They can be used to promote higher-order thinking by having students generate questions about them and hypotheses about what they represent. Students can also be asked to apply standard reading strategies (making a connection, prediction, etc.) to a photo. Or, as mentioned in the earlier Novelty section, an attention-grabbing picture can be a useful lesson introduction.

Most research on the appropriate length of time for students to watch a video relates to post-secondary education or online courses.[34,35] Our interpretation of how to apply them to high school suggests that six minutes would be the absolute longest time and that it would be better to be closer to three minutes. Be sure that the assignment is clear prior to showing the video.

See the Technology Connections section for a link leading to many more ideas on how to incorporate visuals into lessons.

Peak/End Rule

Nobel Prize winner Daniel Kahneman tells about an experiment done in the 1990's when two groups of patients were given colonoscopies.[36] One group "finished" when the procedure was completed. The other group stayed a while longer, believing the procedure was continuing when in fact it had ended so the pain was gone or reduced dramatically. The second group described the procedure afterward as much less painful than the first group did, even though both groups had recorded similar levels of pain during the procedure except for the extra time provided to the second group. Kahneman uses this example to explain that we have an "experiencing self" and a "remembering self."

The "remembering self" consists of the one or two "peak" moments we have had in a situation *combined* with how it ends. (This is known as the "Peak/End Rule.") It is the remembering self that tends to stick with us and the one we use to frame future decisions.

We try to keep this in mind every day, recognizing that how our class ends is likely to have an outsized influence on how our students will remember it and that these feelings are what may strongly impact the attitude they'll have entering class the following day.

---

[34] Lassof, M. (2023, March 28). Research and goldfish: Best practices for determining video length. *SkillSprints.*

[35] Video length: How long should a course video be? (n.d.). UC San Diego Multimedia Services.

[36] Raz, G. (2013, May 24). How do experiences become memories? [Podcast]. *Ted Radio Hour.*

So, we'll often end our class with a short game reinforcing the lesson, or an exercise where students think about how they'll use what they learned elsewhere, or with some kind of activity, perhaps a short low-stakes assessment, where students can reflect on learning something new that day. Or, if there's no time for any of those things to happen, we'll just restate what they learned or say how they can use it elsewhere. At minimum, though, we'll tell them we're happy to have them as students, we'll look forward to seeing them the next day, and we hope the rest of their day goes well. At the very least, those parting comments will remind them we like and care about them, and hope they'll remember that!

ASSESSMENT/REFLECTION

Check for Understanding

We can't assume that because students appeared to be on task during the lesson, or because they didn't ask many questions, or because they nodded their heads when we dumbly asked "Everyone understand?" that everyone "got" the lesson.

A Check for Understanding can be a simple test at the end of a class. However, if you don't do any of these checks or formative assessments before then, you won't have any time left in class to try to fix things.

These are the Checks for Understanding that we try to do periodically during class, and not just at the end:

- We tell students: "Give me a thumbs up, thumbs down, or thumbs in the middle to help know if I've explained things well and you understand it. It's fine to put a thumbs down—that's on me, not you."

- We might also say: "Here's a tiny scrap of paper. Don't put your name on it. Write a one, two or three—one is that you're very clear on _______, two in the middle, or three not clear at all."

- Mini-whiteboards are miracle tools for formative assessment—just ask a question, tell everyone to not lift their boards up before you say to do so, and, voila, you have a check for understanding. Take a picture if you want to be able to reference it later to plan future instruction.

- We mentioned in the previous section how we often will end class with a game. These can also often function as formative assessments. We especially like to use online game tools like Wayground (formerly Quizizz), Blooket or Kahoot, which all give us individual reports on student responses.

LEARNING TRANSFER

We can't end without mentioning again the importance of periodically including in lessons opportunities for students to identify how they might be able to use that day's lesson content in another class, in their life outside of school, or in their future. As we mentioned earlier, sometimes we alert students at the beginning of class that they'll be doing this at the end, and sometimes we just make it an assignment a few minutes before the bell.

What Could Go Wrong

We cannot over-emphasize this enough—this chapter is not a checklist! Not all of our lessons contain all of these elements, and yours shouldn't, either. Just keep them in your back pocket and take a few out when needed.

National-security expert Gregory Treverton has famously distinguished problems in world affairs as either puzzles or mysteries. Puzzles have a clear and logical conclusion. On the other hand, he says[37]:

> A mystery cannot be answered; it can only be framed, by identifying the critical factors and applying some sense of how they have interacted in the past and might interact in the future. A mystery is an attempt to define ambiguities.

Treverton suggests that major strategic errors are made when we think that some mysteries are puzzles.

We believe that his analysis has a lot of relevance to the schools and the classroom, which is why we emphasize that nothing in this book should be viewed as a checklist—especially this chapter!

Your students are unique individuals, who are facing different challenges and stresses each year. Your school community is also unique, and every year you bring greater and different experiences and knowledge to your practice as a teacher.

Revel in the joy of school as a mystery (on good days, at least!) and look at the ideas in this chapter, and in this book, as potential strategies to bring a little light toward how you *might* get a little closer to solving it.

---

[37] Treverton, G. (2007, June). Risks and riddles. *Smithsonian Magazine.*

Chapter Summary

If we only had a few minutes to chat in the teacher faculty room, here's what we'd want you to remember about maximizing learning:

Technology Connections

For lots of different ideas on doing Warm-Up activities, visit *The Best Resources For "Do Now" Activities To Begin A Class* https://larryferlazzo.edublogs.org/2016/09/10/the-best-resources-for-do-now-activities-to-begin-a-class/.

Go to The Best Resources For Learning About Retrieval Practice https://larryferlazzo.edublogs.org/2017/10/22/the-best-resources-for-learning-about-retrieval-practice/ to find many examples of how to use Retrieval Practice in the classroom.

To learn about many different strategies for helping students activate and connect to prior knowledge, visit *The Best Resources For Learning About The Importance Of Prior Knowledge* (& How To Activate It) https://larryferlazzo.edublogs.org/2016/01/09/the-best-resources-for-learning-about-the-importance-of-prior-knowledge-how-to-activate-it/.

Learn about other Inductive Teaching strategies at *The Best Resources About Inductive Learning & Teaching* https://larryferlazzo.edublogs.org/2015/01/16/the-best-resources-about-inductive-learning-teaching/.

For more ideas on using simulations in class, visit *The Best Online Learning Simulation Games & Interactives—Help Me Find More* https://larryferlazzo.edublogs.org/2014/07/23/the-best-online-learning-simulation-games-interactives-help-me-find-more/.

For examples of how to implement the Jigsaw instructional strategy either collaboratively or cooperatively, visit *Here's A Short Slidedeck I Made For Our School On The Difference Between "Cooperative" & "Collaborative" Jigsaws* https://larryferlazzo.edublogs.org/2022/02/25/heres-a-short-slidedeck-i-made-for-our-school-on-the-difference-between-cooperative-collaborative-jigsaws-2/.

Find even more advice on "Teacher Talk" at *The Best Resources Sharing Recommendations About "Teacher Talk"* https://larryferlazzo.edublogs.org/2021/06/29/the-best-resources-sharing-recommendations-about-teacher-talk/.

Learn about more ideas on incorporating visuals into lessons at *The Best Ways To Use Photos In Lessons* https://larryferlazzo.edublogs.org/2010/06/27/the-best-ways-to-use-photos-in-lessons/.

CHAPTER 8

Classroom Climate and Culture

What Is It?

Classroom climate, called classroom management by many, is the glue that holds a class together, and handling it effectively is critical for student learning.[1]

We are believers, as are many researchers, in the effectiveness of creating an *authoritative* climate in class rather than an *authoritarian* or *permissive* one.[2,3]

Qualities of an authoritative climate include having a teacher who is in control of the class and has high expectations but prioritizes student needs and two-way communication. We like to think of it as an attitude suggesting that "we're all in this together."

In authoritarian climates, teachers function as little dictators. Communication is unilateral—from teacher to students. No explanations are necessary.

Permissive climates exist where pretty much anything goes. The few rules that exist are seldom enforced.

It doesn't take having a Ph.D. to know which of these climates researchers suggest leads to the most effective learning environment.

[1] Putra, E., & Yanto, M. (2025). Classroom management: Boosting student success—A meta-analysis review. *Cogent Education,* 12(1), 2458630. https://doi.org/10.1080/2331186X.2025.2458630

[2] Trinkner, R., Cohn, E. S., Rebellon, C. J., & Van Gundy, K. (2012). Don't trust anyone over 30: Parental legitimacy as a mediator between parenting style and changes in delinquent behavior over time. *Journal of Adolescence*, 35(1), 119–132. https://doi.org/10.1016/j.adolescence.2011.05.003

[3] Université du Luxembourg. (2015, June 10). Why boys are performing less well at school, how to fix it. *ScienceDaily*.

Why We Like It

Based on our experience in the classroom, this kind of authoritative attitude just plain works—for us and for our students.

We approach each day with the perspective of "unconditional positive regard," a phrase and concept adapted from psychology by educator Alex Shevrin Venet.[4] As the old saying goes, we view all our students as inherently good people who might be having good days, or might be having bad days (or even weeks or months).

To repeat what we mentioned in Chapter 4, we try to approach our students with the perspective of inquiry, not judgment. We want to learn and want them to be aware of what's making their days good and what is having the opposite effect.[5]

Are we always successful? Of course not! We're only human and often react impatiently out of frustration.

And, sometimes, we need to put our foot down.

But we work hard to look at our students through the lens of "authoritativism," and believe this kind of perspective gives all the ideas we share in this book the best chances to flourish.

The word *discipline* is often connected to punishment or correction. However, if you go to its word root in Latin, you'll see that it's mainly related to "teaching, learning, knowledge."[6] We think teachers are likely to be far more effective in creating a positive classroom environment if they focus more on the latter definition than the former.

Supporting Research

Though we'll highlight research for many of the specific recommendations we'll share in the Application section, there is ample research supporting our overall "praise beats punishment" strategy.[7] Studies suggest that behavior specific praise is the most effective classroom strategy that can "increase engagement and decrease disruptive behavior."[8] In fact, one study found that in classrooms that had the

[4] Gonzalez, J. (2023, September 18). Nothing's going to change my mind: How unconditional positive regard transforms classrooms. *Cult of Pedagogy*.

[5] Terada, Y. (2020, August 7). 7 classroom management mistakes—And the research on how to fix them. *Edutopia*.

[6] *Discipline*. (n.d.). Etymonline. https://www.etymonline.com/search?q=discipline

[7] Wilkins, N. J., Verlenden, J. M. V., Szucs, L. E., & Johns, M. M. (2023). Classroom management and facilitation approaches that promote school connectedness. *Journal of School Health, 93*(7), 582–593.

[8] Gage, N. A., & MacSuga-Gage, A. S. (2017). Salient classroom management skills: Finding the most effective skills to increase student engagement and decrease disruptions. *Report on Emotional & Behavioral Disorders in Youth, 17*(1), 13–18.

highest ratio of praise to reprimand, on-task behavior increased dramatically while classroom disruptions were cut in half.[9]

There is another exceptionally important piece of research that speaks to the importance of many of the recommendations we share in this chapter, as well as in other chapters.

Readers might be familiar with ACEs, Adverse Childhood Experiences. These are traumatic events that occur in children's lives that can negatively impact their health throughout their lives.[10] Note that Alex Venet, who we mentioned in Chapter 1, encourages schools avoid using ACE surveys in schools, so don't feel you need to administer them to your students.[11]

Researchers have also more recently identified PCEs, Positive Childhood Experiences, that have the potential to counteract the negative effects of ACEs.[12] Several of the specific Positive Childhood Experiences highlighted in the research, including having nonparent adults taking an interest in them, feeling supported by friends, having a sense of belonging in high school, and being a participant in community traditions can all be supported by recommendations in this chapter and in others throughout the book.[13]

Application

There are a lot of good ideas in this chapter and in this book. Sometimes it's a matter of throwing a bunch of them at the wall and seeing which ones will stick.

Sometimes you'll find ones that will, and other times they won't.

A few years ago, Larry had two students facing a lot of challenges in one of his classes.

One student was very unfocused, though he had good days. When he had a good day, he was not able to tell Larry what made the difference. During one class, after he had a good day, Larry gave him some food and asked him to sit outside at a picnic table and think for ten minutes about what may have made the difference for him. Ten minutes later, Larry went out and, much to his surprise, the student said he thought the difference was that he worked in a small group with people who didn't distract him. He gave Larry a short list of students who he felt were distracting.

---

[9] Caldarella, P., Larsen, R. A. A., Williams, L., & Wills, H. P. (2023). Effects of middle school teachers' praise-to-reprimand ratios on students' classroom behavior. *Journal of Positive Behavior Interventions, 25*(1), 28–40. https://doi.org/10.1177/10983007211035185

[10] National Center for Injury Prevention and Control. (2025, September 24). *About adverse childhood experiences*. CDC.

[11] Venet, A. S. (2024, January 2). Letting go of ACEs to support trauma-affected students. *Unconditional Learning*.

[12] Klass, P. (2023, August 5). How parents can shape a child's future with small moments of joy. *The Washington Post*.

[13] APA Foundation. (n.d.). *What are PCE's?*

After that day, he only worked with students he chose (Larry approached each one privately to see if they would be okay working with him), and he became much more focused and his groups produced excellent work.

In this case, Larry's strategy stuck. But it's impossible to know exactly why, which is why it's key to be patient and flexible.

Another student in the same class was also not focused and not happy about being in this country. Larry felt they had a good relationship and asked the student what he thought would help him get on track in class. He said he often was very hungry, and food would help. Larry kept crackers in this drawer and told the student to come to his desk at the beginning of class each day, get a few crackers, eat them outside, and come back in. The student was excited! The next day, he came to get his crackers, and went outside to eat them.

He didn't return to class for two months.

When he did return (he said he was gone because of family issues), he apologized and asked if they could try the crackers again—and he promised he would return. Larry agreed, and the student was much more focused for the remaining several months of school.

It was delayed, but the strategy eventually stuck.

If we show students we care, and invite them to problem-solve *with* us, we generally find that something will eventually work, though not always. But it works often enough to give us the energy and optimism to keep on trying when the first, second, or third strategy we try doesn't work.

Here are some of those strategies to try (not listed in any particular order).

TEMPORARY ACCEPTANCE/AGREEMENT, NOT "PLANNED IGNORING"

Planned ignoring is a term used to describe ignoring certain attention-seeking behaviors as a strategy to reduce them from happening again, and it is also very difficult to implement effectively.[14,15] We don't really ignore any inappropriate behaviors in our classes. However, we also don't necessarily punish all of them, either.

If a student has their head down on their desk, we'll ask the rest of the class to do some kind of activity and go over to the student to speak privately with them. We'll quickly ask if they're okay and what time they went to bed the previous night. Depending on their responses, we might send them to the nurse (or call their home), or we might just make an offer to let them nap for five minutes and then we'll come over to wake

---

[14] Behavior Assessment Training. (2024, July 22). Planned Ignoring Positive Behavioral Supports and Interventions. Retrieved from https://stemedresearch.siu.edu/_common/documents/plannedignoring.pdf

[15] Gable, R., Hester, P., Rock, M., & Hughes, K. (2009). Back to basics: Rules, praise, ignoring, and reprimands revisited. *Intervention in School and Clinic*, 44(4), 195–205.

them up. In addition, we often remind our classes that we understand why students can get tired after sitting in classes all day and that if they are sleepy they can go get a drink of water, take a walk down the hall, or stand in the back of the room when they need to.

If we have an occasional student who appears to be uncontrollably obsessed with their cellphone, we might start weaning them away from it by making an agreement that they can be on it for three minutes if they can stay off of it for twenty.

The strategy we use with the sleeping student and the student who seems obsessed with their phone is a persuasive technique sometimes called "reducing the size of the ask."[16] It means that we start off asking for less, and then, later, ask for more.

We've never had issues with other students complaining about "Why can they do it, but not me?" because, in our experience, students get it—they understand why certain students need to be treated differently.

Earlier in our careers, we had similar experiences—and compromises—with individual students who violated classroom rules that we used to have until we realized they were bad ones. One was eating in class, which we have now modified to not eating during whole class instruction because it can be a distraction, but it's okay to do when working on projects in small groups.

Another was listening to music. Though we do a mini-lesson about the potential distraction of listening to music with lyrics,[17] we let students listen to music on their ear buds if they are working individually for an extended period of time.

When a student's behavior interferes with learning by other students, or if they violate agreements we've made with them about their behaviors, all bets are off, and we handle things firmly—no one would ever think our classrooms did not have safe, orderly, and welcoming environments for our students.

But teachers are able to "ignore" certain behaviors and, at the same time, handle them in ways that are respectful to individual students and the entire class. Teachers can also stop some of these problems before they occur by not creating inflexible rules to begin with!

TEACHER LANGUAGE

We've previously discussed the importance of genuine praise for specific actions and of saying "please," "thank you," and "I'm sorry"—and not saying those words sarcastically.

There are also other times when language can be particularly helpful in creating a positive classroom climate.

[16] Berger, J. (2020, April 20). How to persuade people to change their behavior. *Harvard Business Review*.

[17] Ferlazzo, L. (2014, April 15). The best research on listening to music when studying. *Larry Ferlazzo's Website of the Day*.

One is using the word "we" instead of you, as in "What can *we* do to handle this better in the future? How can I support you?" and not "What can *you* do to handle this better in the future?"

Another is asking students "What could you do?" or "What could you have done?" after they exhibited inappropriate classroom behavior instead of "What should you have done?" Using the word "should" carries the clear message that we are judging them. Obviously, we are doing just that. However, using the word "could" instead communicates the message that there is not just one answer, and there isn't one. "Could" promotes a less adversarial tone.

Whenever possible, we've found that our taking some degree of responsibility for our contribution to a problem—no matter how small it might be—can be a huge step in solving classroom issues and diffusing conflict. Whether it's something like, "First, I'm sorry for not being as patient as I should have been" or "I should have been more clear in what I wanted the class to do," modeling that kind of self-awareness can make it easier for students to do the same.

As most parents and teachers know, yelling and using harsh language doesn't usually help situations, and researchers have found that it actually tends to increase inappropriate behaviors in teenagers.[18] That doesn't mean that we never raise our voices in our classrooms—we're human, after all. But the few times we do, it's never targeting an individual student (unless it's a dangerous situation), and it's usually to get the full attention of the class. Since we do it so seldom, it is very effective!

GETTING A CLASS'S ATTENTION

Search online for this topic and you'll find a ton of ideas—some good, some too cute for our taste, and some we think are not very respectful of young adults.

Our standby, which has worked quite well over the years, is to raise one of our arms and say in a slightly elevated volume, "Can I have your attention?" Sometimes we have to do it a couple of times, but it seems to work far more often than it doesn't.

We've also sometimes used a "Three, Two, One" verbal and finger countdown, that is generally equally effective.

But, hey, if neither of those float your boat, check out other online ideas.

HELPING STUDENTS LEARN ABOUT THE BENEFITS OF SELF-CONTROL

We have had some success in helping our students learn about the long-term benefits of being able to delay gratification.

---

[18] Efstathiou, J. (2013, September 4). Using harsh verbal discipline with teens found to be harmful. *Society for Research in Child Development*.

For many years, we did this by teaching about the famous Marshmallow Test where children were given a marshmallow and told that they would receive a second one if they didn't eat the first one before the researcher returned to the room. Researchers tracked the lives of those children, and suggested that those who showed more self-control gained greater success during the rest of their lives. TED Talks has a wonderful video about it that students enjoy and, of course, students loved us replicating the experiment by using candy with them![19]

However, several researchers in recent years have raised questions about that experiment, though they and many other studies have still found that people gain benefits by developing the ability to delay gratification.[20,21]

So, now, we have replaced teaching about the Marshmallow Experiment with either giving students an article or showing a video describing the benefits of exhibiting self-control and tips for developing it. We then ask students to write a short essay about the article or video and respond to an AWPE (Analytical Writing Placement Examination) prompt, a style used by the University of California to assess the writing skills of incoming students. It's an excellent frame for any kind of prompt. One for self-control would look something like this:

> In the above article (or in the video you just watched), what is the author (or video-maker) saying about the value of self-control and how to develop that skill? To what extent do you agree with what they are saying? To support your opinion, be sure to include specific examples drawn from your own experience, your observations of others, or any of your reading.

Figure 8.1 Essay Graphic Organizer can help students plan this short essay, or for any other topic using the AWPE style.

In the Technology Connections section, you'll find a link that will lead you to many videos and articles that can be used with this strategy.

One of the advantages of doing a lesson like this is that it can be referred back to many times during the school year!

[19] de Posada, J. (2009, February). Don't eat the marshmallow! [Ted Talk].

[20] Watts, T. W., Duncan, G. J., & Quan, H. (2018). Revisiting the marshmallow test: A conceptual replication investigating links between early delay of gratification and later outcomes. *Psychological Science*, 29(7), 1159–1177. https://doi.org/10.1177/0956797618761661

[21] Salley, E. (2024, December 26). Patience pays off: Delayed gratification and executive function in children. *The Executive Function Blog*.

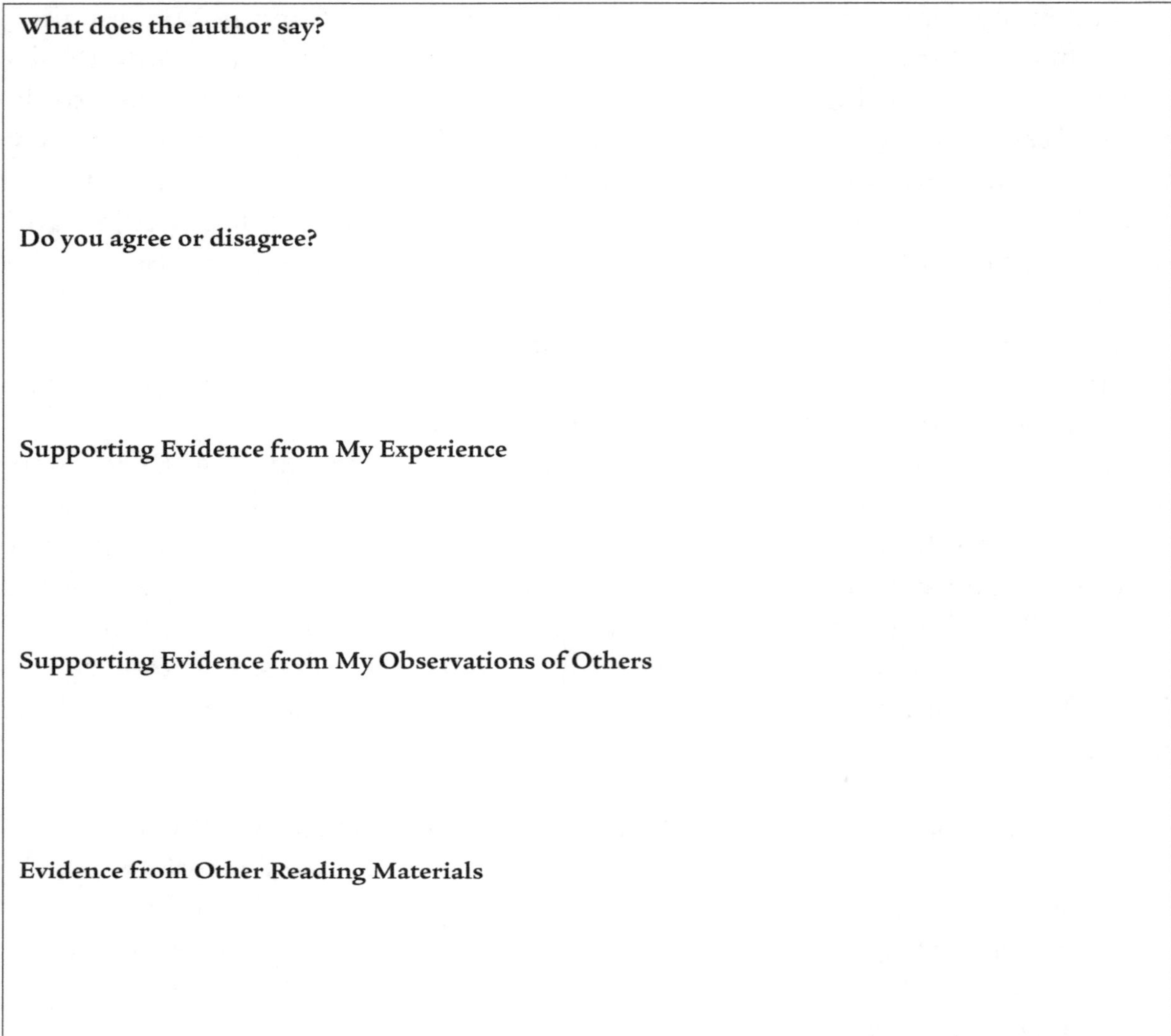

Figure 8.1 Essay Graphic Organizer

SHARING GOOD NEWS

Though perhaps not a classroom management strategy per se, having people share positive things that have happened to them—and then having others react enthusiastically to that sharing—has been shown to help build a sense of community and trust, as well as giving energy to the person doing the sharing.[22,23]

We periodically have students write down on a Friday three good things that they experienced during the week and share them with their classmates. Based on

[22] Barker, E. (2010, August). What's an easy way to strengthen your relationships? *Barking Up the Wrong Tree.*

[23] Seppala, E. (2012, December 25). Share your good news, and you will be better off. *Scientific American.*

our experiences, the researchers are correct—this exercise does seem to build trust and community!

"BREAKING THE PLANE"

"Breaking the Plane" is the catchy—and easy to remember—phrase educator Doug Lemov uses to remind teachers to not spend all our time standing in front of the class.[24] The "plane" refers to the line formed by all the student desks in the front row, assuming that's how your desks are arranged.

We find it's easy to spend *a lot* of time up there—the document camera, the whiteboard, and our desks are all there! However, research, and our own experience, shows that a teacher's physical proximity to students can influence behavior and motivation, so we need to constantly remind ourselves to "Break the Plane."

FRESH STARTS

We've found that Resets, or Fresh Starts, can help students who aren't doing very well find the motivation to improve, and research supports our experience.[25]

It can be a useful strategy for a student who, for example, has an F in class during the first month or two of school and who can get "reset" to an A. In our experience, at least, it's highly unlikely they'll make the radical change to stay at that level but, often, it's enough of a nudge to get them working considerably harder at learning.

And, even if it doesn't, we've found that the offer itself builds up the deposit in our relationship "bank," and potential classroom management problems are decreased.

CLASSROOM RULES

We mentioned earlier that we feel we've had "bad" classroom rules in the past around eating in class and listening to music. We've generally found that the fewer the rules, the easier it is to enforce them and the more likely students are going to pay attention to them.

For years now, our rules have been: Be respectful and don't touch other people's stuff.

[24] Lemov, D. (2015, December 10). What is 'breaking the plane'? *Doug Lemov's Field Notes*.

[25] Dai, H. (2019, February 4). Research explores how "fresh starts" affect our motivation at work. *Harvard Business Review*.

WALK AND TALKS

Sometimes, a situation arises where a teacher needs to have a deeper conversation with a student than the minute or two that they can manage when there's a class full of students.

That's where Walk-and-Talks (a phrase and strategy developed by Jim Peterson, the exceptional principal at our former school) come in.

These conversations take place during the teacher's prep period. We've had many over the years. We make arrangements with another teacher who has our student during that time to pull them out for 5 or 10 minutes to. . . walk-and-talk with them.

These are less threatening or intimidating than a sit down, since we're walking side-by-side. We often begin with a big picture question: "What do you want to be doing five years from today?" or "What brings you joy?" Then, we'll often ask for their ideas about how we can better support them? Next, we'll bring up whatever the elephant in the room is—the primary reason that precipitated the conversation—grades, behavior, etc.

That is a quick-and-dirty summary of what happens in these "Walk-and-Talks." See a link in the Technology Connections section for more detailed plans.

ASKING FOR ADVICE

Sometimes when one of our students might be exhibiting challenging behavior, we've applied (with minor modifications) a strategy some researchers have found effective: asking them to offer advice to any younger person, or a younger family member, or to a future child of their own who was exhibiting the same type of behavior.[26] More often than not, their advice is spot-on, and a positive change results. In fact, we also often use this same strategy when students come to us for relationship, family, interpersonal, or professional advice.

Other times, we might change this strategy up a bit and, first, ask students for the name of someone they respect. Just asking that question often startles them, because they might be expecting a reprimand instead. After they give us the name—a family member, a famous athlete, anybody—we then follow-up and ask the student what advice that person would give them now about how to handle the situation.

CLASSROOM SEATING

There are *so* many different ways to configure student desks in a classroom, though we prefer the "standard" desks in rows. One reason we use it is because our rooms

---

[26] Fessler, L. (2022, July 20). Psychologists have surprising advice for people who feel unmotivated. *Quartz.*

are small, and we don't really have much choice considering our class sizes. Another is because we—and researchers—have found that it's the layout resulting in fewest disruptions primarily because it reduces the chances of students looking at, and communicating with, others during inappropriate times.[27,28]

A major critique of this kind of arrangement is that it's easier for those seated in the back to be disengaged. We agree with that criticism, which is a major argument for the importance of "Breaking the Plane."

The bottom line for us, though, is that we think pretty much any arrangement *can* work, as long as the teacher is regularly circulating throughout the classroom and every student is easily accessible to the teacher. In addition, it's critical for teachers of most grades (maybe less so for more mature high school juniors and seniors) to strategically assign seats—and reassign them when student behavior warrants it.

If we have to move a student because of disruptive behavior, we also make sure that we always give them two choices (we've previously discussed the importance of choice). And, if either of those choices would require another student to move, we clear it with them earlier and make it entirely optional. We find that most students are amenable to giving up their seats after we explain it's a vote of confidence in their self-discipline but, if they're not, we just find another alternative.

In years that we're not entirely exhausted and feel a bit ambitious, we might ask each student to list their name, along with the names of four other students to whom they'd like to sit near. We explain that there is no guarantee that we can accommodate all their wishes, and we explain in some instances we won't because we don't think it's good idea to have certain students sit near each other, but we usually are able to develop a seating chart where everyone has at least one or two of their choices nearby.

We should also emphasize that even though we use the standard row arrangement, we often have students work in small groups and then they are welcome to move the desks in whatever way they want. We just ask them to put them back to their original positions at the end of the period.

See the Technology Connections for additional research and ideas about classroom seating.

SHOWING CURIOSITY

Teachers will need to engage with students countless times who are exhibiting challenging behavior. Doing so in a confrontative manner and leading with blame will typically result in student defensiveness and other non-preferred reactions.

---

[27] Terada, Y. (2025, August 22). 11 smart student desk layouts. *Edutopia*.
[28] Terada, Y. (2025, August 18). Research-based tips for optimal seating arrangements. *Edutopia*.

Researchers, and our experiences, point toward approaching these kinds of conversations with curiosity: "It seems to me you're not very happy in class—what's going on?" or "There seems to be some tension in our relationship—what can we do to reduce it?" or "You seem pretty tired today—how many hours of sleep did you get last night?"[29]

Obviously, there are some immediately disruptive behaviors or safety issues that need to be confronted. In those situations, we can still demonstrate curiosity well after the fact—later that day, or the following day, after the situation has been depolarized.

More often than not we find that mildly disruptive behaviors are better handled in the near term (and, as we mentioned, more severe disruptions in the slightly longer term) by leading with curiosity. We believe that students tend to feel more respected by teachers and can be less challenging in the future when we treat them as individuals who, like us, can have complex stories and reasons behind behaviors.

CHOOSE YOUR BATTLES

Abraham Lincoln once wrote[30]:

> When I was a boy on the farm in Illinois there was a great deal of timber on the farm which we had to clear away. Occasionally we would come to a log which had fallen down. It was too hard to split, too wet to burn, and too heavy to move, so we plowed around it.

We also think it's also a good classroom management guide. We need to, as the old Civil Rights anthem says, "keep our eyes on the prize" and not get sucked into distracting conflicts. Sometimes, you just have to choose your battles and plow around.

If a student keeps on forgetting to bring a pencil to class, we just give them one from a big box of golf pencils we buy at the beginning of each school year. If they don't have paper or a Chromebook, we have extra. Who knows why they didn't bring them, and there's definitely no guarantee punishment is going to "teach them responsibility" (many of our students already have far greater responsibilities at home than we ever had). We've got bigger fish to fry, like helping them develop intrinsic motivation, a love of learning, and mastery of the content.

---

[29] Delizonna, L. (2017, August 24). High-performing teams seed psychological safety: Here's how to create it. *Harvard Business Review*.

[30] Widmer, T. (2001, November 17). Lincoln and the Mormons. *The New York Times*.

By the way, if for some reason you still question why teachers should have that perspective, it's also supported by specific classroom management research.[31,32]

A corollary to the idea of picking your battles is this community organizing adage: Sometimes the only worse thing than losing a fight is winning one.

In organizing, that can mean you've won a political fight, but have drained every last ounce of energy from your organization, and now it's hollowed-out.

In teaching, it has informed our strategy about carefully selecting which "fights" (rules, classroom routines, student comments) we choose to enforce—and when. There are ones that are critical to effective learning taking place. And there are ones that are *not* critical to that goal.

> *Of course, this organizing maxim can also apply to avoiding power struggles with students—we teachers can never really win one. It may appear like we have, but the resentment created will likely poison the atmosphere.*

DON'T TAKE THINGS PERSONALLY

Try not to take things personally.

Students can be mean—they're kids and often not in control of their emotions. That doesn't mean you can't tell them about how what they said or did made you feel, but get over it and move on. They likely won't remember it the next day, and it's best if we don't, either.

TRYING TO REDUCE THE ENDLESS LOOP OF NEGATIVE ATTENTION THROUGH CUES

Research and many teachers' experiences—including our own—show that often the more negative attention you focus on a student will result in more behavior problems, not fewer ones.[33] Of course, just because we know it works that way

---

[31] Reinke, W. M., Herman, K. C., & Newcomer, L. (2016). The brief student–teacher classroom interaction observation: Using dynamic indicators of behaviors in the classroom to predict outcomes and inform practice. *Assessment for Effective Intervention, 42*(1), 32–42. https://doi.org/10.1177/1534508416641605

[32] Ford, T., Hayes, R., Byford, S., et al. (2019). The effectiveness and cost-effectiveness of the Incredible Years® Teacher Classroom Management programme in primary school children: Results of the STARS cluster randomised controlled trial. *Psychological Medicine, 49*(5), 828–842. https://doi.org/10.1017/S0033291718001484

[33] Reinke, W. M., Herman, K. C., & Newcomer, L. (2016). The brief student–teacher classroom interaction observation: Using dynamic indicators of behaviors in the classroom to predict outcomes and inform practice. *Assessment for Effective Intervention, 42*(1), 32–42. https://doi.org/10.1177/1534508416641605

doesn't mean that many of us stop ourselves from doing it! That same research finds that highlighting positive student behavior tends to result in more of that happening.

If we find ourselves in a kind of endless loop of giving negative attention, we generally try a first step of having a conversation with the student that starts this way:

> I think I'm calling your name out and getting on your case too much. I'm not feeling good about it, and I suspect that you aren't, either. Sometimes what I've done in the past is, instead of calling out students' names, we arrange a sign—like my tapping on the desk once, or saying a word—that reminds the student to get refocused. Could we try something like that? What would be a sign that you'd like me to give?

That conversation, applying the sign, and combining it with a lot of praise for specific positive behaviors, usually—though, unfortunately, not always, succeeds in turning things around.

STORYTELLING

Storytelling can be a strategy for connecting present actions to some kind of bigger picture in an effort to help students—and others—learn a lesson of some kind.[34] These stories can be short-and-sweet, and can be far more effective than a reprimand by reframing the moment.

To students who are feeling frustrated, we have shared stories about when we've been tempted to give up during challenging experiences, and what made us continue. To students who have issues with self-control, we've shared stories of past students who had similar experiences, what they did to change, and how they felt about it. And, once you develop relationships with students and learn what athletes and public figures they look up to, it's usually pretty easy to find inspirational stories from their lives about how they overcame multiple challenges, as well.

CALLING HOME

What teacher among us has not called a student's parent/guardian to express concern about a student's behavior?

---

[34] Grenny, J. (2017, September 25). Great storytelling connects employees to their work. *Harvard Business Review*.

We've made a simple modification to this strategy that has worked exceptionally well. Instead of saying we're going to call home that night to tell their family about a misbehavior, we say we're going to call home in three days, and it's their behavior during that time that will determine what we are going to say.

Nine times out of ten, the student will behave well, and we'll have positive things to say on the call. And, more often than not, this sort of breaks the cycle, and the student's behavior will continue being positive, or at least less disruptive, for an extended period of time.

And, if their behavior begins to worsen again, and we have to call home with a concern, the parent/guardian is likely to be much more receptive that time around since the first time we called we had a positive report to share!

LIGHT TOUCHES

Studies have shown that a supportive touch on the shoulder can result in a student being twice as likely to volunteer in class than if he or she did not receive that touch.[35] Library users who are touched rate the library more favorably, and people dining at restaurants who are casually touched by waiters or waitresses feel more positively about their experience and leave higher tips. Further studies have shown that a light touch on the upper arm can increase compliance substantially, and two light touches can increase it even more.[36]

Of course, teachers have to be careful using this tactic—some students, for a variety of reasons, do not want to be touched, and some cultures have strict gender rules about it. We've found that as long as we do it lightly and quickly, in a public environment, and are respectful of students' comfort levels, this kind of touch can help build a connection between us and a student.

Hugs, of course, are a different kettle of fish. If we feel a hug is appropriate (if a student is in distress, or if a student just received good news) we *always* first ask if we can give them a hug, and then they are always side hugs, not face-to-face.

LEADING WITH THE BIGGER PICTURE

Anytime we're experiencing challenging behavior from a student, every ounce in our being wants to directly deal with it. In the case of student safety or major disruptions, we obviously have to do just that.

At other times, however, it may be more of an issue that doesn't reach being an all-class disruption. Rather, it may be a major issue for that particular student that doesn't necessarily require immediate action but does call for a serious private intervention.

[35] Carey, B. (2010, February 22). Evidence that little touches do mean so much. *The New York Times*.
[36] Dean, J. (2023, February 18). What does it mean if someone touches your arm? *PsyBlog*.

We have found one strategy that almost always improves the situation—sometimes just in the short term, though often for the long term.

It's actually a two-steps strategy.

First, we need to find 10 or so minutes to talk with the student one on one. Most of the time, that means doing a "walk-and-talk" (see that section earlier in this chapter). Usually, that means arranging with the student's teacher for us to take them out for a walking conversation during our prep period.

Second, we think carefully about how we begin the conversation itself. It's never about the immediate classroom behavior situation. We recognize that the behavior is often just a symptom of a greater issue, so we try to get at *that* issue.

For a student who refuses to read in class, we might say:

> We'll talk about your not reading in class later. I want to talk about the truly important issue—you're a super smart person and you tell me you want to go to college. Help me understand what is difficult for you about reading so we can develop ideas on how I can support you so you can get into college. You not realizing your potential would really be depriving the world of a gift.

For a student who is not doing work in class, we might say:

> We can talk about our classwork a little later. The much more important issue is I know you want to go to college, and I see your grades have dropped a lot in all your classes this year. I'd like to know what's going on and how I can support you.

In other words, a student may be expecting us to harangue them about their behavior. Instead, we begin by downplaying that, and focus on their *assets* and how we can work together to amplify them.

Near the end of our conversation, almost as an after-thought, we'll talk about the specific classroom issues, how they make us feel, and how we can work that out, which we almost always do.

When we first consider how to deal with these kinds of problems, our first impulse may be to lash out. But we've learned from experience—and extensive research that very little positive resolution generally comes from that kind of strategy.[37,38,39]

Leading with the bigger picture has a bigger pay-off.

[37] Starr, D. (2018, April 21). What hospitals can teach the police. *The New York Times*.

[38] Gallo, 2024.

[39] Seppälä, E. (2015, May 7). Why compassion is a better managerial tactic than toughness. *Harvard Business Review*.

AVOIDING "AVOIDANT INSTRUCTION"

What is avoidant instruction and should we. . . . avoid it?

Avoidant instruction is emphasizing what people, including students, cannot do—you *can't* chew gum, you *can't* talk in class, etc.

Obviously, there are times we teachers need to do some of this kind of avoidant instruction.

Researchers, however, suggest that it's more effective to emphasize what people *can* do instead of what they can't.[40]

For example, when students ask to go to the restroom in the middle of a lesson, we'll often say, yes, in five minutes. Or, if we're going on a field trip, we'll often lead with a list of things they *can* do on the trip, and then follow it up with a list of don'ts.

Oftentimes we teachers are in situations where we have to send an avoidant instruction message. But we find it helpful to try to look for opportunities to say yes instead of no and believe it contributes to a healthier classroom culture.

"IF YOU'RE GOING TO POLARIZE, ALWAYS DE-POLARIZE, AS SOON AS YOU CAN"

In community organizing this means that, yes, political fights require polarization. However, it's likely your opponent is still going to be around after that political fight is over.

So, don't humiliate today's opponent, and figure out ways to re-engage with them as quickly as possible in case they can be an ally in the next fight.

In teaching, this adage has reminded us to never do something that would embarrass a student—(and, if we do, make sure we publicly apologize) and, when tension does happen between a student and us, we work toward "depolarizing" it as soon as possible (by the end of the class period, by the end of the day, at the beginning of class the next day—at the latest).

What Could Go Wrong

It's very possible that you may try every one of the strategies listed in this chapter, and there still may be a student you are not able to reach. If that's the case, don't beat yourself up over it. Sometimes situations call for sending a referral to the office, or two of them, or even three of them.

Other options could be to talk to that student's other teachers (or guidance counselor) to learn if they are having any better luck and, if so, to learn what they're

---

[40] Russell, C., & Grealy, M. A. (2010). Avoidant instructions induce ironic and overcompensatory movement errors differently between and within individuals. *Quarterly Journal of Experimental Psychology, 63*(9), 1671–1682. https://doi.org/10.1080/17470210903572022

doing and/or to ask them if they can put a good word in for you. In those situations, we've even sometimes had them facilitate a three-way meeting as a "mediator" of sorts with us and the student.

Asking advice from parents and guardians is also an option. Find out from them when their child has done well in school and how their teachers at that time worked with them.

If that student participates in sports, enlisting their coach as your ally can work wonders!

All we teachers can do is try our best. An advantage to trying the different ideas in this chapter is that all your students see that, even though you're not "soft," you're also not reaching for the "stick" first.

If you've tried these strategies and still have to go the discipline route, it's highly unlikely that student is going to be receiving much sympathy from their classmates. A little peer pressure has the potential of going a long way.

Finally, what happens if you're reading this book later in the school year and you have an entire class that is basically out-of-control, which is a situation Larry found himself in several years ago? Fear not! Larry adapted a suggestion from his principal at the time that involved an extrinsically-based point system that moved into developing student intrinsic motivation and allowed him to completely turn things around. You can read about it at a link in the Technology Connections section or in one of his books, such as *Helping Students Motivate Themselves*.

Chapter Summary

If we only had a few minutes to chat in the teacher faculty room, here's what we'd want you to remember about classroom climate:

Technology Connections

For even more classroom management ideas, visit *The Best Posts On Classroom Management* https://larryferlazzo.edublogs.org/2010/07/23/my-best-posts-on-classroom-management/.

Find many articles and videos that can be used to teach students about the value of delaying self-gratification at *The Best Posts About Helping Students Develop Their Capacity For Self-Control* https://larryferlazzo.edublogs.org/2010/06/03/my-best-posts-about-helping-students-develop-their-capacity-for-self-control/.

Learn more about handling "Walk-and-Talks" at *Guest Post: "Walk & Talks" Are Extremely Effective Way To Connect With Students—Here's A "How-To" Guide* https://larryferlazzo.edublogs.org/2016/03/13/guest-post-walk-talks-are-extremely-effective-way-to-connect-with-students-heres-a-how-to-guide/.

Learn about research, and more ideas, about classroom seating at *The Best Resources On Classroom Seating Strategies* https://larryferlazzo.edublogs.org/2017/03/02/the-best-resources-on-classroom-seating-strategies/.

Read how Larry turned around one of his classes that had gotten completely out of control at *Have You Ever Taught A Class That Got "Out Of Control"?* https://larryferlazzo.edublogs.org/2009/02/23/have-you-ever-taught-a-class-that-got-out-of-control/.

CHAPTER 9

Providing Effective Student Feedback

What Is It?

There are few, if any, aspects of a teacher's job as important as giving students helpful feedback.[1]

In fact, since so much research and our own experiences also support the value of peer assessment and self-assessment,[2] perhaps it's better to frame it as:

Education researcher Dylan Wiliam recommends that teachers aim for a quarterly distribution of feedback[3]:

Are there really any parts of a teacher's job more important than creating the conditions where students can receive—as well as give themselves—helpful feedback?

- 25% of the feedback students get comes from teacher to them individually
- 25% of the feedback students get comes from teacher to the entire class
- 25% of the feedback students get is from a student to a classmate (or classmates)
- 25% of the feedback students get comes from themselves

This seems to us to be a helpful "aspirational" goal that we don't always reach. We also use those categories as a framework for the Applications section.

In addition, we've added a fifth kind of feedback in the Application section—technological feedback. Though, as we've discussed in previous chapters, we're not

[1] Hattie, J., & Timperley, H. (2007). The power of feedback. *Review of Educational Research*, 77(1), 81–112. https://doi.org/10.3102/003465430298487

[2] Visible Learning. (2024, November). *Self-reported grades meta-analyses*.

[3] Schimmer, T. (2023, May 16). Exceptions prove the rule | Dylan Wiliam | Cumulative effect. *Tom Schimmer Podcast*. [Podcast].

big fans of tech use *in* the classroom, we do believe that certain online learning tools, particularly those that utilize adaptive learning, can be useful for home use. We're less positive about other forms of AI feedback but, as we discussed in our chapter on tech, we have offered it sometimes as an option for students.

We should also point out that we'll be including a discussion on grading in this chapter because it, too, obviously functions as "feedback."

Why We Like It

We like practically all the kinds of feedback that we feature in this chapter because the reason we do our job is to help students learn, and providing feedback that students actually want to pay attention to is a critical part of making that happen.

The only practice we talk about that we're not big fans of is grading. How many teachers really *like* to grade? Some studies show that grading, in many ways, is a far, far less helpful form of feedback than oral or even written comments because then students almost entirely focus on the grade itself.[4] So our discussion on grading is similar to our earlier discussion on Artificial Intelligence in most classrooms—offering suggestions on how to minimize its harm to both teachers who have to give grades and students who have to receive them.

Supporting Research

Though there is a vast quantity of research on feedback, education researcher Dylan Wiliam points out that the majority of it is only about college students, which reduces its usefulness to those of us in K-12 teaching.[5] In addition, the Harvard Business Review regularly discusses research on feedback in the workplace.[6]

However, that doesn't mean that it's non-existent.

We will cite research at various points in the Applications section supporting our specific recommendations. Here, though, we'll share a couple of points that could apply to many of the practices we recommend.

Interestingly—at least, it's interesting to us—studies show a similar positive impact on K-12 students whether they receive the kind of feedback we discuss in this chapter during the time they are learning, right after their learning, or a week

[4] Lipnevich, A. A., & Smith, J. K. (2008). Response to assessment feedback: The effects of grades, praise, and source of information. *ETS Research Report Series*, 2008(1). https://doi.org/10.1002/j.2333-8504.2008.tb02116.x

[5] Wiliam, D. (2021, June 11). Let's look again at research on feedback. *TES Magazine*.

[6] See: https://hbr.org/search?term=feedback

after their learning.[7] We're not arguing with those results but, based on our experience, we tend to believe that sooner is better.

Another important point raised in research that is not specific to K-12 environments but is nevertheless important to consider is that feedback done badly can have major detrimental effects on learning.[8,9] Who among us hasn't been the recipient of poorly done feedback that was not helpful to us in the short or long term?

We're not sure that there is a pithy and universal set of feedback guidelines that teachers can keep in mind that will help our students and not harm them. But, based on research and our own experience, we are confident that most teachers likely won't go wrong with the specific strategies we recommend in the next section.

Application

Though, as we just mentioned, we're not sure that there is a truly "universal" criteria to bear in mind when providing feedback to students, we do think there are three key elements to keep in mind when applying any of the recommendations in this section.

Most feedback, and especially any that might be less-than-positive, is likely not going to be very effective if students don't feel that the person giving them that feedback truly values them as individuals.[10] That research makes sense to us—if the key to successful feedback is getting the person to change, why would they listen to someone who they don't believe truly cares about their growth, development, and success?[11]

Secondly, we always want to try and have an attitude of framing feedback, even the critical kind, with a positive twist. Tom Landry, the famous Dallas Cowboys football coach, supposedly only had his players watch film of their executing good plays and not the ones where they blew their assignments. He felt that they could learn far more from reinforcing what they did well than reviewing what they did badly.[12]

That practice may not *always* be possible in the classroom, but we *can* often highlight where a student did something the correct way previously or, if they didn't,

[7] Colin, J., & Quigley, A. (n.d.). Teacher feedback to improve pupil learning. *Education Endowment Foundation*. (Page 19)

[8] Kluger, A. N., & DeNisi, A. (1996). The effects of feedback interventions on performance: A historical review, a meta-analysis, and a preliminary feedback intervention theory. *Psychological Bulletin*, 119(2), 254–284. https://doi.org/10.1037/0033-2909.119.2.254

[9] Wiliam, D. (2016). The secret of effective feedback. *Educational Leadership*, 73(7), 10–15.

[10] Berinato, S. (2018, February). Negative feedback rarely leads to improvement. *Harvard Business Review*.

[11] Wiliam, D. (2018). *Embedded Formative Assessment* (Second Edition). Solution Tree Press.

[12] Buckingham, M., & Goodall, A. (2019, April). The feedback fallacy. *Harvard Business Review*.

show a model of how it could be done correctly, instead of just saying, "You did this wrong." Or, when pointing out a mistake, we *can* lead by saying "It's important that *we* do (this) in (this situation)" instead of saying "*You* didn't do this right."[13] Or, we can keep in mind what educator Dan Meyer suggests about "mistakes"—using them as windows to access student thinking and reflecting on what question they were answering correctly in their minds and then using that answer as a jumping off point for a conversation.[14] These are a few kinds of actions, though not the only kinds, that communicate to students that our feedback—both positive and critical— is an affirmation of our confidence in, and our care about, them.

And, thirdly, we think it's important for students—and teachers—to not look at feedback as a one way street. We need to model for our students that we, too, are continually learning and are eager for *their* feedback. We've previously discussed doing weekly surveys where students share how they're feeling about their lives and about our classes, and we've mentioned the regular anonymous evaluations we ask students to complete about our teaching. We also invite student feedback during multiple other times and, most importantly, model *not* reacting defensively. We strongly believe that this kind of teacher modeling increases the odds that students will take our feedback to them more seriously than they would otherwise.

TEACHER TO INDIVIDUAL STUDENT

Agentic Feedback

"Agentic feedback" is a term used to describe a feedback process where it is a partnership between teacher and student and not just a process where the teacher is the all-knowing distributor of wisdom.[15] It's very similar to the ideas of Dylan Wiliam, who recommends that teachers frame their feedback as "detective work."[16]

The idea is that teachers just don't tell students what they've done wrong. Instead, we provide guidance and challenge students to figure out the specifics.

For example, if a student turns in an essay or story without a good hook at the beginning, instead of doing the work for them and telling them a hook they could use, we might ask them to again review the sheet where we had learned the different types of hooks, ask them if they see any one of them in their essay and, then, assuming the answer is "no," ask them to choose one model and write one.

---

[13] Lemov, D. (2018, February 12). Coaching words: You don't, you didn't, you must, we will. *Doug Lemov's Field Notes.*

[14] Meyer, D. (2018, November 20). That isn't a mistake. *Dy/Dan.*

[15] Mutoni Griffiths, C. (2023). Useful feedback, more than praise, helps students flourish. *Scientific American.*

[16] Barton, C. (2022, March 29). *Dylan Wiliam.* [Podcast].*Tips for Teachers.*

Wiliam describes a teacher who writes out and cuts-up short comments about student essays, puts students in groups of four, returns their essays to them, and then challenges the group to connect up each comment to the appropriate essay.[17]

Or a teacher can tell a student they have done a great job using supporting details to support their topic sentence in one paragraph. Then ask them if they can tell in which paragraph that is the case and then apply the same skills in the others.

Using this kind of agentic feedback process is a way to voice confidence in the abilities of students and can be a strategy that helps provide them with choices, both of which can enhance student motivation.[18]

Concept Attainment is a way to provide this kind of agentic feedback to the entire class, and we explained how that works in Chapter 7: Maximizing Student Learning and will revisit it again later in this chapter.

Helping Students Feel Like They Matter

Researchers and, again, our own experience, find that providing feedback, especially agentic feedback that is more of a conversation, helps students feel like they genuinely matter.[19] In other words, teachers are taking time to connect and care with the student.

One way to make feedback even more meaningful is by helping students understand how what they are doing can be applied in other contexts. For example, when we give feedback to students on their oral presentations, it's easy for us to give examples of how they'll be using their speaking skills in college (especially now that more and more classes there are using oral exams or presentations to thwart AI use) or in professional venues.

Another way to raise the bar of feedback is by using what psychologists Geoffrey Cohen and David Yeager call "wise feedback."[20] In their studies, students became more engaged in following through on the feedback they received if their instructor prefaced it by saying something like, "I'm giving you these comments because I have very high expectations and I know that you can reach them."[21]

---

[17] Wiliam, 2016.

[18] Mutoni Griffiths, 2023.

[19] Pacheco, R. (2025, January 24). Why feedback can make work more meaningful. *Harvard Business Review*.

[20] Yeager, D. S., Purdie-Vaughns, V., Garcia, J., et al. (2014). Breaking the cycle of mistrust: Wise interventions to provide critical feedback across the racial divide. *Journal of Experimental Psychology: General*, 143(2), 804–824. https://doi.org/10.1037/a0033906

[21] Office of Inclusive Excellence in STEM. (n.d.). *Wise Feedback and Assessment*. University of Colorado Denver, College of Liberal Arts and Sciences.

Praising Effort and Process, Not Intelligence

Many educators are, by now, familiar with the "growth mindset" concept developed by Carol Dweck. In the context of providing feedback, applying a growth mindset means that we make a point of praising effort or process ("Your working hard at revising this essay is really paying off, and this kind of 'sticktoitiveness' is going to help you in college and at work in the future") instead of "intelligence" ("You are such a great writer!"). Research has found that praising intelligence can reduce students' future achievement and perseverance because they become hesitant to take risks and make—and bounce back from—mistakes. In other words, they fear that errors won't make them look "smart" and they may even believe that having to work hard at learning something could indicate that they are "dumb" because they believe it should come naturally to them.[22,23]

As Professor Dweck has put it, praise for intelligence instead of praise for effort sends the wrong message.[24] People who are praised for being smart "don't want to risk their newly minted genius status," . . . Praise for effort keeps people engaged and willing to work hard.[25]

When it comes to having to offer constructive criticism, "yet" is the magic word, as in "Your claim here doesn't seem quite there *yet*. Looking at the examples we reviewed, how do you think we can strengthen it?"

Plussing

"Plussing" is a feedback strategy popularized by Pixar, the animated movie studio.[26]

It's not rocket science, but it's a simple strategy to keep in mind that goes along with everything else we've said so far.

Simply put, when giving feedback, don't use the word "but" and replace it with "and" or "what if." So, instead of telling a student, "I see you have a lot of good information on your slides, *but* it's just too overwhelming for the viewer," say "I see you have a lot of good information on your slides. *What if* you took out two-thirds of it and put a visual there, instead?" or "I see you have a lot of good information on your slides, and I wonder if it might look better if some of it was replaced by an image?"

According to author Peter Sims, the idea is to "build and improve on ideas without using judgmental language."[27]

---

[22] Dweck, C. (2015, January 1). The secret to raising smart kids. *Scientific American*.

[23] Dweck, C. (2007, October 1). The perils and promises of praise. *Educational Leadership*, 65(2), 34–39.

[24] Rock, D. (2011, November 10). Praise leads to cheating. *Harvard Business Review*.

[25] Glei, J. (2013, March 18). Talent isn't fixed and other mindsets that lead to greatness. *Behance*.

[26] Lee, D. (2020, July 20). What is Pixar's Plussing? [YouTube]. *DavidLeeEdTech*.

[27] Ferlazzo, L. (2013, April 6). Quote of the day: Giving feedback. *Larry Ferlazzo's Website of the Day*.

Is There Value in Giving Written Comments as Feedback?

We're not huge fans of providing written feedback to students because we're not convinced most will read it—one-on-one conversation is more our style.

Nevertheless, researchers have found that some students do read comments, though it's important to keep in mind what we discussed earlier—much research on feedback has been on post-secondary students, not K-12 classes.

The limited research that there is on K-12 students have found that students are more likely to pay attention to comments reflecting the kind of more positive frameworks we've previously discussed in this section and, importantly, if specific time is set aside in class for them to review teacher comments on their work.[28,29]

Grading & Assessments

Ah, grading.

We're not sure that any other topic in education provokes more angst among students, families, teachers, and administrators.

We urge everyone to relax and take a chill pill. We know that this is more easily said than done, especially in environments where there is an extreme degree of family involvement or administrative focus on grades. But we suggest that it's worth a try.

Grading has never been one of our big teaching worries, and our students have seemed to do just fine in our classes, in their future college coursework, and in their subsequent professional careers. Those in our International Baccalaureate (IB) classes have also done well in their IB assessments, which must be reviewed and marked by teachers all across the world.

We don't have a prescription for how teachers *should* grade.

We will, however, share some important elements of how we handle grading, which is really another form of feedback to students, though we think in many ways it's the lowest. We think the real key for a successful grading strategy is if your students think it's fair and if you're not spending enormous amounts of time doing it. If both of those things are true, then we would subscribe to, "If it ain't broke, don't fix it." However, if one or both of those things are not true, we would recommend you consider how we handle grades or, at least, visit the link in the Technology Connections section to explore other grading ideas.

---

[28] Brandmo, C., & Gamlem, S. M. (2025). Students' perceptions and outcome of teacher feedback: A systematic review. *Frontiers in Education, 10*, 1572950. https://doi.org/10.3389/feduc.2025.1572950

[29] Elliott, V., Baird, J., Hopfenbeck, T., et al. (2016). A marked improvement? A review of the evidence on written marking. *Education Endowment Foundation*. (Page 5)

Here are a few of the grading strategies we use:

Grading Less: We do fewer assignments that require grades. Instead, we do many more formative assessments and provide opportunities for peer and self-assessment.

We discuss peer and self-assessment later in this chapter. Here, we'll spend some time reviewing formative assessment.

Formative assessments are ongoing practices that help both the teacher and student evaluate and reflect on how they are both doing and what changes either or both might need to make to become a more effective teacher and learner. *Formative* assessments are often contrasted with *summative* assessments. Summative assessments are the mid-term and final exams, benchmarks, and state tests that we give. They're designed to, at least theoretically, identify what a student has learned and what she/he hasn't learned.

To quote education researcher Robert Marzano from *The Art and Science of Teaching*, formative assessments "might be one of the more powerful weapons in a teacher's arsenal."[30]

Formative assessments are low-stakes and provide evaluative feedback to both students and teachers. Some that we use include asking questions and having students respond on mini-whiteboards that they hold up, clozes (fill-in-the-blank passages) to help gauge vocabulary knowledge, reading fluency assessments (where students orally read passages to use and we can evaluate prosody), and online games like Wayground and Blooket. (A quick word here: though we use lots of different online games, we've begun to favor Blooket and others that let students "steal" points from others to move up the public leaderboard. Though it doesn't alter the internal scores for assessment, this feature ensures that you can't publicly see who really answered the fewest questions correctly.)

These formative assessment strategies obviously inform the feedback that we teachers can provide students. However, as we mentioned earlier, an often underappreciated role of formative assessments is to also help students inform *themselves*.

This student agency aspect of formative assessment does not happen automatically or magically and requires teacher support. We'll discuss how to make it happen later in this chapter.

See a link in the Technology Connections section to learn even more about formative assessments.

Eliminating Zeros: Our district, like many others, eliminated the zero grade and replaced it with 50%, which makes a ton of sense to us. How does it make sense to have a grading system from 60 to 100% use intervals of 10%, and then the next

---

[30] Marzano, R. J. (2007). *The Art and Science of Teaching: A Comprehensive Framework for Effective Instruction*. ASCD. (Page 13)

interval be 60% to zero? Not only is it fairer, it's helped motivate students so they don't feel like they can't dig out of a huge hole.

This change hasn't resulted in anyone passing our classes who, without it, would have failed.

We've also always allowed our students to resubmit assignments for higher grades.

If these practices sometimes mean a student gets an A, when in other circumstances they might have gotten a B—big deal.

What's wrong with giving our students some grace?

We understand that not all teachers agree with this perspective. For more evidence for why it works, though, visit a link found in the Technology Connections section.

Redo/Retest: Research, and our own experience, shows that offering students the chance to redo assignments and tests for higher grades enhances learning and reduces failures, and doesn't appear to negatively impact students' efforts or motivation the first time around.[31] Students don't always take us up on our redo/retest offers, but many do. As a result, they learn more (remember our comments elsewhere in this book about the value of retrieval practice), feel more positive about the class, and we build up collateral in our relationship "bank." What's not to like?

Student Self-Grading: See the student self-assessment section later in this chapter for ideas on how we incorporate student self-reflection in the grading process.

TEACHER TO THE ENTIRE CLASS

Another way to provide actionable feedback to students is through offering Whole Class Feedback. Many teachers have already been doing this for years. It entails the teacher identifying common challenges that many students may be facing and teaching or reteaching that skill to the entire class at the same time.

The teacher could be identifying these issues in "real time" by circulating throughout the classroom as students are working on a project or worksheet or by reviewing student work that had previously been submitted.

When reteaching, we cannot overemphasize a point that we've made in earlier chapters—don't teach the concept or skill the same way you taught it the first time! If that method had worked, you wouldn't have to be reteaching it!

Instead, we recommend taking advantage of a resource you have the second time around that you didn't have before—student work.

One way is by using a form of inductive learning that we discussed in Chapter 7: Strategies for Maximizing Learning called Concept Attainment. Just identify student work examples that are "good" ones and others that are "not so good," always

---

[31] Goodwin, B., & Rouleau, K. (2020). Grading to encourage re-learning. *Educational Leadership*, 78(1).

asking students for permission to use them but without publicly identifying who did which one. It almost goes without saying that using this instructional strategy well necessitates creating a growth mindset classroom culture where students can celebrate making mistakes as learning opportunities. Students then work in pairs identifying why the ones under the "Good" heading are…good, and why the ones under the "Not So Good" or "Bad" heading are…not so good.

Another effective strategy we use often is just slapping a good example of student work (with their permission) on the document camera and either asking the class to write on mini-whiteboards why it's good (our preferred way) or, if we don't have time to use whiteboards, just explaining to students why it's an excellent example.

STUDENT TO CLASSMATES (PEER ASSESSMENT)

Peer assessment, done with careful planning that includes teacher modeling, can be a productive activity that helps everybody in the classroom. Researchers have found that it improves academic performance while at the same time promoting student agency and autonomy, which enhance intrinsic motivation.[32,33] Research has also found that the act of providing peer feedback in some cases was more of the trigger for improved performance than hearing the feedback.[34] We don't quite understand how they can tell that difference, but neither are we trained education researchers. But that finding does make sense to us.

We have primarily used peer assessment for student writing, but it can obviously be used in all subjects and for many different kinds of student work. Logistically, we've usually done it in a "speed-dating" style, but it can also be done more simply with three or four different partners (it's important to have more than one-or-two peer reviewers just in case some are not very helpful), or sometimes even taping essays around the classroom (sometimes with names folded over so that the authors can't be identified) and having students leave comments on them (sometimes anonymously) using sticky notes. When we do the last method, we also give students time to review *all* the comments left on *all* the papers.

The keys to increase the chances of it being helpful and not reverting to students providing vague positive comments or, worse, demoralizing ones, have been providing clear guidelines, organizing a simple process, and offering examples of good and bad comments (sometimes through the concept attainment process) while showing

---

[32] Yan, Z., Lao, H., Panadero, E., et al. (2022). Effects of self-assessment and peer-assessment interventions on academic performance: A meta-analysis. *Educational Research Review*, *37*. https://doi.org/10.1016/j.edurev.2022.100484

[33] Double, K. S., McGrane, J. A., & Hopfenbeck, T. N. (2020). The impact of peer assessment on academic performance: A meta-analysis of control group studies. *Educational Psychology Review*, *32*(2), 481–509. https://doi.org/10.1007/s10648-019-09510-3

[34] Dunn, P. (2024, April 3). An unsung benefit of peer feedback. *Inside Higher Ed*.

the class a model essay. It's also important to provide time after the peer review process for students to process the comments they received and reflect on how they'll use them. Another prerequisite for success is to have created a growth mindset class culture where students feel safe in providing and hearing constructive critique (see Chapter 6: Emphasizing Students' Assets Not Deficits for more ideas on teaching students about a growth mindset).

Often, we've asked students to focus their feedback more narrowly (e.g., introductions), especially during the first times we do it, while later in the school year we've left it more open after students have developed more experience and have a greater comfort level with the process.

We've used various guidelines over the years, including:

- Ron Berger from EL Education recommends *Be kind* (and provide thoughtful praise), *Be specific*, and *Be helpful*.[35] We provide multiple sentence starters for students to use. For example:

  - Kind: I like how you________ because ___________

  - Specific: In the first/second/third paragraph I wonder if you could _________________? or I'd like to know more about ___________ here.

  - Helpful: I think it might be worth your time to look at the teacher example or rubric, or look at what (name of other student) has done.

- We learned a different three-part sequence from Jennifer Serravallo called Praise, Question, Polish.[36] Again, we provide sentence starters like:

  - Praise: I liked how you ___________ because __________;

  - Question: I wonder___________;

  - Polish: I wonder if it can be strengthened if you ___________________.

- Figure 9.1 Peer Review of TOK Essay Outlines is a form Larry has used with his classes. It has four parts:

  - One where students have to write down areas where they are specifically looking for help,

  - then they list helpful advice they received,

  - next they share helpful advice that they gave, and,

  - finally, they need to complete an anonymous Google Form saying how helpful or not helpful they found the process.

[35] Clark, J. (2025, July 24). Peer Feedback. *DistillED*.

[36] Serravallo, J. (2017). *The Writing Strategies Book: Your Everything Guide to Developing Skilled Writers*. Heinemann.

1. Think of at least three areas where you could use help in your essay. Write them as questions (like, "I'm having a hard time developing a counterclaim for this claim—do you have any ideas?" or "Where do you think I can find an example to support this claim?" or "What is your advice for how I can write a better thesis statement?.")

   My Question Requesting Help One:
   My Question Requesting Help Two:
   My Question Requesting Help Three:

2. As you "speed-date," explain at least one of the problems you are having to your partner (don't just ask them the question—give them some background information and context.) If you have time, ask them as many of the questions as you can. Write down here helpful advice you receive from your partners. You don't have to write down everything everyone says, though:

   Helpful Advice I Received One:
   Helpful Advice I Received Two:
   Helpful Advice I Received Three:
   Helpful Advice I Received Four:
   Helpful Advice I Received Five:

3. What are two examples of helpful advice that you gave to someone during this exercise? The "Suggested Sequence for Writing Your TOK Essay" is at the bottom of this document— you might want to refer to it when you're giving advice. You'll also have textbooks that you can refer to, as well as previous assignments we did in Google Classroom, plus remembering feedback Mr. Ferlazzo has given to you about YOUR essay:

   Helpful Advice I Gave One:
   Helpful Advice I Gave Two:

4. After you are done speed-dating, please complete the anonymous survey on Google Classroom helping Mr. Ferlazzo know if this was helpful or a waste of time.

Figure 9.1 Peer Review of TOK Essay Outlines.

We have had success, and not-so-much success, with each of these strategies. The common denominator determining which way it has gone has been the amount of time we have put into modeling the process beforehand—the more prep time, the more success. In addition, we have learned the hard way that, as we mentioned earlier, it is best to encourage students to focus their feedback more narrowly at the beginning of the year.

See the Technology Connections section for a link to many other resources on peer assessment, including various guides and forms for students to use.

STUDENT TO SELF (SELF-ASSESSMENT)

Neither teachers, nor other students, are going to often be present to provide feedback when students are doing academic work—or, in fact, any other kind of work, either—outside of school. Given that reality, developing self-assessment skills will be critical for all students' long-term success. Substantial research supports this position and while, at the same time, emphasizing that teacher modeling and other scaffolds are essential to make self-assessment work.[37,38]

There are various instructional strategies we've used over the years to strengthen students' self-assessment skills, including:

- "Plus, minus, interesting" is an activity we learned from education researcher Dylan Wiliam.[39] It's a useful introduction to self-assessment that asks students to say something that was easy about the assignment, then something that was difficult, followed by something that they found interesting. Wiliam also recommends another simple question: What would you do differently if you had to do the assignment again? He suggests, and we agree, that both of these activities help students begin to develop their own critical eyes.

- Research, and our own experience, supports the idea that sharing examples of previous student work, highlighting what makes them good and what they might be missing, and then having students use them to self-assess what they produce, can be an effective self-assessment strategy.[40] We've been very pleased with how this activity has worked with our classes. We've never used rubrics much, but if you do, research suggests that they will work best after you first show these examples, and then co-create the rubrics with your students.[41]

- We've previously discussed the motivational importance of students actually seeing the learning progress they are making. Effective strategies to make this happen include sharing a list of vocabulary words at the beginning of a unit where they mark which ones they know and then they revisit the same list at the end of the unit; or giving students at the end of the year the opportunity to revise essays they wrote at the beginning of the year; or having them record themselves reading a text in September, and then have them listen to that and redo it in June so they can see how much their prosody has improved. All these strategies, and others with the same goal in mind, contain a self-assessment component.

- We've had students use various forms to grade themselves. Figure 9.2 Student Self-Assessment One and Figure 9.3 Grade Reflection are two examples.

---

[37] Panadero, E., Jonsson, A., & Botella, J. (2017). Effects of self-assessment on self-regulated learning and self-efficacy: Four meta-analyses. *Educational Research Review*, 22, 74–98. https://doi.org/10.1016/j.edurev.2017.08.004

[38] Yan, et al. (2022).

[39] Wiliam (2016).

[40] Lemov (2015).

[41] Panadero, et al. (2017).

If I disagree with you, we will meet individually & you can make your case

NAME ____ Period __________

Personal Grade Reflection—Answer and Give supporting examples (you may write on back)

1. Do you initiate working and learning most or all of the time in this class, or does Mr. Ferlazzo have to push you a lot?

2. Do you take risks and try challenging tasks in this class even if you make mistakes (and learn from them). Or do you "play it safe" most of the time?

3. Do you try to teach other students if you understand something more than they do? Do you just give them the answer, or do you help them learn? Or do you only focus on your own work and ignore students who need help?

4. When you don't feel like doing the assignment, most of the time do you do your best anyway, or do you try to put it off and/or not do your best or not do it at all?

5. Are you respectful of your classmates and Mr. Ferlazzo? In other words, do you listen when they are speaking, are you serious when you are presenting to the class and thoughtful when asking questions of presenters?

6. Think about the answers you made to the last four questions, and think about the quality of your schoolwork this quarter—tests, classwork, computer assignments, etc. What grade do you think you deserve and why?

Originally published in The Student Motivation Handbook by Larry Ferlazzo, Routledge 2023 Reprinted with permission

Figure 9.2 Student Self-Assessment One

Name: Period:

Researchers have found that several qualities are important for a person to be a successful learner. Please answer each question. Then, take some time to reflect on all of your answers and give yourself the grade that you believe you have earned in this class. If the grade you decide is higher than I believe is appropriate, we will meet and you will have an opportunity to convince me that you are correct.

In the seven years students have graded themselves, I have either agreed with their grade or believed they earned a higher one than they had thought 90% of the time. Five percent of the time where there has been the other kind of difference students have persuaded me to go along with their position.

(continued)

SELF-CONTROL: How do you act in class? Do you pay attention when your classmates and/or Mr. Ferlazzo is speaking or do you often talk with a neighbor or text during those times? Can you restrain yourself from eating at inappropriate times, or are you unable to stop yourself even when it distracts you and your classmates from a learning task?

PERSEVERANCE: Do you do your best work most of the time? Do you give your best effort even when you are not that interested in the learning task? Or do you typically do the least amount you believe you can get away with?

CONSCIENTIOUSNESS: Do you do your homework and classwork on time? Do you keep track of your assignments? Is your class folder or binder organized and up-to-date?

CURIOSITY: Do you work to find something of interest in whatever we are studying, even though on the surface it might not "grab you." Do you think of thoughtful questions to ask your classmates during presentations, to write down when you are reading, or to ask Mr. Ferlazzo? Do you try to "stretch yourself"?

ETHICS: Have you generally acted ethically? In other words, have you done your own work and not copied from a classmate or plagiarized from a book or from the Internet when you could have done so and would likely not have been discovered?

GIVING: Adam Grant, an author and researcher, suggests that people are generally one of three types: givers, takers and matchers. Givers tend to help others without always expecting something in return; Takers tend to look out for themselves and take advantage of others; and matchers tend to only give when they can expect to get something back. Grant suggests that people who are Givers are the ones who are most successful in life. In this class, have you tended to be a giver, taker or matcher?

MASTERY: How well do you think you've learned the concepts we have explored in class? Have you "mastered" it? In other words, do you know enough of the key ideas to be able to explain it to others and to apply them to your own life?

FINAL GRADE: Reflect on your answers to all of the previous seven questions. What grade do you believe you have earned in this class? Feel free to provide any additional evidence to support your position that you have not described earlier.

Figure 9.3 Grade Reflection

Source: Reproduced from Larry Ferlazzo, 2023 / with permission of Taylor & Francis

We've agreed with the grades students have given themselves between 90% and 95% of the time during our careers and, where there is disagreement, offer students an opportunity to make their cases to us. Occasionally, we've been convinced.

- We've had our classes use different versions of Figure 9.4 Essay Self-Assessment to analyze first drafts of essays and other projects prior to having an individual conference with us. It pushes students to consider if they are truly showing us the best work they are capable of doing at that time. Here, as in all of these examples, teacher modeling is essential.

Name ____ Period ____________

1. On a scale of 1 to 5, with 1 being the lowest and 5 being the highest, I would rate my Hook as a __________ because _______________________________.
I think I need/don't need (circle one) help on it.

2. On a scale of 1 to 5, with 1 being the lowest and 5 being the highest, I would rate my Introductory Paragraph as a __________ because _________________.
I think I need/don't need (circle one) help on it.

3. On a scale of 1 to 5, with 1 being the lowest and 5 being the highest, I would rate my Topic Sentences as a __________ because ____________________.
I think I need/don't need (circle one) help on it.

4. On a scale of 1 to 5, with 1 being the lowest and 5 being the highest, I would rate my Supporting Details as a __________ because____________________.
I think I need/don't need (circle one) help on it.

5. On a scale of 1 to 5, with 1 being the lowest and 5 being the highest, I would rate my Conclusion as a __________ because ____________________________.
I think I need/don't need (circle one) help on it.

Figure 9.4 Essay Self-Assessment

- Students setting their own goals and tracking their progress is a self-assessment strategy we have used many different times in many different forms. The constant biggest challenge has always been to find the time needed for students to regularly review their progress towards achieving them and make any needed readjustments. Figure 9.5 Goal Setting Form

---

Name ____

NEXT YEAR

1. My school goal for next year is ___________________________________.

2. My outside-of-school goal for next year is ______________________.

3. Next year, I want my friends to describe me by saying I am ___________

____.

4. Next year, I want my teachers to describe me by saying I am __________

____.

5. Next year, I want my parents/family to describe me by saying I am

____.

10 YEARS FROM NOW

6. In 10 years, I want to ___________________________________.

7. In 10 years, I want my friends to describe me by saying I am

____.

8. In 10 years, I want my parents/family members to describe me by saying I am

____.

20 YEARS FROM NOW

9. In 20 years, I want to ___________________________________.

10. In 20 years, I want my partner/wife/husband/friends to describe me by saying I am ___________________________________.

11. In 20 years, I want my children (if I have them) to describe me by saying I am

____.

Figure 9.5 Goal-Setting Form One

Things I can do NOW to help achieve these goals:

1.

2.

3.

When I don't feel like doing these things, actions I can take to help me get back on track:

1.

2.

3.

When I don't feel like doing these things, actions my teachers can take to help me get back on track:

1.

2.

3.

One is an example of one sheet our students have used. Figure 9.6 Goal Setting Form Two is another version that we've had students in our English Language Learner classes use monthly to set goals and then they've completed Figure 9.7 Goal Review Form weekly.

See a link in the Technology Connections section for more ideas on student self-assessment.

Name ____ Date ____________

1. These are things I've done well to learn English during the past month (circle all that apply):

Worked hard and was not distracted

Helped my classmates

Attended Zero Period English class before school

Practiced English at home (did computer work, watched English language movies/videos/tv shows, spoke English with family and friends, read a book in English)

Studied and did well on tests

2. These have been the scores on my last four Friday tests:

__________ __________ __________ __________

3. I want the scores on my next four Friday tests to be:

__________ __________ __________ __________

4. These are actions I'm going to take to learn English better (circle all that apply):

Work on the computer 15 minutes at home each school day on Quill, Raz Kids, ESL Video, Brainpop, Adobe Express, Blooket, Quizizz, Wordwall, other (write here) ____________________

Attend Zero Period English class before school

Work harder in class and not be distracted

Be an assistant peer tutor (help classmates focus more, help classmates understand things)

Study on my own before the Friday test

Read a book and complete the "Reading a Book" form

Speak English with my family and friends

Watch English language movies/videos/television shows

Figure 9.6 Goal-Setting Form Two

Name: ____

1. What did you do to learn English in the past week? Check all that apply:
    ☐ Worked hard and was not distracted.
    ☐ Helped my classmates.
    ☐ Went to the 7:45 a.m. class.
    ☐ Practiced English at home (did work on the computer, watched English language videos, spoke English with friends/family, read a book in English).
    ☐ Studied a lot for the test.

2. What was your goal for today's test?

3. What was your actual score in today's test?

4. Did you meet your goal?

5. Look at your goal for next week's score. You can keep it the same, or change it. If you want to change it, cross out the old goal and write the new one. Write your goal for next week here, too.

6. What can you do to learn English in the next week? Check all that apply.
    ☐ Work harder and not be distracted.
    ☐ Help my classmates.
    ☐ Go to the 7:45 a.m. class.
    ☐ Practice English at home (do work on the computer, watch English language videos, speak English with friends/family, read a book in English).
    ☐ Study a lot for the test.

7. Do you have other ideas of actions you can take to learn English, or ideas on how Mr. Ferlazzo can help you learn English?

Figure 9.7 Goal Review Form

TECHNOLOGICAL FEEDBACK

We mentioned earlier in this chapter our use of online games as a fun and useful formative assessment tool. As we discussed in Chapter 4: Tech Has Its Place, but Also Has to Be Kept in Its Place, apart from games and Chromebooks for writing, we've been trying to minimize its use in the classroom.

However, as we also described in that chapter, we often encourage the use of online tech tools for practice at home. In particular, we're fans of "adaptive" tools that adjust questions depending on which questions students answer correctly. Researchers have found that the most effective ones for learning provide additional feedback apart from if the answer was right or wrong—they provide some explanation.[42] Few have done that in the past, but we assume that by the time you read this book most or all will have incorporated Artificial Intelligence capabilities to do just that.

A link in the Technology Connections section will lead you to the online adaptive tools that we've had our students use.

Speaking of technological feedback, we also shared in Chapter 4 how we very, very carefully sometimes offer students a process they can use to receive feedback from ChatGPT or Google Gemini on their writing. And again, we say, be sure to check carefully the feedback they get to avoid the introduction of new errors.

What Could Go Wrong

We've shared many different ways to offer students feedback—don't feel like you have to use all or most of them! Experiment! Some kinds of feedback will work with some students and some classes, and others might feel less authentic to you and be less successful for them.

We would like to offer one very clear note of caution—as generative AI tools become more and more sophisticated, its allure in providing more and more student feedback may become seductive to teachers. What teacher wouldn't like an additional several hours a week to do lesson planning, play with their kids, read a book, or take a nap? We hope teachers resist that temptation for most assignments, though obviously AI can have its place in low-stakes activities like online games and adaptive learning practice or if students choose to get initial feedback on assignments as part of a carefully constructed process.

We hope you agree.

But nothing will convince us that genuine feedback is anything but a human-to-human endeavor that is an irreplaceable part of the learning process.

---

[42] Sibley, L., Fabian, A., Plicht, C., et al. (2025). Adaptive teaching with technology enhances lasting learning. *Learning and Instruction, 99.* https://doi.org/10.1016/j.learninstruc.2025.102141

Chapter Summary

If we only had a few minutes to chat in the teacher faculty room, here's what we'd want you to remember about feedback:

Technology Connections

Explore different grading strategies at *The Best Resources On Grading Practices* https://larryferlazzo.edublogs.org/2013/01/09/the-best-resources-on-grading-practices/.

Learn more strategies for formative assessments at *The Best Resources For Learning About Formative Assessment* https://larryferlazzo.edublogs.org/2010/08/22/the-best-resources-for-learning-about-formative-assessment/.

Visit Do We Give A Zero Or 50% For Work Not Turned-In? Here Are Some Useful Commentaries https://larryferlazzo.edublogs.org/2018/09/29/do-we-give-a-zero-or-50-for-work-not-turned-in-here-are-some-useful-commentaries/ for more information on this issue.

For more ideas on facilitating peer review, visit *The Best Ideas On Peer Review Of Student Writing* https://larryferlazzo.edublogs.org/2019/05/12/the-best-ideas-on-peer-review-of-student-writing/.

Go to *The Best Resources On Student Self-Assessment* https://larryferlazzo.edublogs.org/2018/07/24/the-best-resources-on-student-self-assessment/ for more ideas on student self-assessment.

The Best Free Online Tools Using Adaptive Learning https://larryferlazzo.edublogs .org/2023/01/01/the-best-free-online-tools-using-adaptive-learning/ will share some of our favorite online tools for student practice at home.

Cultural Responsiveness, Not Cultural Tokenism

What Is It?

Culturally Responsive Teaching was coined by educator Geneva Gay.[1] Also known as Culturally Relevant Pedagogy, it has three key components according to education researcher Gloria Ladson-Billings.[2] One, there is a focus on student learning, high expectations, and rigorous academic instruction. Two, there's a recognition, welcoming, and prioritizing of students' cultural identities. Thirdly, there's support for assisting students to develop critical thinking skills to analyze problems around them, including society's inequities, and consider ways to address them, as well as teachers doing their own analyses and taking their own actions on the inequities they see in their own schools.

Much of what we've already discussed in this book is part and parcel of culturally responsive teaching, including building relationships, developing student agency, providing "wise" feedback, and supporting an intrinsic motivation to learn.

In other words, culturally responsive teaching isn't just a list of strategies. It's a mindset, or a stance, that reflects how educators view the world, their students, and their students' families. We hope that in reading this book you've seen this kind of consistent "worldview" that recognizes our students as unique individuals who bring gifts to the table and sees our job as helping them maximize what they can achieve with those gifts—and help them find even more talents that they may not even know they possess.

---

[1] University of Washington College of Education. (2020, July 7). Geneva Gay: A legacy of elevating multicultural education to prominence.

[2] Fay, L. (2019, August 7). Researcher Gloria Ladson-Billings on culturally relevant teaching, the role of teachers in Trump's America & lessons from her two decades in education research. The 74.

Notwithstanding this perspective, there are some additional ways that we have not mentioned already that can support the cultural identities of students and their families and ensure that their experiences are fully integrated in day-to-day instruction. And we'll share them here.

The facts of the matter are that 80% of public school teachers in the United States are white, and 56% of those enrolled in K-12 public schools are students of color.[3,4] In addition, researchers have found that white teachers often have the same biases that many white people tend to have—including lower expectations of students of color.[5] Culturally responsive teaching is one way that we can combat these biases, because ignoring them doesn't make them go away.

We also need to recognize that whiteness has been centered in every major American institution for hundreds of years and is already a major part of everything that already happens in our schools. Being culturally responsive doesn't mean that we pay less attention to our white students because of the primacy of white culture. It is important to highlight that white students can *also* benefit greatly from all the strategies we've already discussed in this book and from the ones we'll share in this chapter.

As teachers of English Language Learners, we often say that good ELL teaching is better teaching for everyone else because it makes learning more accessible for everybody. The same is true for Culturally Responsive Teaching—it makes the learning environment better for everyone.

Culturally Responsive Teaching is *not* the same as Critical Race Theory, though some have made that claim. Culturally Responsive Teaching is a pedagogical practice to enhance student learning. Critical Race Theory, on the other hand, is an academic theory used in higher education to analyze systemic racism.[6]

Why We Like It

We've seen that Culturally Responsive Teaching results in students who are more engaged with academic work and are clearly more motivated to learn.

[3] Schaeffer, K. (2024, September 24). Key facts about public school teachers in the U.S. Pew Research Center's Short Reads.

[4] Statista. (2024, March). Share of students enrolled in K-12 public schools in the United States in 2022, by race/ethnicity and state. www.statista.com/statistics/236244/enrollment-in-public-schools-by-ethnicity-and-us-state

[5] Will, M., & Najarro, I. (2022, April 18). What is culturally responsive teaching? Education Week: Teaching.

[6] McDavid, M., & Groth, E. (2022, January 30). Know the difference between culturally responsive teaching and critical race theory. [YouTube]. League of Women Voters.

And we've also directly experienced how utilizing it has changed *us* as teachers and as human beings. It has forced us to examine our own biases and how they may play out in the classroom. Culturally Responsive Teaching has greatly enriched our lives as it has allowed us to learn more deeply about the lives of our students and their families.

Supporting Research

Multiple studies have found that the use of Culturally Responsive Teaching has helped *all* students improve academic achievement, school attendance, graduation rates, and critical thinking skills.[7] Research surveying students directly has found they particularly value how Culturally Responsive Teaching helps them learn about other cultures.[8] In addition, studies demonstrate that students in classes where Culturally Responsive Teaching is being implemented have a greater sense of belonging in school.[9]

Application

SUPPORTING STUDENTS' CULTURAL IDENTITIES

Though many of the activities throughout this book and in this chapter provide opportunities for students to express their cultural identities and learn from one another, one specific related assignment can be to have students create some version of an "Identity Self-Portrait."

There are many different ways to make this happen, and a link in the Technology Connections section will lead you to several lesson plans and examples.

Various versions of these kinds of assignments are also called "self-portraits," "ethnographies," and "Language Portraits." All provide a guide—a list of questions or a graphic organizer—where students share the most important parts of their self-identity. They then visually display their responses, share them with classmates, followed by posting them on classroom walls.

[7] National Education Association & Law Firm Antiracism Alliance. (2022). The very foundation of good citizenship: The legal and pedagogical case for culturally responsive and racially inclusive public education for all students.

[8] Byrd, C. M. (2016). Does culturally relevant teaching work? An examination from student perspectives. Sage Open, 6(3), 2158244016660744. https://doi.org/10.1177/2158244016660744

[9] Muñiz, J. (2019, September 23). 5 ways culturally responsive teaching benefits learners. New America.

"WINDOWS, MIRRORS, AND SLIDING DOORS"

Dr. Rudine Sims Bishop famously described the importance of using, and providing access to, diverse books in the classroom by describing their roles as "windows, mirrors, and sliding doors."[10] In other words, it's critical for books to act as windows so readers can see different experiences; it's equally important for them to be mirrors so readers can see their own experiences in them; and, finally, they are sliding doors so readers can actually step inside and be immersed in them.

Yes, this speaks to the importance of having diverse classroom libraries for our students. But it also applies to many other aspects of classroom life and its environment, including:

- What is hanging on the classroom's walls? Are images (of people or other representations) reflective of students' cultures? Key words or identity self-portraits chosen by students to represent themselves? Different languages? Representative holidays and traditions?

- Are diverse guest speakers (both in occupation and race) invited to speak to the class (don't ignore students' families as resources)?

- In addition to books, are short stories and other writings used in class representative of different cultures? We particularly like the Shared Journal Process developed by Dr. Amanda Branscombe and others where students regularly write about events in their lives and share them with classmates.[11] After sharing, students would write and draw what they liked or connected to in their own journals. Though it can be used in all classes, we found it especially helpful in our English Language Learner ones. Figure 10.1 My Journal is the graphic organizer we have students use to plan their writing.

See a link in the Technology Connections section for more resources on how to support "windows, mirrors, and sliding doors" in your classroom. Dr. Deb Reese has expanded on Dr. Sims Bishiop's to incorporate the idea of curtains, or the things that some cultures keep private. Considering such topics for your students is important when you want to tap into prior cultural knowledge.[12]

[10] New York State Office of Cultural Education. (2025, July 14). DEI Toolkit: Mirrors, Windows, and Sliding Glass Doors. Available at: https://nyslibrary.libguides.com/dei

[11] Ferlazzo, L. (2020, March 10). Culturally responsive teaching is not a quick fix. Classroom Q & A with Larry Ferlazzo.

[12] Writing the Other. (2016, October 12). Mirrors, windows, sliding glass doors, and curtains, from: writing Native American characters. [YouTube.]

<table>
<tr><td>Where did it happen?</td></tr>
</table>

<table>
<tr><td>Who was there?</td></tr>
</table>

<table>
<tr><td>When did it happen?</td></tr>
</table>

<table>
<tr><td>What happened?
First,
Then,
Finally,</td></tr>
</table>

<table>
<tr><td>How Did I Feel About What Happened?</td></tr>
</table>

<table>
<tr><td>What Did I Learn From What Happened?</td></tr>
</table>

Figure 10.1 My Journal

CONNECTING TO PRIOR CULTURAL KNOWLEDGE

In Chapter 6: Emphasizing Students' Assets, Not Deficits, we discussed Funds of Knowledge and shared several ways we utilized them in classroom lessons.

Some ways we've done the same with students' cultural knowledge have been:

- While in refugee camps, many Hmong women created "story cloths" (embroidery that told stories about their lives). In a series of lessons, our Hmong students created their own hand-drawn versions of story cloths and helped the non-Hmong students to do the same. We then used their creations as springboards to learn the English words needed to talk and write about these stories. Students were more engaged in this language-learning activity because it mirrored, valued, and respected an important part of their home culture.

- Students retold fables and folktales from their cultures in their own words prior to writing their own.

- We've used the concept of "Historical Empathy" to help students teach each other. Historical Empathy is the idea of trying to better understand the context and beliefs of people in the past, without necessarily agreeing with them.[13] We were studying the California Missions established by Spain in one of our US History classes and were discussing how many more Native Americans ran away to escape them than organized rebellions. Many of our students said they thought they would have actively fought against the colonizers if they had lived then. However, our Hmong students, whose families had barely escaped with their lives fleeing from the North Vietnamese through the jungle, were very clear that they believed running away in the face of overwhelming power and living was far superior to fighting and dying in the face of likely death. After hearing from their Hmong classmates about their experiences, everyone else in the class changed their mind.

TRANSLANGUAGING

Translanguaging means honoring students' use of their home languages as a way to help them learn English and understand the academic content that's being taught.

It doesn't really mean "translating," though translating some words could be a part of it. It's a pedagogical strategy where we view students' home languages as an asset they can use to more actively engage with the lesson we are teaching.

It's about strategically using a student's home language as a *scaffold* to help them achieve English language acquisition success, in addition to being a scaffold for an English language learner to learn *higher-level academic content* that they might not be able to access yet in English.

It could mean letting students use Google Translate or talk to a classmate in their home language to gain a better understanding of a word or concept, or encouraging students to share home language words or expressions that could connect to a lesson, or have classmates teach each other words in their respective home languages, or many other activities.

See a link in the Technology Connections section to learn more about what translanguaging could look like in the classroom.

---

[13] Ferlazzo, L. (2025, October 10). The best resources for learning & teaching about historical empathy. Classroom Q & A with Larry Ferlazzo.

FREIRE'S LEARNING SEQUENCE

We learned an excellent strategy from an old Peace Corps teacher training manual on how to apply some of Brazilian educator Paulo Freire's pedagogical ideas.[14] We often use this "learning sequence" in preparation for students' writing an argument essay. It looks like this:

1. Show a picture or short video clip portraying a national or international problem or a common challenge students might face. We've shown a video clip from *Les Miserables* where a character is arrested for stealing bread to feed his family or an image of schoolyard bullying, etc.

2. Next, ask students to share what they believe is happening. What is the problem they think is being portrayed?

3. Then, ask students what they think caused the problem.

4. This is followed by asking students if they, members of their family, or friends have ever experienced a similar problem.

5. Next, students can share how they or their family/friends responded to the problem.

6. Then, students talk about other ideas they might have about how to respond to the problem.

7. Finally, each student has to decide which response to the problem they think is the best one and why; then they're ready to complete a graphic organizer that leads to writing an essay.

PRONOUNCING STUDENT NAMES CORRECTLY

We can't say it enough times: taking the time to learn how to pronounce each of your student's names is essential to relationship building, and if you get it wrong, keep practicing until you get it right!

Researchers have affirmed what just makes sense: mispronouncing students' names can cause embarrassment and shame, and it certainly doesn't communicate respect.[15]

Write it out phonetically, record your student saying it so you can listen and practice on the drive to school—whatever it takes, just do it!

[14] Peace Corps Information Collection & Exchange. (1992). Teaching English as a foreign language.

[15] Mitchell, C. (2016, May 16). A teacher mispronouncing a student's name can have a lasting impact. PBS News.

MAKING FAMILY AND COMMUNITY CONNECTIONS

We've discussed in prior chapters the value we've found in developing strong connections to the families of our students, including through going on home visits. As a result of these visits, where we have asked family members for their ideas on how our school could support them *and* if they knew of other neighborhood residents who they believed could be allies in making those ideas realities, we have worked closely with families on several community projects.

These have included starting a community garden on school grounds and also organizing a home computer project where our district provided desktops and home internet access to families so they could study English together.

Obviously, not all home visits and phone conversations have to lead to those kinds of major projects. But we are advocates of parent engagement, where families are viewed as full partners with schools, as opposed to parent involvement, where schools view them as more passive participants in their child's education.[16]

This kind of communication is made more possible with the advent of efficient AI-moderated translation tools, like Google Translate.

Another way we facilitate family connections is by having students write a weekly letter or email, in their home language, to parents/guardians telling them about what they did and learned in school. See Figure 10.2 Parent Guardian Letter Guide

Date ________________

Dear Mom/Dad/Uncle/Aunt/_______________

This week was (good, great, challenging, difficult, bad) because______________.

The three best things that happened in school this week were:

_________________________________ because ___________________.

_________________________________ because ___________________.

_________________________________ because ___________________.

The most interesting thing I learned in school this week was _______________.

It's interesting to me because _______________________________________.

A not-so-great thing that happened this week was ___________________________.

That wasn't so great because ____.

A goal I have for next week is ____

because ____.

What's a question you would like to ask me about my week?

Figure 10.2   Parent Guardian Letter Guide

[16] Ferlazzo, L. (2012, March 27). The difference between parent "involvement" & parent "engagement." Education Week Opinion.

for an English draft of this kind of letter. We ask students to bring their letters back to us (or forward the email response they received) with a question their family asked them about it and a signature.

The letter doubles as a student reflection and also as a retrieval practice opportunity!

BEING TRAUMA-INFORMED

Trauma-Informed Practices (TIP) are a set of principles designed to support students, and others, who have been impacted by trauma. Many of the practices we have discussed in this book and this chapter, including showing compassion, cultivating a growth mindset, building positive relationships, fostering a sense of belonging, demonstrating flexibility, and prioritizing restorative practices are just a few elements of being trauma-informed.[17]

There are also many other direct intersections between being trauma informed and being culturally responsive, including making family connections and supporting student identity.

In Chapter 8: Classroom Climate and Culture, we briefly mentioned ACEs, Adverse Childhood Experiences, a list of common traumatic events experienced by children. Students might demonstrate signs of trauma, including "acting out" behaviors or their reverse, withdrawal, absenteeism, being distracted, and many more.[18]

Making a referral to a trained counselor is our recommended first-line of response, along with teachers acting on the many suggestions we include in this book.

A good example of culturally responsive/trauma-informed teaching happened in Larry's classroom one year.

The majority of students in his Newcomers English Language Development class were refugees from Central America, many of whom experienced trauma with a capital "T" in their home countries and in their journey to the United States.

One day Larry saw a first-person account written in accessible English about gang violence in El Salvador. He had individual conversations with students to see how they would feel reading such a piece. Would it hit "too close to home" or would they want to try reading it. All said they wanted to read it, but when he brought copies to class, one student, "Alfredo" said he wanted to read it alone in the corner.

---

[17] NEA. (2023, September). Trauma-informed Practices. Professional Excellence Tools & Tips.

[18] REL Appalachia Cross-State Collaborative to Support Schools in the Opioid Crisis (CCSSOC). (2020). Common Trauma Symptoms in Students and Helpful Strategies for Educators. Institute of Education Sciences.

So, Alfredo took his copy of the article, moved his desk to one of the corners and positioned it so he had his back to the rest of us. We began reading it together with students leaping at the chance to interject their own comments and connections to the article. At one point, Larry could tell—even from just seeing his back—that Alfredo was having a hard time. Larry asked students to continue to read as partners and went over to see him. Alfredo then took out his phone and began to show Larry photographs of all his friends who had been killed by gang violence in El Salvador and told him their stories.

Afterward, all students, including Alfredo (who had previously not been very interested in academic work), asked that we read and write as much as possible about what was happening in Central America.

Respecting students by first asking their permission to bring in an article on such a personal issue, *acknowledging* the different ways they might want to react to it, and *listening* to their personal commentaries all combined to form a more cohesive classroom community and provide superior opportunities for highly-engaging academic lessons.

Leading with our ears instead of our mouths works with students experiencing trauma—and with most others, too!

It's important to note that community wide trauma can affect our students, too. A nearby immigration raid, a local police shooting, a wildfire requiring wide-spread evacuations, a political assassination, and flooding are just a few of the broader traumatic events that could affect large numbers of students. Though, again, we recommend enlisting trained counseling support, this could also be time for the Community Building Circles we discussed in Chapter 5: Developing Classroom Conditions Where Students Can Motivate Themselves.

See a link in the Technology Connections section for many more resources on trauma-informed instruction.

CULTURAL COMMEMORATIONS AND HOLIDAYS

Black History Month, Hispanic Heritage Month, Women's History Month, Asian American and Pacific Islander Heritage Month, Arab American Heritage Month, and others can be excellent opportunities to spotlight the different cultures present in your classroom.

Please keep two elements in mind, however. One, if you are going to do activities to recognize them, do it thoughtfully and seriously, don't just show a five minute video and share cultural food.

Prior to the commemoration, do research to explore the many possible lesson plans and projects available online *and* engage students in conversations to hear their ideas about what should happen in class. In fact, we often have students help us teach the class about their

Avoid superficiality!

cultures. And, too, make sure that your recognition of these cultures are not limited to the commemorative periods! Culturally Responsive teaching is about integrating students' cultures into the classroom all throughout the year!

When it comes to holidays, we're advocates of celebrating and recognizing as many of them as possible! For example, introduce Christmas, Hanukkah and Eid al-Fitr; acknowledge your students' diversity, don't try to hide it.

LEARN ABOUT YOUR STUDENTS' LANGUAGES, CULTURAL/RELIGIOUS BELIEFS AND TRADITIONS

Learning more about your students is not only respectful, but can be extremely helpful when it comes to instruction. For example, knowing that adjectives often come after nouns in Spanish can help inform a teacher why a Spanish heritage speaker is making that error in English. Or knowing that some cultures discourage socializing among different genders might assist a teacher better navigate small group instruction. Teachers having this kind of knowledge can also help them respond to potential inadvertent disputes among students.

One year, a group of students in one of Larry's classes was scared of visiting the restroom because they felt it was inhabited by bad spirits. They were willing to bring a shaman in to perform a ritual that made it safe again.

Learning about these cultures doesn't necessitate lengthy research—just asking your students about them should do the trick.

TEACHERS APPLYING A CULTURAL ANALYSIS TO THEIR OWN CLASSES AND SCHOOLS

So far, we've spoken about Culturally Responsive Teaching mainly in the context of actual instructional strategies.

But it also requires us teachers to examine ourselves.

We're definitely not fans of self-flagellation. However, we do recognize that all of us have implicit biases, unconscious attitudes that affect how we act.

We're not going to recommend that all of us attend district-sponsored training on implicit bias, though. Based on our experiences with any kind of district-sponsored professional development, it would probably put us all to sleep instead of helping us learn anything!

Instead, we're fans of the approach recommended by education researcher and culturally responsive teaching pioneer Gloria Ladson Billings, who suggests that instead of going to this kind of training, teachers sit down and look at their data for their school and look at:

- who's being suspended
- who's attending advanced classes

For their individual classes ask:

- who am I disciplining the most
- who do I have challenging relationships with

And then examine the question: "How do we explain it?"[19]
Ladson Billings offers:

> People's explanations will help you understand why certain things are happening. If their explanation is, 'Well, you know, we have all these poor kids,' OK, the poverty is not gonna stop next week. Are we saying because the children are poor, they are incapable of X, Y or Z?

Our school, and we as teachers, have found this kind of exercise to be extremely helpful and has led to both institutional and individual changed behaviors.

Another way to answer the question, "How do we explain it?" is by asking *students* themselves. Our school has had several professional development sessions led by student panels discussing various topics, including what is working—and what is not working—for them in classrooms.

For additional ideas on how to examine institutional and educator implicit bias, and respond to them in effective ways, visit the link in the Technology Connections section.

What Could Go Wrong

The goal of Culturally Responsive Teaching is not to teach about students' cultures.

The goal of Culturally Responsive Teaching is to honor, respect, and utilize students' cultures to more effectively promote instructional equity and academic rigor for everyone.

It is a strategy, not a goal.

Confusing the two can be a common error made by many well-meaning educators.

Try not to be one of them. If you have questions, reach out to your administrator or your school's or district professional development. If that's not a viable option, there are multiple organizations linked in the Technology Section you can reach out to or referenced in Chapter 11.

[19] Fay, L. (2019, August 7). 74 interview: Researcher Gloria Ladson-Billings on culturally relevant teaching, the role of teachers in Trump's America & lessons from her two decades in education research. The 74.

Chapter Summary

If we only had a few minutes to chat in the teacher faculty room, here's what we'd want you to remember about cultural responsiveness:

Technology Connections

Find lesson plan ideas for specific assignments on students' self-identities at *Some Of The Best Resources On Supporting & Valuing Students' Identities* https://larryferlazzo.edublogs .org/2024/02/16/some-of-the-best-resources-on-supporting-valuing-students-identities/.

For more ideas and resources to ensure that you have a diverse classroom library and classroom environment, visit *A Beginning Collection Of Resources About Books As "Windows, Mirrors & Sliding Glass Doors"—Please Suggest More* https://larryferlazzo .edublogs.org/2019/06/21/a-beginning-collection-of-resources-about-books-as-windows-mirrors-sliding-glass-doors-please-suggest-more/.

Find more ideas about translanguaging at *The Best Resources For Learning About Translanguaging* https://larryferlazzo.edublogs.org/2022/07/17/the-best-resources-for-learning-about-translanguaging/.

Go to "Best" Lists Of The Week: Responding To Student Trauma https://larryferlazzo .edublogs.org/2018/06/14/best-lists-of-the-week-responding-to-student-trauma/ for more information on Trauma-Informed instruction.

Implicit Bias Training Doesn't Seem To Work—So What Should Teachers & Others Do, Instead? https://larryferlazzo.edublogs.org/2021/10/06/a-look-back-implicit-bias-training-doesnt-seem-to-work-so-what-should-teachers-others-do-instead-2/ contains ideas and resources on what schools and teachers can do about implicit biases.

For plenty of additional ideas on how to implement Culturally Responsive Teaching in many different subjects and grade levels, visit *The Best Resources About "Culturally Responsive Teaching" & "Culturally Sustaining Pedagogy"—Please Share More!* https://larryferlazzo.edublogs.org/2016/06/10/the-best-resources-about-culturally-responsive-teaching-culturally-sustaining-pedagogy-please-share-more/

CHAPTER 11

Teacher Self-Care and Sustainability

What Is It?

Larry retired from teaching while writing this book. In the months following his retirement announcement, many of his colleagues would come up to him and say how envious they were.

He was a bit perplexed—in previous years, he had always felt happy for teachers who were retiring, but never envious. After all, he taught at a great school, and in most ways felt like he was working in an ideal situation with minimal stress.

Larry's wife Jan, however, regularly (and lovingly) told him he was clueless and living in a fantasy world—not questioning that the school where he worked was great, but that he was experiencing minimal stress.

Of course, as in most things, Jan was correct. In the first two and a half months following his retirement, Larry easily lost 20 pounds, slept regularly through the night for the first time in years without waking up worrying about something related to school, and his eyesight even improved—he no longer had to wear reading and computer glasses.

Teaching in public education is stressful—whether we realize it or not. The American Teacher Survey, conducted annually by RAND, shows that compared to similar working adults, teachers report experiencing less well-being in every element measured.[1] And who knows how many more are clueless like Larry was and are not doing well, but don't realize it? The same survey also finds that most teachers are working an average 49 hours per week.

---

[1] Woo, A., Doan, S., Levine, P. R., & Steiner, E. (2025). *Teacher Well-Being, Pay, and Intentions to Leave in 2025*. RAND Education and Labor.

District and school administrators can also be often clueless when it comes to teacher care. At one point, our school district sent us all a breathless email grandly announcing that free chair massages would be available at the Central Office to all staff during a two week period—from 9:00 AM to 3:00 PM.

Why We Like It

This chapter will share a few practices that we think might help teachers reduce stress and stay in the classroom for a longer period of time. We can't say we have been consistent practitioners of everything on the list, but they've all worked for us when we've had the self-discipline to act on them.

None of the strategies in this chapter are substitutes for having a strong teachers' union to ensure that district and administration demands are kept in check, planning and collaborative time is protected, and that teachers receive fair wages and benefits. But they can be helpful additions.

Supporting Research

Though there is somewhat limited research available on teacher self-care, studies that have been done find that teacher stress is negatively associated with academic achievement by their students.[2] Other research finds that teacher self-care is no substitute for improved working conditions that are controlled by administrators and policymakers, and we wholeheartedly agree.[3]

Application

DON'T GRADE EVERYTHING

Grading can take up an enormous amount of teachers' time. Larry remembers seeing a video on social media recording a dog going to every window in a house following their owner who was walking around it. Larry captioned it "Unfinished grading following me around this weekend" and it was reshared *many* times by other educators.

---

[2] McMakin, D., Ballin, A., & Fullerton, D. (2023). Secondary trauma, burnout, and teacher self-care during COVID19: A mixed-methods case study. *Psychology in the Schools, 60*(5), 1442–1458. https://doi.org/10.1002/pits.22764

[3] Hilligoss, A., Carpenter Estrada, T., Graham, M., et al. (2025). Exploring teacher self-care in an age of burnout and anxiety. *Arts Education Policy Review*, 1–14. https://doi.org/10.1080/10632913.2025.2497408

Here are some strategies we use:

- **Prioritize doing formative assessments,** like the ones described in Chapter 9: Providing Effective Student Feedback, that just require observation (like mini-whiteboards) or viewing technology-assisted evaluation (like online learning game results), and not formal grading by the teacher. Not only does that reduce time teachers spend grading, but researchers suggest that "right now, we don't know anything that has a bigger impact for a smaller cost than classroom formative assessment."[4]

- **Create more time for peer review and assessment,** which we also discussed in Chapter 9: Providing Effective Student Feedback.

- **Provide verbal feedback as students are working in the classroom.** We discussed in that same chapter our preference for constantly circulating around the classroom and giving oral feedback on student work, instead of waiting until it was turned in.

- **Utilize a self-assessing process for students,** like the ones described in that same chapter. If you use rubrics, have students use them as checklists prior to turning in work.

- **Group presentations means grading one assignment for multiple students.** In previous chapters, we've discussed the value of collaboration (students working with others to improve the quality of their own individual work) as opposed to cooperation (a group of students all working together on the same project). In acknowledgment of that difference, we'll often have students work Jigsaw-like collaboratively on individual aspects of a bigger project that they have to turn in, and then work collaboratively to make a class presentation. For example, students have to work in a group to present about an entire textbook chapter, but each student is responsible for answering questions in writing about just a few pages that they were responsible for reading. Or, the group makes a presentation on a historical figure, but each student was individually responsible for writing about one aspect of their life.

CREATE A PROFESSIONAL LEARNING NETWORK

A Professional Learning Network (PLN) is simply a group of other educators—IRL (In Real Life) or online—who you can learn from, give advice to, and offer support to and receive it, as well.

---

[4] Wiliam, D. (2022, November 2). The role of leaders in promoting more effective assessment. *Nurture*.

Nothing beats having a mentor or collaborator on your school site, as the two of us know well. It's also a wide world out there, too, with Facebook groups of educators galore, and teacher hashtags on every other social media platform, too.

But, please, as we've previously stated, never say anything negative about your students or their families in writing anywhere, and certainly never share photos of your students without express written permission from their parents or guardians.

But while keeping those guidelines in mind, there are hundreds of thousands of educators accessible and willing to freely provide resources and advice. Why not take advantage of that kind of expertise?

FOCUS MORE ON "INPUT"

Larry's grandson has just begun student teaching as we are finishing writing this book. He recently told Larry he was giving his students their first test and was very worried that if they did not score well that it would indicate that he had been a bad teacher.

No, no, no. . . .

It is true that teachers are the most important school-based factors in influencing student academic achievement. It is also true that there is overwhelming research finding that out of school factors like racial inequality, family income, food and health insecurity, and parental educational attainment have a far, far greater influence on student school success.[5]

Given these conclusions, basing teacher evaluations on student test scores is a questionable practice, as is teachers beating themselves up if it doesn't appear that all their students have learned everything they have been taught.

Annie Dukes is a cognitive scientist who calls a misplaced focus on outcomes such as test scores a "resulting" cognitive bias that rewards results that might have nothing to do with the actions that we took and punishes other results that might have been the result of circumstances entirely out of our control.[6]

Education researcher Larry Cuban suggests that, instead, we should consider focusing on supporting the input of "good teaching" that reflects the best research-based instructional practices.[7]

[5] Hanover Research. (2019). *Factors Influencing Student Learning*. Utah Learning through Effective, Actionable, and Dynamic Education (ULEAD).

[6] Duke, A. (2018). *Thinking in Bets: Making Smarter Decisions When You Don't Have All the Facts*. Penguin Publishing Group.

[7] Cuban, L. (2020, August 5). Remote delivery of instruction–COVID-19 and re-opening schools. *Larry Cuban on School Reform and Classroom Practice*.

Of course, that leads us to wondering who decides which are the "best" instructional practices. We're biased, but we think the ones described in this book are a good start.

But, for this chapter's purposes of teacher self-care, we hope that you are willing (and that your administrators and district teacher evaluation policy) to distance yourself from connecting your success as a teacher to your students' results on district assessments and state tests.

For more information on the idea of distinguishing outputs from inputs, see a link in the Technology Connections section.

CLASSROOM ROUTINES AND CLASSROOM "JOBS"

Researchers have found that classroom routines help raise student academic achievement.[8] They also can make a class run a lot smoother and reduce teacher stress.

If students know how to handle the Warm-Up (Do Now) when they enter the class, or how "speed-dating" works to share their work with classmates, or how dividing up for Jigsaw projects work, teachers don't have to explain and re-explain procedures repeatedly.

See a link in the Technology Connections section for more ideas about classroom routines.

Class "jobs" can serve a similar function. Typical jobs in our classrooms are unofficially helping with attendance, putting fruit out for students (Larry brings a variety of fruit several days a week), making sure borrowed Chromebooks are plugged in and recharging at the end of each class, and distributing textbooks or papers. Sometimes we offer weekly "fruit snacks" as student "pay," but students often forget about it and do it freely without compensation just because they want to help and like the responsibility. And, importantly for us, these student jobs mean fewer jobs that we have to do!

HANDLING PARENT/GUARDIAN COMPLAINTS

We're a fan of proactivity, and having students write letters or emails home each week, as we discussed in Chapter 10: Culturally Responsive Teaching, is a key way we make that happen for parent communication.

That doesn't mean we don't end up having to make some phone calls home about student behavior or grades, or that we haven't very occasionally received a parent complaint about our teaching. We think following the recommendations we've shared in this book are generally a pretty good recipe for minimizing those problems from arising.

[8] Barshay, J. (2022, July 11). The paradox of 'good' teaching. *The Hechinger Report's Proof Point*.

But, if and when they do, we listen, acknowledge their concerns, look for something in the situation we can apologize for to deescalate the situation, invite them to share their ideas for resolving the problem, and communicate that we're partners in helping their child be successful. We also alert our administrator to what's going on and ask for their help, if necessary.

But we don't beat ourselves up about it, we certainly don't take it out on the student; we try to learn from the situation and move on.

FORGET ABOUT A "PINTERESTY" CLASSROOM DECOR

The social media platform Pinterest is filled with classroom images where teachers have invested an incredible amount of time, energy, and money into elaborate decorations.

Even though some studies suggest these kinds of flashy environments can be distracting to students' attention, we agree with critics like psychology professor Dan Willingham who says that even if that's true, students will quickly get used to them and their distractibility will diminish.[9] He also points out that we shouldn't shortchange many teachers' intentions behind these decorations—that they want their classroom to feel welcoming.

But does it really take teachers' hours and dollars to create classroom walls that feel inviting to students?

Our answer is "no" to that question. In fact, we begin most school years with bare walls and start filling it up with student work and student suggestions. Why shouldn't they be co-creators of their classroom environment? In addition to filling up the space with student examples, we often invite input from classes on "decorations" that might be helpful to student learning, like interactive word walls and sentence starters, and have students create them. And it's easy to regularly change the decor by making it a classroom "job" for several students.

See a link in the Technology Connections section for other ideas for classroom walls.

AVOID TOXIC NEGATIVITY

There will never be any shortage of things to complain about if you are a public school teacher and we, too, have sometimes felt a need to orally "vent" to a trusted colleague, personal friend, or family member.

But if you're going to go that route more than occasionally, please also try to keep in mind the Gandhi story we recounted in Chapter 6: Emphasizing Students'

[9] Willingham, D. (2014, June 5). Bare walls and poor learning? The trouble with the latest headlines. *RealClear Education*.

Assets, Not Deficits—look at every problem as an opportunity, not as a pain in the butt. This attitude does not mean we have to buy into toxic positivity (see the next section). But it will help not drag us down into a spiral of continuous negativity that creates the possibility of us not being a helpful presence to our students, colleagues, friends, or family members. The reality is that nobody likes a whiner, and being perceived as one is not going to help you, either.

This doesn't mean you should not be honest with administrators or colleagues about challenges you are experiencing in the classroom. Asking for assistance, or pointing out possible shortcomings in what's happening at school, are actions to be admired and encouraged, not to be hidden. It's in no one's interest for a teacher to fail or be unhappy, so colleagues and administrators should be happy to provide assistance.

And it also doesn't mean that teachers shouldn't voice critiques of school curriculum, policies, or structures. When educators do so, though, we suggest you keep in mind advice offered by legendary community organizer Saul Alinsky, who founded the organization where Larry worked for nineteen years prior to becoming a teacher: *The price of a successful attack is a constructive alternative.*

Criticism without an alternative action recommendation is unlikely to help move anything toward a positive resolution.

It also sounds cliche, but it's not unusual to find that the teachers' lounge during lunchtime functions as a misery club. If that's the case at your school, we'd recommend you eat at your desk.

Finally, we don't want anything we have said in this section to mask these next two important points:

We just suggest that when pursuing this necessary accountability, keeping some of the suggestions we've made in mind might increase the odds of success. For example, these problems might offer opportunities to bring colleagues to fight together, and challenging them requires the development of alternative visions.

AVOID TOXIC POSITIVITY

Toxic positivity can mean unrealistic insistence on maintaining a positive perspective no matter what.[10] In the

Teachers are not being toxically negative by holding administrators and districts accountable for not providing equitable learning opportunities for all students, including students of color, English Language Learners, or students with disabilities.

Teachers are not being toxically negative by holding administrators and districts accountable for providing safe, healthy, and sustainable working conditions for you and your colleagues. As the saying goes, "Teachers' working conditions are students' learning conditions."

[10] Quintero, S., & Long, J. (2022). Toxic positivity: The dark side of positive vibes. *The Psychology Group.*

school environment, it can mean justifying unfair work expectations by claiming teaching is a calling that requires going "above and beyond."

It can mean masking unrealistic or unjust school policies by hyping Teacher Appreciation Week with loudly promoted free pizza or coffee for teachers.

Or, it can mean, as our district did one year, bringing all teachers together for a pep talk from a former teacher/present author who explained to us that we could do all the great things she did in the classroom, just without the financial and resource support she had received.

Or, it can mean collective humming on Zoom, as our district once organized as part of a work-day, instead of giving teachers more time to prepare their rooms.

Bottling up frustrations can be damaging to mental health.[11] And not speaking out about injustice can be damaging to our students.

There is a medium between toxic negativity and toxic positivity. It's about looking at situations with clear eyes, approaching problems with a professional attitude, and recognizing that critiques of policies and actions don't have to be, or be perceived as, personal attacks.

Hiding from problems can breed toxic positivity and denial. It can try to make teachers feel like they are the problem when challenges arise, when in fact, it is more likely that their causes are more systemic and institutional.[12]

Constant dwelling on problems without action toward resolution can produce toxic negativity and depression.

There's a line between the two, but we don't think it's necessarily that fine of one.

We think it primarily takes teachers having confidence in their judgment and in their "gut."

SUBTRACT WHEN ADDING

When schools add things to teachers' plates—whether it's a student extracurricular activity, another meeting, more topics to cover in the curriculum, or a new district initiative—very seldom is anything taken away.[13]

Though it's logical to believe that teachers have only so much time and mental bandwidth available, "addition by subtraction" is seldom practiced by administrators, nor demanded by teachers.

[11] Cousins, L. (2022, August). Can always staying positive be bad for our health? *HCF*.

[12] Noonoo, S. (2021, September 13). How toxic positivity demoralizes teachers and hurts schools. *EdSurge*.

[13] Noonoo, S. (2022, December 2). Why schools should stop adding and adopt a 'subtraction mindset.' *Edutopia*.

We think changing that attitude can be a major positive development for teacher self-care.

DON'T GET SUCKED INTO BEING "DATA-DRIVEN," GO FOR "DATA-INFORMED," INSTEAD

Data, data, data.

It's one of the most-used words in education.

We don't really have a problem with it. We find data very helpful to our teaching. But it's the word that often follows it—"driven." We think being "data-driven" can lead to all sorts of decisions that are harmful to students and to teachers. Being "data-informed," on the other hand, can bring the advantages of data without its harmful baggage.

Teachers can be brow-beaten with data, typically from a narrow number of sources that produce numbers that can be easily quantified, usually from assessments they have had no part in creating, and often displayed to them in infamous "data walls."[14,15]

Being consumed by data with little context in this way can suck the life out of a teacher, and give administrators an excuse to ignore anything else they don't want to take into consideration.

Being data-informed, on the other hand, can lead to beneficial results for both students and for teachers.

If schools are data-driven, they might make decisions like keeping students who are borderline between algebra and a higher-level of math in algebra so that they do well in the algebra state test. Or, in English, teachers might focus a lot of energy on teaching a strand that is heavy on the tests—even though it might not help the student become a life-long reader. In other words, the school can tend to focus on its institutional self-interest instead of what's best for the students.

In schools that are data-informed, test results and other measures are just a few pieces of information that can be helpful in determining future directions. There are countless other data points, including teacher observation, formative assessments, oral presentations, classroom discussions, individual conversations, just to name a few, that can help us make a better determination of how we can best serve students.

In fact, a major study from Harvard found that many schools who embrace so called data-driven instruction often did not analyze the data correctly, incorrectly

---

[14] Mellon, E. (2011, December 29). "Data room" keeps teachers, students focused on goals. *Houston Chronicle*.

[15] Hall, L. (2016, May 19). This ed-reform trend is supposed to motivate students. Instead, it shames them. *The Washington Post*.

identified the causes of the student data they used, and did not identify effective strategies to respond to what they felt they learned from the data.[16,17] A different report from the federal Institute of Education Sciences had similar findings.[18]

Many things just can't be measured and placed in a graph as a data point. Can you measure helping to ignite a student's desire to learn about US History? Can you measure the impact on a student's life of seeing an adult model handling conflict calmly? Can you measure the effect of a student beginning to learn the basics of self-control? Can you measure how a student's life is changed after writing a coherent essay for the first time in his life—as a tenth grader?

We would encourage teachers to push back against any kind of technocratic data-driven culture that might be driving you up the walls and, instead, encourage your administrators to prioritize a data-informed approach that prioritizes teacher judgment. We recognize that a school's principal might be pressured by a district's data-driven priorities, but the best administrators we've known have always viewed one of their core responsibilities as shielding their staff from dumb Central Office decisions.

See the Technology Connections section for more information on the difference between being "data-driven" and being "data-informed."

What Could Go Wrong

Not all of our recommendations in this chapter are within a teacher's full control. Focusing more on input, instead of output, being data-informed instead of data-driven, and subtracting when adding are just three that will likely require administrator support.

So, to avoid receiving a negative evaluation or worse, teachers might want to consider avoiding fully implementing some of these strategies before you get "buy-in" from administrators.

How to do that is the question.

Here are some of our suggestions:

- **Play the long game.** If you're relatively new to your school, focus on developing relationships and allies among your colleagues and administrators.

---

[16] Barshay, J. (2022, February 28). Researchers blast data analysis for teachers to help students. *The Hechinger Report's Proof Point.*

[17] Geller, A. (2021, September 17). Should you cancel teacher data team meetings? You might be surprised. *SmartBrief.*

[18] What Works Clearinghouse [Mathematica Policy Research]. (2009). Using student achievement data to support instructional decision making. *U.S. Department of Education IES.*

Learn their interests and goals. Don't push your ideas—look for opportunities to help others get theirs implemented. Don't talk too much at meetings (or gossip)—look for times when you can offer thoughtful comments and questions. Become a solid team player. And if you're not new to your school, but haven't done these things already, it's time to start!

- **Go one at a time.** Based on what you've learned about your colleagues and administrators, identify one—yes, just *one*—of the ideas you'd like to have implemented at school. Begin to raise the idea in individual conversations, but be in a "listening" mode, and not a "selling" one. For example, the district has just unveiled yet another new initiative for teachers to implement, perhaps begin by asking a colleague, "I read an article saying that a big challenge in education is that we add lots of things to teachers' plates, but never take anything off them. I thought that was interesting. What do you think?"

- **Have a similar approach in conversations with your administrators.** In Larry's work as a community organizer, he and his colleagues would approach meetings with decision-makers believing that the decision-makers would likely have one of several attitudes:

  - One, they didn't know that a problem existed; in that case, all it took was telling them about it.

  - Two, they knew the problem existed, but didn't know how to solve it; if that was the situation, they just had to present a solution or two.

  - Three, they were genuinely sympathetic, but didn't have all the power needed to prove what Larry's group wanted; if they had this position, then it took a strategic discussion about how to build the necessary leverage over the people with the power.

  - Four, maybe they didn't know about the problem or maybe they did, but either way they thought our solution was a bad one and they flat-out opposed it.

  No matter which response it was, it was always important to achieve clarity to plan next steps, and this holds true with your school administrator, too. Recognize that your first meeting, or even meetings, with administrators will be exploring the idea, not trying to get a decision.

- **Learn from those conversations.** Refine your arguments based on those conversations, or even decide to drop your idea and choose another one. Perhaps you'll learn that the issue is more one for bargaining in a union contract, and that realization will affect who you should meet with sooner rather than later.

- **Don't go it alone.** Once you've taken these actions, and decide it's time to move forward by bringing it to local union leadership, or to local or district administrators, consider bringing a respected ally to that conversation.

We don't mean to suggest that following these steps will guarantee success, but they will certainly increase the odds of getting an agreement.

For more ideas on how to build influence and affect change, see a link in the Technology Connections section.

Chapter Summary

If we only had a few minutes to chat in the teacher faculty room, here's what we'd want you to remember about teacher self-care:

Technology Connections

For more information on the idea of focusing on inputs instead of outputs, visit *The Best Resources On The Idea Of Evaluating Teacher "Input" Instead Of Student "Output"* https://larryferlazzo.edublogs.org/2017/07/16/the-best-resources-on-the-idea-of-evaluating-teacher-input-instead-of-student-output/.

Visit *The Best Resources On The Value Of Classroom Routines* https://larryferlazzo.edublogs.org/2025/10/17/the-best-resources-on-the-value-of-classroom-routines/ for more information about. . .classroom routines.

See *The Best Ideas About How To Use Classroom Walls—Please Recommend More Resources* https://larryferlazzo.edublogs.org/2018/01/18/the-best-ideas-about-how-to-use-classroom-walls-please-recommend-more-resources/ for ideas on "decorations" that don't require much teacher time, energy, or money.

For more ideas on how to be data-informed, instead of being data-driven, go to *The Best Resources Showing Why We Need To Be "Data-Informed" & Not "Data-Driven"* https://larryferlazzo.edublogs.org/2011/01/28/the-best-resources-showing-why-we-need-to-be-data-informed-not-data-driven/.

For more tips on how to build influence to effect change at school or anywhere else, go to *The Best Posts & Articles On Building Influence & Creating Change* https://larryferlazzo.edublogs.org/2012/04/16/the-best-posts-articles-on-building-influence-creating-change/

Index

A

Abbott Elementary, 107

ACEs. *See* Adverse Childhood Experiences (ACEs)

"acting out" behaviors, 195

actionable feedback, 32–33

active citizenship, 31

advanced learning, 49

"Advanced Learning For All" activity, 46

Adverse Childhood Experiences (ACEs), 145, 195

advice, 152

agency, 22

   reinforcing of, 34

   sense of, 23

   student, 21, 23, 37

   writing about values, 98–99

agentic engagement, 23

agentic feedback, 166–167

AI Guidelines for TOK Essays, 80–81

"AI-proofing," 83

Alinsky, S., 207

American Teacher Survey, 201

Analytical Writing Placement Examination (AWPE) prompt, 149

anchor charts/word walls, 64

application

   asset-based instruction

     community assets lesson, 117–118

     of ELLs, 112–113

     feedback, 117

     funds of knowledge, 110–111

     growth mindset, 118–119

     rubrics, 113–115

     stories, 111–112

     teacher expectations, 116–117

     "Wall of Fame," 116

classroom climate and culture, 145–146

   advice, 152

   attention, 148

   avoidant instruction, 159

   battles, 154–155

   "Breaking the Plane," 151

   calling home, 156–157

   curiosity, 153–154

   Fresh Starts, 151

   leading with picture, 157–158

   negative attention, 155–156

   planned ignoring, 146–147

   polarization, 159

   rules, 151

   seating, 152–153

   self-control, 148–150

   sharing good news, 150–151

   storytelling, 156

   teacher language, 147–148

   touches, 157

   walk and talk, 152

culturally responsive teaching

   commemorations and holidays, 196–197

   family and community connections, 194–195

   Freire's learning sequence, 193

   knowledge, 191–192

   learning, 197

   pronouncing student names, 193

   supporting students' cultural identities, 189

   teachers, 197–198

   translanguaging, 192

   trauma-informed practices (TIP), 195–196

   "windows, mirrors, and sliding doors," 190

differentiated instruction, 42–43

   advanced learning, 49

   anchor charts/word walls, 64

   audio support for text, 45

   bookmarks with hints, 60

   class routines, 65–66

   closed captioning for video/ modifying speed, 59

   connecting to prior knowledge, 60

   content, 43–44

   easier text/videos, 46–47

   extra credit, 46, 63

   formative assessments, 49–51

   graphic organizers, 52

   independent reading, 47

   Jigsaw, 44–45

   literature circles, 47–48

   multilingual support, 45–46, 57–58, 63

application (*continued*)
  online adaptive learning technology, 47
  options for culminating projects, 61–62
  options to move, 65
  pre-teaching vocabulary (frontloading), 58–59
  recommended sequences/ checklists, 53–55
  reteach, 60
  seating arrangements, 64
  sentence starters, 52
  small groups/working independently, 51–52
  student-created test questions, 63
  supportive class culture/ SEL, 64–65
  text engineering, 44
  time flexibility, 55
  using visuals, 48–49, 59
  voice typing, 51
  writing frames and structures, 53
  Zeigarnik effect, 55–56
instructional strategies
  assessment/reflection, 138
  goal of lesson, 122
  hook, 125–127
  instruction, 127–138
  learning transfer, 139
  retrieval practice, 123–125
  warm-up, 122–123
relationship, 6
  classmates, 15–16
  classroom, 12
  demonstrate personal vulnerability, 8–9
  generous with praise, 8
  greetings to students, 6–7
  humor, 7–8
  listen and respond to students, 10–12
  "looping," 15
  noticing students, 15
  practice common courtesy, 9–10
  student events, 13
  student names, 7
  supportive "hard" conversations, 13–14
  teach engaging lessons, 14

self-motivation
  agency, 98–99
  autonomy, 93–94
  competence, 95–98
  relatedness, 100–101
  relevance, 102–105
student agency
  actionable feedback, 32–33
  democratic citizenship, 31–32
  enhanced discovery learning, 33
  goal-setting, 24–25
  learning, 30, 34–35
  metacognitive reflection, 29–30
  operations into opportunities, 25
  opinion vs judgment, 35–36
  peer tutoring and mentoring, 25–27
  providing students choice, 30–31
  reactance, 36
  self-talk, 28–29
  Student Leadership Teams, 29
  students access prior knowledge, 33–34
  "teaching others" strategy, 27–28
  wait time, 35
student feedback, 165–166
  student to classmates (peer assessment), 172–174
  student to self (self-assessment), 174–182
  teacher to entire class, 171–172
  teacher to individual student, 166–171
  technological feedback, 183
teacher self care and sustainability
  "addition by subtraction," 208–209
  avoid toxic negativity, 206–207
  avoid toxic positivity, 207–208
  classroom routines and jobs, 205
  data, 209–210
  focus, 204–205
  grading, 202–203

  handling parent/guardian complaints, 205–206
  "Pinteresty" classroom decor, 206
  professional learning network, 203–204
tech
  classroom, 73–76
  generative AI, 77–85
  handling student cellphone use, 76–77
  use, 76
Arab American Heritage Month, 196
The Art and Science of Teaching (Marzano), 170
Artificial Intelligence (AI), in classroom, 50, 73, 164, 183
Asian American and Pacific Islander Heritage Month, 196
aspirational goal, for students, 24
assessments
  check for understanding, 138
  formative assessments, 203
  multilingual support for, 63
  peer, 172–174
  short low-stakes, 138
asset-based instruction, 107–108, 119–120
  application
    community assets lesson, 117–118
    ELLs, 112–113
    feedback, 117
    funds of knowledge, 110–111
    growth mindset, 118–119
    rubrics, 113–115
    stories, 111–112
    teacher expectations, 116–117
    "Wall of Fame," 116
  supporting research, 109
  Technology Connections, 120
assets, 158
  asset-based lens, 108
  asset-based pedagogy, 107
  asset-based words, 113
  community, 117–118
  of ELLs, 112–113
  stories, 111–112
assignments, 189
athletic activity, 65
audio support for text, 45

authoritative climate, in class, 143
authoritativism, 144
autonomy, student to motivate, 90
  choices, 93–94
  student voice, 94
avoidant instruction, 159
AWPE prompt. *See* Analytical Writing Placement Examination (AWPE) prompt

B
backward design and planning, 122
banking model, of schooling, 22
Berger, R., 173
Billings, E., 44
Billings, G. L., 197–198
Bishop, R. S., 107, 190
Black History Month, 196
Blooket (online game), 170
Bloom's Taxonomy, 46
Bond, C., 84
"bookmarks with hints," 60, 64
Branscombe, A., 190
"Breaking the Plane," 151
Bruner, Jerome S., 97, 130
Bryan, C., 36
building connections for classroom, 102–103
Bunch, G. C., 39
"2 by 10" strategy, 17–18

C
CER-OR rubric, 115
Character Lab, 102, 103
charts
  anchor, 64
  KWL, 34, 128
ChatGPT, 84, 183
"check for understanding," 50, 138
Chetty, R., 109
Choice Board for ELL Newcomers, 62, 94
Choice Theory, 23
Civil Rights, 7, 40, 154
Civil Society, 32
classmates, 6, 25, 34
  students
    to develop relationships with, 15–16
    peer assessment, 172–174

classroom, 12, 22, 23, 33, 35, 43, 71
  building connections for, 102–103
  climate and culture (*see* classroom climate and culture)
  community, 6
  "do now/warm-up" activity in, 47
  dynamics, 3
  ELL, 78, 118
  ELL US History, 75
  feedback, 11
  games, 136
  IB Theory of Knowledge, 53, 74, 78, 169
  Intermediate/Advanced English Language Learners, 45
  jobs, 205
  K-12, 23
  management (*see* classroom climate and culture)
    strategy in, 36
  movement activities in, 135–136
  non-ELL, 78
  pie-in-the-sky view of, 3
  Pinterest, 206
  routines, 65–66, 205
  self-motivation, 89–92, 105–106
    application, 93–105
    supporting research, 92–93
  teachers, 134, 171–172
  technology in (*see* tech (technology))
  visuals in, 48–49
  working in, 203
classroom climate and culture, 143–144, 159–160
  application, 145–146
    advice, 152
    attention, 148
    avoidant instruction, 159
    battles, 154–155
    "Breaking the Plane," 151
    calling home, 156–157
    curiosity, 153–154
    Fresh Starts, 151
    leading with picture, 157–158
    negative attention, 155–156
    planned ignoring, 146–147
    polarization, 159
    rules, 151
    seating, 152–153
    self-control, 148–150

    sharing good news, 150–151
    storytelling, 156
    teacher language, 147–148
    touches, 157
    walk and talk, 152
  supporting research, 144–145
  Technology Connections, 161
closed captioning for video, 59
cognates, 113
cognitive choices, of student, 30, 31
Cohen, G., 167
Cohen, T., 13
cold calling work, teachers, 134
collaborative vs cooperative learning, 133
community
  assets lesson, 117–118
  building activities, 100–101
  school-based problem, 31
competence, student to motivate, 90
  letters to students, 97–98
  mental imagery, 96–97
  positive reinforcement, 95–96
  progress principle, 95
  "The Progress Principle," 95
  scaffolding, 97
Concept Attainment, 130–131, 167, 171
connecting to prior knowledge, 60
"Connection"/"Community-Building" Circles, 94
conscientiousness, 177
content, 43–44
  advanced learning, 49
  assessments, 75
  audio support for text, 45
  easier text/videos, 46–47
  extra credit, 46
  independent reading, 47
  Jigsaw, 44–45
  literature circles, 47–48
  multilingual support, 45–46
  online adaptive learning technology, 47
  text engineering, 44
  visuals, 48–49
cooperative vs collaborative learning, 133
COVID pandemic, 74
critical feedback, 32
Critical Race Theory, 188

Critical Thinking Dialogue Ethnic Studies, 132
criticism, 207
Cuban, L., 204
culminating projects, options for, 61–62
cultural commemorations and holidays, 196–197
cultural knowledge, 191–192
culturally relevant pedagogy. *See* culturally responsive teaching
culturally responsive teaching, 107, 187–189
  application
    cultural commemorations and holidays, 196–197
    cultural knowledge, 191–192
    family and community connections, 194–195
    Freire's learning sequence, 193
    learning, 197
    pronouncing student names, 193
    supporting students' cultural identities, 189
    teachers, 197–198
    translanguaging, 192
    trauma-informed practices (TIP), 195–196
    "windows, mirrors, and sliding doors," 190
  supporting research, 189
  Technology Connections, 199–200
curiosity, 153–154, 177
currency, 1
curriculum, 75

D
data, 209–210
Deci, E., 89
democratic citizenship, 31–32
demonstrate personal vulnerability, 8–9
designed differentiation, 40
Dewey, J., 121
Dialogue Journal idea, 26
differentiated instruction, 39–41, 66
  application, 42–43
    advanced learning, 49
    anchor charts/word walls, 64
    audio support for text, 45
    bookmarks with hints, 60
    class routines, 65–66
    closed captioning for video/ modifying speed, 59
    connecting to prior knowledge, 60
    content, 43–44
    easier text/videos, 46–47
    extra credit, 46, 63
    formative assessments, 49–51
    graphic organizers, 52
    independent reading, 47
    Jigsaw, 44–45
    literature circles, 47–48
    multilingual support, 45–46, 57–58, 63
    online adaptive learning technology, 47
    options for culminating projects, 61–62
    options to move, 65
    pre-teaching vocabulary (frontloading), 58–59
    recommended sequences/ checklists, 53–55
    reteach, 60
    seating arrangements, 64
    sentence starters, 52
    small groups/working independently, 51–52
    student-created test questions, 63
    supportive class culture/ SEL, 64–65
    text engineering, 44
    time flexibility, 55
    using visuals, 59
    visuals, 48–49
    voice typing, 51
    writing frames and structures, 53
    Zeigarnik effect, 55–56
  supporting research, 42
  Technology Connections, 67–69
direct communication, 102
discipline, 144
"do now/warm-up" activity, in classes, 47
Dragnet: "Just the facts" (TV series), 12
Dukes, A., 204
Dweck, C., 32, 65, 118, 168
  "The Power of Yet," 108

E
easier text/videos, 46–47
ed tech. *See* tech (technology)
educators, 5, 21, 202
effective classroom management, "keystone" of, 4
  strategy, 144
"effective" instructional strategies, 92
effective self-assessment strategy, 175
"empowerment," in context of student agency, 22
English Language Learner (ELL), 39, 45, 51, 57, 59, 63, 71, 72, 82, 83, 85, 109, 113, 129, 134, 188, 190
  assets of, 112–113
  classrooms, 25, 26, 73, 78, 96, 118, 132, 134–135, 180
  Newcomers in class, 45, 112, 125, 131
  students, 26, 28, 46, 104, 110
  US History classes, 75
English-proficient classes, 135
English-proficient students, 26, 72, 73, 83, 96, 112, 130, 132
enhanced discovery learning, 33
enhancing student learning, 27
environment, learning
  anchor charts/word walls, 64
  class routines, 65–66
  options to move, 65
  seating arrangements, 64
  supportive class culture/ SEL, 64–65
Essay Graphic Organizer, 149–150
Essay Self-Assessment, 178
"Establish, Maintain, and Restore" approach, 19
ethics, 177
"ethnographies," 189
excellent differentiation strategy, 46
excellent formative assessment tools, 11
"experiencing self," 137
extensive credible research, 73
extra credit, 46
  for more advanced projects, 63
extrinsic motivation, 90

F

feedback, student, 117, 163–164, 183–184
  actionable feedback, 32–33
  agentic feedback, 166–167
  application, 165–166
    student to classmates (peer assessment), 172–174
    student to self (self-assessment), 174–182
    teacher to entire class, 171–172
    teacher to individual student, 166–171
    technological feedback, 183
  supporting research, 164–165
  Technology Connections, 184–185
Ferlazzo, L., 1–2, 6–7, 9, 16, 17, 24, 28–29, 41, 47, 55, 60, 61, 75–78, 81, 86, 89, 91, 96–98, 101, 110, 112, 118, 123, 126, 129, 135, 145, 146, 160, 195–197, 201–207, 211
  class evaluations, 11
  community organizer, 12, 31, 35
  ELL students, 104
  generative AI, 83
  Google Form survey to learn, 10
  Helping Students Motivate Themselves, 160
  "How can we do this better?, " 26
  IB Theory of Knowledge classes, 25, 26, 53, 65, 74
  Small Learning Communities, 15
  "transactional" vs "transformational, " 3
  The Washington Post, 14
feudalism, 110
formative assessments, 49–51, 76, 170, 183, 203
free voluntary reading, 47
Freire, P., 22, 92
  learning sequence, 193
frequent partner/small group work, 135
frontloading, 58–59
fuhgeddaboutit, 36
Funds of Knowledge, 110–111, 191

G

Gallup-Walton Family Foundation survey, 5

Gay, G., 187
gender identity, 7
generative Artificial Intelligence, 44, 59, 76
  chatbot, 47
  in education, 78–85
Glasser, W., 136
Goal Review Form, 182
Goal-Setting Form, 179–181
goal-setting, for students, 24–25
Google
  Classroom, 11, 16, 63, 66
  Docs, 51, 82
  Form, 8, 43, 94
  Gemini, 183
  Maps Street View, 118
  Translate, 28, 57, 73, 192, 194
Grade Reflection, 175–176
grading & assessments, 169–171, 202–203
"Gradual Release of Responsibility" model, 28
graphic organizers, 52
Gras, M., 60
growth mindset, 118–119, 168
guardian complaints, 205–206
guided discovery process, 33
guiding principles for teaching, 33

H

handling
  parent/guardian complaints, 205–206
  student cellphone use, 76–77
Harvard Business Review, 17, 164
Hattie, J., 27
heliocentrism, 44
Helping Students Motivate Themselves (Ferlazzo), 160
Hernandez, I., 111
higher-level academic content, 192
Hispanic Heritage Month, 196
Historical Empathy, 192
Hoekstra, L., 115
"homophily, " 5
"hook" strategy, 125–127, 130
Hull-Sypnieski, K., 47, 74, 76–78, 101
"Human Scavenger Hunt, " 15
humor, 7–8

I

IB-evaluated assessments, 74
"Identity Self-Portrait, " 189

IEP. *See* Individualized Education Program (IEP)
IKEA effect, 22
independent reading, 47
Individualized Education Program (IEP), 40, 61, 66
inductive teaching methods, 128–131
institutional barriers, 108
instructional process, with ELLs, 74
instructional strategies, 42, 104, 121, 129, 132, 139–140, 172, 175, 197
  application
    assessment/reflection, 138
    goal of lesson, 122
    hook, 125–127
    instruction, 127–138
    learning transfer, 139
    retrieval practice, 123–125
    warm-up, 122–123
  supporting research, 122
instructions, for students
  activating and connecting, to prior knowledge, 127–128
  cold calling, 134
  collaboration vs cooperation, 133
  fun, 136
  inductive teaching, 128–131
  movement, 135–136
  peak/end rule, 137–138
  relevance, 136
  simulations, 131–132
  teacher talk, 134–135
  visuals, 136–137
  wait time, 133
  written and oral directions, 127
interactional differentiation, 40
Intermediate and Advanced English Language Learners, 45, 53, 130
International Baccalaureate Theory of Knowledge, 53, 74, 78, 169
International New Year's Traditions Data Set, 130
intrinsic motivation, 90, 126
introductory letters, 10

J

Jigsaw method of instruction, 27, 44–45, 133, 205
Johnson, L., 126
Jones, K., 124

K

K-12
    classroom, 23, 169
    environment, 122, 165
    public schools, 188
    students, 164, 169
    teaching, 164
Kahneman, D., 137
"keep our eyes on the prize" (Civil Rights anthem), 154
Kennedy, J. F., 129
"keystone, " of effective classroom management, 4
kindness, 101
knowledge, funds of, 110–111
KWL charts, 34, 128

L

Ladson-Billings, G., 187
Landry, T., 165
language
    learning
        activity, 192
        classes, 131
    teacher, 147–148
"Language Portraits, " 189
"Lead Mentor" for coordination, 25
"Lead Peer Tutors, " 25
learning, 30, 34–35, 75, 197
    about students, 43
    advanced learning, 49
    environment
        anchor charts/word walls, 64
        class routines, 65–66
        options to move, 65
        seating arrangements, 64
        supportive class culture/SEL, 64–65
    strategies for maximizing, 121, 139–140
        application, 122–138
        supporting research, 122
        Technology Connections, 140–141
    teacher-student relationships for, 4
    transfer, 139
"learning menus" online, 62, 94
Learning Network, 32
Lemov, D., 151
lesser-tech strategy, 76

Letter of Recommendation Request Form, 84–85
Levine, E., 13
Lexile levels, 46
LGBTQ +, 100
Lincoln, A., 154
literature circles, 47–48
"looping" strategy, 5, 15
"Lost Einsteins" research, 109

M

Macbeth Retrieval Grid, 124
Machine Learning (ML), 44, 73
machine translation tools, 57
Mann, H., 31
Marshall, M., 13
Marshmallow Test on self-control, 126, 149
Marzano, R., 3, 4, 14, 33, 50
    The Art and Science of Teaching, 170
maximizing learning, strategies for, 121, 139–140
    application
        assessment/reflection, 138
        goal of lesson, 122
        hook, 125–127
        instruction, 127–138
        learning transfer, 139
        retrieval practice, 123–125
        warm-up, 122–123
    supporting research, 122
    Technology Connections, 140–141
McTighe, J., 122, 126
    Understanding by Design, 122
mental imagery, 96–97
"mental model, " students, 127
metacognitive reflection, 29–30
Meyer, D., 113, 166
mini-whiteboards, 50
modifying speed, 59
motivation transformations, 91
movement activities, in class, 135–136
multilingual support for assessments, 45–46, 57–58, 63
My Journal, 190, 191

N

Napolitano, J., 108
Natural Disasters, 41
negative attention, through cues, 155–156

neuroplasticity, 30
Newcomer and Intermediate classes, 63
Newcomer English Language Learner students, 16
Newcomers English Language Development class, 195
non-ELL
    classrooms, 78
    students, 112
non-tech class, 75
"numbered off" groups, 135

O

online
    adaptive learning technology, 47
    courses, 137
    games, 50, 76
    simulations, 132
    text, 45
operations into opportunities, 25
opinion vs judgment, 35–36
options
    for culminating projects, 61–62
    to move, 65
organizational choices, of student, 30
"outcome" goal, for students, 24
"out of control" class, 91

P

parallel text, 57
parental relationships, 4–5
Parent Guardian Letter Guide, 194
Parent Teacher Home Visit Project, 110
PCEs. *See* Positive Childhood Experiences (PCEs)
Peace Corps teacher training manual, 193
peak/end rule, 137–138
pedagogical philosophy, 121
peer review and assessment, 172–174, 203
Peer Review of TOK Essay Outlines, 173–174
peer tutoring and mentoring, 25–27
"performance" goal, for students, 24
permissive climate, in class, 143
perseverance, 168, 177

personal greetings, to students, 6–7
personalized feedback, 81
personal/professional "equilibrium," 2
Peterson, J., 152
Pierson, R.
    Kids don't learn from people they don't like, 4
Pink, D., 95
Pinterest, 206
piquing students' curiosity, 104
planned ignoring, 146–147
PLN. *See* Professional Learning Network (PLN)
"Plus, minus, interesting" activity, 175
plussing strategy, 168–169
polarization, 159
Positive Childhood Experiences (PCEs), 145
positive reinforcement, 95–96
positive self-concepts, 34
post-secondary education, 122, 137
practice common courtesy, 9–10
"praise beats punishment" strategy, 144
"praise-to-reprimand ratio," 8
praising effort/process, 168
pre-teaching vocabulary (frontloading), 58–59
Preview-View-Review, 57–58
primary challenges teachers, 16–18
primary teaching strategies, 28
"prior knowledge," 110
private relationship, 1, 2
proactive, 21
proactive precaution, 81
Problem-Based Learning assignment, 31, 93
"procedural" choices, of student, 30–31
process
    bookmarks with hints, 60
    closed captioning for video/ modifying speed, 59
    connecting to prior knowledge, 60
    formative assessments, 49–51
    graphic organizers, 52
    multilingual support, 57–58
    pre-teaching vocabulary (frontloading), 58–59

recommended sequences/ checklists, 53–55
    reteach, 60
    sentence starters, 52
    small groups/working independently, 51–52
    time flexibility, 55
    using visuals, 59
    voice typing, 51
    writing frames and structures, 53
    Zeigarnik effect, 55–57
products, 61
    different options for culminating projects, 61–63
    extra credit for more advanced projects, 63
    multilingual support for assessments, 63
    student-created test questions, 63
professional "equilibrium," 2
Professional Learning Network (PLN), 203–204
"The Progress Principle," 95
"Progress Ritual," 95
project-based learning activity, 30, 93, 94
psychological needs, 136
public relationship, with students, 1, 2

R
Rabin, T., 50
RAND, 201
reactance, 36
reciprocal/transformational relationships, 3
recommended sequences/ checklists, 53–55
"reducing the size of the ask," 147
Reese, D., 190
Reeves, D., 61
relatedness, student to motivate, 90
    being kind, 101
    encourage sense of belonging, 100–101
    small group learning, 101
"relationship bank," with students, 13

relationships, 1
    application, 6
        classmates, 15–16
        classroom, 12
        demonstrate personal vulnerability, 8–9
        generous with praise, 8
        greetings to students, 6–7
        humor, 7–8
        listen and respond to students, 10–12
        "looping," 15
        noticing students, 15
        practice common courtesy, 9–10
        student events, 13
        student names, 7
        supportive "hard" conversations, 13–14
        teach engaging lessons, 14
    parental, 4–5
    positive, 3
    private, 1, 2
    public, 1, 2
    reciprocal/transformational, 3
    remember about, 19
    student, 1
    supporting research, 4–5
    teacher-student, 1, 3–5, 7–8, 14, 15, 17, 19
    Technology Connections, 19–20
relevance, 136
    student to motivate, 90
        connecting lessons to student interests, 104–105
        linking lessons to personal goals, 102–104
        piquing curiosity, 104
"remembering self," 137
Remind, 16
Report Card: Student Perspective on U.S. Schools (2025), 5
research, of teacher-student relationships, 4–5
responding, to students, 10–12
"resulting' cognitive bias, 204
reteach, 60
retrieval practice, 28, 123–125
Riley, B., 73
Ross, Gail, 97
routines, class, 65–66
rubrics, 61, 113–115, 175

rules, classroom, 151
Ryan, R., 89

S
scaffolding, in classroom, 33, 97, 192
school
  banking model of, 22
  context, 8
  suspensions, 18
Schwab, S., 57
Schwartz, J., 63
Scrivner, N., 115
seating arrangements, 64
SEL, 64–65
self-assessing process for students, 203
self-assessment strategy, 174–182
self care and sustainability, 201–202, 210–212
  application
    addition by subtraction, 208–209
    avoid toxic negativity, 206–207
    avoid toxic positivity, 207–208
    classroom routines and jobs, 205
    data, 209–210
    focus, 204–205
    grading, 202–203
    handling parent/guardian complaints, 205–206
    "Pinteresty" classroom decor, 206
    professional learning network, 203–204
  supporting research, 202
  Technology Connections, 212–213
self-control, 177
  benefits of, 148–150
self-determination theory, 89, 92–93, 126
self-fulling prophecy, 109
self-generation of relevance, 102
self-motivation, 89–92, 105–106
  application, 95–98, 100–101
    agency, 98–99
    autonomy, 93–94
    competence, 95–98
    relatedness, 100–101
    relevance, 102–105

supporting research, 92–93
Technology Connections, 105–106
self-portraits, 189
self-talk, 28–29
sense
  of agency, 23
  of belonging, 100–101
  of community and trust, 150
sentence starters, 52
Shared Journal Process, 190
short anonymous Google Forms, 11
short low-stakes assessment, 138
Sims, P., 168
simulations, 131–132
small group learning, 101
small groups/working independently, 51–52
Small Learning Communities, 15
Special Education teachers, 73
"speed-dating" style, 95, 102, 118, 136, 172, 205
storytelling strategy, 156
strategies for maximizing learning, 121, 139–140
  application
    assessment/reflection, 138
    goal of lesson, 122
    hook, 125–127
    instruction, 127–138
    learning transfer, 139
    retrieval practice, 123–125
    warm-up, 122–123
  supporting research, 122
  Technology Connections, 140–141
strength-based instructional strategies, 108
student agency, 21–23, 37
  application
    actionable feedback, 32–33
    democratic citizenship, 31–32
    enhanced discovery learning, 33
    goal-setting, 24–25
    learning, 30, 34–35
    metacognitive reflection, 29–30
    operations into opportunities, 25
    opinion vs judgment, 35–36

peer tutoring and mentoring, 25–27
    providing students choice, 30–31
    reactance, 36
    self-talk, 28–29
    Student Leadership Teams, 29
    students access prior knowledge, 33–34
    "teaching others" strategy, 27–28
    wait time, 35
  empowerment in, 22
  of formative assessment, 170
  supporting research, 22, 23–24
  Technology Connections, 38
student feedback, 163–164, 183–184
  application, 165–166
    student to classmates (peer assessment), 172–174
    student to self (self-assessment), 174–182
    teacher to entire class, 171–172
    teacher to individual student, 166–171
    technological feedback, 183
  supporting research, 164–165
  Technology Connections, 184–185
students, 41, 42, 44, 65, 66, 111, 123, 137, 172, 179, 192
  absent in classrooms, 15
  access prior knowledge, 33–34
  act in annoying ways, 14
  agency (*see* student agency)
  Artificial Intelligence use, 71
  autonomy for engagement and motivation, 61
  benefits of self-control, 148–150
  cellphone, 71, 86
  choices, 30–31, 93–94
  to classmates (peer assessment), 172–174
  of color, 100
  confidence levels, 95
  cultural identities, 189
  develop relationships with classmates, 15–16
  ELL, 110
  events, 13

feedback (*see* student feedback)
goal-setting process, 103
Google Docs, 82
IB Theory of Knowledge, 53, 74, 78, 169
instructions for
  activating and connecting, to prior knowledge, 127–128
  cold calling, 134
  collaboration vs cooperation, 133
  fun, 136
  inductive teaching, 128–131
  movement, 135–136
  peak/end rule, 137–138
  relevance, 136
  simulations, 131–132
  teacher talk, 134–135
  visuals, 136–137
  wait time, 133
interests, 104–105
K-12, 164, 169
leadership teams, 29, 94
learning about, 43
letters to, 97–98
listen and respond to, 10–12
"looping" strategy, 15
"mental model," 127
names, 7
non-ELL, 112
opportunities for, 101
pattern-seeking opportunities, 128
personal greetings to, 6–7
positive relationships with, 16–18
pronouncing names, 193
public relationship with, 1
relationship, 1
to self (self-assessment), 174–182
self-assessing process for, 203
self-grading, 171
self-motivation, 89–92, 105–106
  application, 93–105
  supporting research, 92–93
student-created test questions, 63
supportive touches in, 157
teaching, 21–22
text supports, 45
values, 99
verbal feedback as, 203

voice, 94
"warm-up" activity for, 122–123
Student Self-Assessment One, 175–176
student-teacher relationships, 3–5, 7–8, 14, 15, 17, 19
study strategy, 28
substantial research, 19, 42, 129, 174
  on teacher expectations, 116
sufficient support, 117
Suggested Sequence for Writing Your TOK Essay, 53–55
summative assessments, 49, 170
supporting research
  asset-based instruction, 109
  classroom climate and culture, 144–145
  culturally responsive teaching, 189
  differentiated instruction, 42
  instructional strategies, 122
  relationship, 4–5
  self-motivation, 92–93
  student
    agency, 23–24
    feedback, 164–165
  teacher self care and sustainability, 202
  tech, 72–73
supportive class culture, 64–65
supportive touch, in student, 157
sustainability, 201–202, 210–212
  application
    addition by subtraction, 208–209
    avoid toxic negativity, 206–207
    avoid toxic positivity, 207–208
    classroom routines and jobs, 205
    data, 209–210
    focus, 204–205
    grading, 202–203
    handling parent/guardian complaints, 205–206
    "Pinteresty" classroom decor, 206
    professional learning network, 203–204
  supporting research, 202
  Technology Connections, 212–213

T
teachers, 32, 34, 40, 43, 46, 131, 153, 197
  to class, 171–172
  classrooms, 134
  cold calling work, 134
  credential programs, 121
  of English Language Learners, 188
  expectations, 116–117
  extra credit, 46
  faculty room, 19
  language, 147–148
  primary challenges, 16–18
  self care and sustainability (*see* teacher self care and sustainability)
  to student
    agentic feedback, 166–167
    grading & assessments, 169–171
    helping students, 167
    plussing, 168–169
    praising effort/process, 168
  talk, 134–135
  "teacher-proof," 75
  time for engineering, 44
  "transactional" vs "transformational," 3
teacher self care and sustainability, 201–202, 210–212
  application
    addition by subtraction, 208–209
    avoid toxic negativity, 206–207
    avoid toxic positivity, 207–208
    classroom routines and jobs, 205
    data, 209–210
    focus, 204–205
    grading, 202–203
    handling parent/guardian complaints, 205–206
    "Pinteresty" classroom decor, 206
    professional learning network, 203–204
  supporting research, 202
  Technology Connections, 212–213
teacher-student relationships, 1, 3–5, 7–8, 14, 15, 17, 19

teaching, 25, 27–28
  careers of students, 23
  guiding principles for, 33
  inductive methods, 128–131
  K-12, 164
  Marshmallow Test, 149
  students, 21–22, 30
"teaching others" strategy, 27–28
tech (technology), 71, 86
  application
    classroom, 73–76
      generative AI, 77–85
      handling student cellphone
        use, 76–77
      use ed tech, 76
  supporting research, 72–73
  Technology Connections, 87
technocratic data-driven
    culture, 210
technological feedback, 183
Technology Connections
  asset-based instruction, 120
  classroom climate and
    culture, 161
  culturally responsive teach-
    ing, 199–200
  differentiated instruction, 67–69
  relationships, 19–20
  self-motivation, 105–106
  strategies for maximizing
    learning, 140–141
  student
    agency, 38
    feedback, 184–185
  teacher self care and sustainabil-
    ity, 212–213
  tech (technology), 87
TED Talks, 149

text
  engineering, 44
  supports students, 45
Theisen-Homer, V., 2
Think-Pair-Share, 35, 134–135
time flexibility, 55
TIP. *See* Trauma-Informed
    Practices (TIP)
TOK Class Guidelines for Use of AI
    In Writing, 78–79
TOK Essay Sequence, 53–55
TOK Exhibition Checklist, 55, 56
Tomlinson, C. A., 39, 40, 52
Trabelsi, W., 73
traditional teaching methods, 131
"transactional" vs "transforma-
    tional" teachers, 3
"translanguaging," 113, 192
Trauma-Informed Practices
    (TIP), 195–196
Treverton, G., 139
"turning operations into
    opportunities" goal, 25

U
"unassisted discovery," 33
Understanding by Design (McTighe
    and Wiggins), 122
US
  Census surveys, 31
  Civil War, 111, 126

V
Venet, A. S., 41, 61, 144–145
verbal feedback, as students, 203
visuals, 59, 136–137
  in different content
    classes, 48–49

voice
  student, 94
  typing, 51

W
"wait time," 35, 133–134
walk-and-talks strategy, 152, 158
"Wall of Fame," 116
Walqui, A., 39, 44
"warm-up" activity, for stu-
    dents, 122–123
Watson, A., 124, 125
Wayground (online game), 170
weekly Google Form survey,
    10–12
Whole Class Feedback, 171
Wiggins, G., 122, 126
  Understanding by Design, 122
Wiliam, D., 6, 42, 163, 164,
    166–167, 175
Williams, R., 82
Willingham, D., 206
Women's History Month, 196
Wood, D., 97
word walls, 64
Wormeli, R., 2
Write-Pair-Share, 35
writing and thinking process, 91
writing frames and structures, 53
written and oral directions, for
    students, 127

Y
Yeager, D., 36, 167

Z
Zeigarnik Effect, 55–57